Routledge Guides to the Great Books

The Routledge Guidebook to Aquinas' *Summa Theologiae*

The Routledge Guidebook to Aquinas' Summa Theologiae introduces readers to a work which represents the pinnacle of medieval Western scholarship and which has inspired numerous commentaries, imitators, and opposing views. Outlining the main arguments Aquinas utilizes to support his conclusions on various philosophical and theological questions, this clear and comprehensive guide explores:

- the historical context in which Aquinas wrote;
- a critical discussion of the topics outlined in the text including theology, metaphysics, epistemology, psychology, ethics, and political theory;
- the ongoing influence of the *Summa Theologiae* in modern philosophy and theology.

Offering a close reading of the original work, this guidebook highlights the central themes of Aquinas' masterwork and is an essential read for anyone seeking an understanding of this highly influential work in the history of philosophy.

Jason T. Eberl is the Semler Endowed Chair for Medical Ethics and Professor of Philosophy at Marian University in Indianapolis, USA.

D1594044

THE ROUTLEDGE GUIDES TO THE GREAT BOOKS

Series Editor: Anthony Gottlieb

Routledge Guides to the Great Books

The Routledge Guidebook to Aquinas' *Summa Theologiae*

Jason T. Eberl

Routledge
Taylor & Francis Group

LONDON AND NEW YORK

First published 2016
by Routledge
2 Park Square, Milton Park, Abingdon, Oxon OX14 4RN

Simultaneously published in the USA and Canada
by Routledge
711 Third Avenue, New York, NY 10017

Routledge is an imprint of the Taylor & Francis Group, an informa business

British Library Cataloguing in Publication Data
A catalogue record for this book is available from the British Library

Library of Congress Cataloging in Publication Data
Eberl, Jason T.
The Routledge guidebook to Aquinas' Summa Theologiae / Jason T. Eberl.
pages cm.—(The Routledge guides to the great books)
Includes bibliographical references and index.
1. Thomas, Aquinas, Saint, 1225?–1274. Summa theologica. I. Title.
BX1749.T6E24 2015
230'.2—dc23
2015021394

ISBN: 978-1-138-77716-3 (hbk)
ISBN: 978-1-138-77719-4 (pbk)
ISBN: 978-1-315-72842-1 (ebk)

Typeset in Times New Roman
by Book Now Ltd, London

For Eleonore

Keep hold of instruction; do not let go;
guard her, for she is your life

—Proverbs 4:13

The teacher excites the student's intellect toward knowledge of the things which she teaches, as an indispensable mover leading the intellect from potentiality to actuality.

—Thomas Aquinas, *De veritate*, q. 11, a. 1 *ad* 12

SERIES EDITOR'S PREFACE

"The past is a foreign country," wrote a British novelist, L. P. Hartley: "they do things differently there."

The greatest books in the canon of the humanities and sciences can be foreign territory, too. This series of guidebooks is a set of excursions written by expert guides who know how to make such places become more familiar.

All the books covered in this series, however long ago they were written, have much to say to us now, or help to explain the ways in which we have come to think about the world. Each volume is designed not only to describe a set of ideas, and how they developed, but also to evaluate them. This requires what one might call a bifocal approach. To engage fully with an author, one has to pretend that he or she is speaking to us; but to understand a text's meaning, it is often necessary to remember its original audience, too. It is all too easy to mistake the intentions of an old argument by treating it as a contemporary one.

The *Routledge Guides to the Great Books* are aimed at students in the broadest sense, not only those engaged in formal study. The intended audience of the series is all those who want to understand the books that have had the largest effects.

AJG
October 2012

PREFACE

At first glance, a "guidebook" to Thomas Aquinas' *Summa theologiae* seems quite unnecessary. Yes, it's a *voluminous* work: over 1.5 million words filling about 3,000 pages in the standard English translation! Nevertheless, Thomas intended this work for "beginners" and the text is systematically organized so that readers can easily follow the flow of subjects from one to the next in the neo-Platonic "*exitus-reditus*" structure that he evidently employs. Yes, you read that correctly. Although Thomas is typically understood as the Christian theologian who "baptized Aristotle," he was just as strongly influenced by Augustine of Hippo, a neo-Platonist who is one of the four early "Doctors of the Church" whose company Thomas was later to join. Thomas' enduring influence is in fact partially due to his ability to *synthesize* Augustinian theology with Aristotelian philosophy, as well as incorporate elements from the thought of other neo-Platonic philosophers, Jewish theologians, and Arabic commentators on Aristotle. Thomas possessed encyclopedic knowledge of past scholarship and was not afraid to utilize philosophical and theological views from all these seemingly disparate sources. He did not, however, merely present summaries of others' arguments, but made his own creative contributions to the lively debates that characterized 13th-century scholasticism. All this is why the *Summa*, despite its somewhat simple and clear structure, rewards careful scholarly attention, while also potentially frustrating novice readers not versed in the myriad figures, movements, and theories Thomas critically engages or uses to formulate his own arguments.

Since the *Summa* is only *deceptively* easy to approach, an informative guidebook is not merely helpful but arguably *necessary* to glean the most one can from the text, to understand the background premises of Thomas' arguments, and thus to critically engage his views informatively, fairly, and effectively—whether one ultimately agrees or disagrees with his conclusions. Unfortunately, for all the reasons just given, no single volume can offer a comprehensive exposition and illumination of the entire corpus of the *Summa*. Hence, in the present volume, certain topics, themes, and arguments will be more emphasized than others relative to their inherent complexity, their foundational role for other arguments Thomas makes, or their historical impact in the development of philosophical theology; although some part of each of the "treatises" that compose the *Summa* will be discussed. Adhering to the style of other "guidebooks" in this series, citations within the main text will be omitted. Instead, "Suggestions for further reading" will be provided at the end of each chapter for readers interested in delving more deeply into various aspects of the *Summa* and relevant background information. Before embarking upon our exploration of the text itself, it will be helpful to have some preliminary biographical and contextual information to understand how and why Thomas wrote the *Summa* in the first place and why it still enthralls readers over 700 years later. Later, having finished our journey through the *Summa*, we will examine in greater detail some of Thomas' metaphysical and ethical views that scholars continue to interpret, reconstruct, and defend in response to both perennial philosophical questions and emergent issues of importance to both religious and secular thinkers.

My keen interest in the person and thought of Thomas Aquinas may have been somewhat predestined by virtue of sharing my middle-name with him and having been baptized at St. Thomas Aquinas Catholic Church in East Lansing, Michigan. I later dressed as Thomas for "Patron Saint Day" at St. Vincent de Paul Catholic School in Phoenix, Arizona, when I was in the first grade. My affinity for Thomistic thought matured during my undergraduate studies at the University of San Diego and while writing my master's thesis on Thomas' interpretation of Aristotle's *De anima* at Arizona State University. I am immensely grateful to all of my professors at these institutions—particularly Linda Peterson, John Donnelly, and Michael White—who nurtured my initial formation as a Thomistic philosopher. I wish to express my deepest gratitude to Eleonore Stump, who generously and maternally shepherded my journey from relative neophyte to dedicated scholar of Thomistic thought during my doctoral studies at Saint Louis University. I dedicate this volume to her with my prayer for continued blessings upon herself, her family, and her continuing scholarship of which the entire philosophical and theological community is the beneficiary.

More immediately, my work in writing this volume has been supported by my colleagues in the Department of Theology & Philosophy and the College of Osteopathic Medicine at Marian University, and the Department of Philosophy at Indiana University-Purdue University Indianapolis. At Routledge, I wish to thank Andy Humphries, who first brought this project to my attention, as well as Siobhán Poole, Iram Satti, Rebecca Shillabeer, and Lucy Vallance for their advice and assistance in bringing this volume to fruition. I owe a tremendous debt of gratitude to Gaven Kerr at Queen's University in Belfast, Ireland, who read and offered insightful feedback on the entire manuscript. Although we have yet to meet in person, connecting through social media has allowed us to cultivate a relationship as colleagues and friends over our mutual passions for Thomas Aquinas and heavy metal music.

Nothing I have accomplished since beginning graduate studies nearly 20 years ago would have been possible without the loving support of my wife, Jennifer, my daughter, August, and my extended family from both sides of our marital union. As my daughter leaves for college in the fall of 2016, I hope and pray she will discover and be able to realize her vocational passion just as I have been blessed to realize mine.

Part I

GENERAL INTRODUCTION

1

THOMAS AQUINAS' LIFE, WORK, AND IMPACT

THE LIFE OF THOMAS

Thomas was born into a somewhat large, aristocratic family in southern Italy near Naples. He is called "Aquinas" as a branch of his family once held the county of Aquino, which is part of the Kingdom of the Two Sicilies in Italy. The family's castle was—and still is today—located in the town of Roccasecca, and it was here that Thomas was born around 1225—give or take a year. At this time, Thomas' family had some degree of political clout due to their geographical location at the boundary of the power struggle between Emperor Frederick II and the papacy; the allegiances of various family members, including Thomas' father and some of his brothers, shifted between emperor and pope. This complex political landscape no doubt influenced Thomas' treatise *On Kingship to the King of Cyprus* (*De regno*), in which he draws a clear distinction between secular and religious spheres of authority; although he reserves ultimate moral authority to the papacy for reasons that will become evident when we discuss the *Summa*'s treatise on law.

As was customary for the youngest son of an aristocratic family, Thomas left Roccasecca at the age of five or six to enter the Benedictine Archabbey of Monte Cassino and then later the Benedictine house of studies in Naples. Given his family's social position and his already evident intellectual acumen, Thomas' father, Landolfo, probably expected that his son would rise through the ranks of the Benedictine Order to become the abbot of Monte Cassino, a position of immense ecclesiastical power at the time. Like many rebellious youths, however, Thomas disrupted his father's plans for him by abandoning the well-established Benedictines to join the newly founded Order of Preachers—informally known as the "Dominicans" after their founder, St. Dominic (1170–1221)—adopting the white habit with black cloak around April 1244. The Dominicans were one of two *mendicant* orders founded in the 12th century—the other being the Franciscans. As mendicants, members of both orders took vows of absolute poverty while devoting themselves to a life defined by their order's particular charism: service to the poor for the Franciscans and preaching for the Dominicans. Intellectually gifted members of both orders, however, could attain seats of academic leadership in the emerging universities, which we will discuss in further detail below.

A month after he entered the Dominican Order in Naples, Thomas' mother, Theodora, went there in an attempt to dissuade him from his Dominican vocation. By the time she arrived, though, Thomas' superiors had secreted him to Rome and were preparing to send him further away from his family's influence. Just north of Rome, however, Thomas was accosted by a party led by his brother, Rinaldo. Peaceful by nature, Thomas did not physically fight his captors and went willingly, ensuring only that he was able to take his breviary—a book of daily prayers, known as the "Liturgy of the Hours," required for clergy and members of religious orders. The only remarkable feature of his arrest is that his captors were unable to remove his Dominican habit—one of the hagiographical moments of Thomas' life intended to demonstrate his unswerving vocation. He was brought back to Roccasecca and kept under "house arrest" for over a year. Although one may be tempted to the image of a "friar in distress" locked away in the castle tower, Thomas was by no means mistreated by a family who, after all, loved him dearly. He enjoyed the freedom of the castle grounds, received visitors—including fellow Dominicans—and was able to carry out his studies of the Bible and other texts expected of him by the order. There is, of course, the (in)famous story of his older brothers pulling an atypical sibling prank and sending a prostitute to Thomas' room, whom he allegedly chased away with a hot iron from his fireplace and then vowed himself to perpetual chastity. Finally, unable to convince him to abandon his vocation, Thomas' family allowed him to return to the Dominicans. This incident, however, did not sour Thomas' relationship with his family, as there are records of his visiting some of his siblings during his travels and even arranging for financial assistance to his family in a time of dire need. Just before he died, in fact, Thomas resided for brief recuperative periods at his sister Theodora's and his niece Francesca's respective homes.

Upon his return to the Dominicans, Thomas was sent to begin his formal studies. First, in Paris for about three years, Thomas completed his education in the liberal arts—logic, grammar, rhetoric, arithmetic, astronomy, geometry, and music—as well as encountering Aristotelian philosophy. Later, in Cologne, Thomas was under the tutelage of the Dominican master Albert the Great (*c.* 1193–1280). In a final, but certainly not mean-spirited, snub at his family, Thomas turned down an offer directly from Pope Innocent IV to become the abbot of Monte Cassino, despite being a Dominican, in order to study with Albert. For four years, Thomas worked closely with Albert, performing tasks such as organizing the latter's course notes, including his lectures on Aristotle's *Nicomachean Ethics*, the influence of which is evident in Thomas' own later commentary on that work. During this time, Thomas also began to deliver his own lectures to his Dominican brethren on Sacred Scripture. It was apparently around this time that Thomas acquired the dubious nickname "the Dumb Ox" from his peers, ridiculing him for his stout stature and taciturn nature. Thomas disdained idle speech, but rather believed that every word uttered should be in the service of God. Albert, justifiably impressed when his star pupil handily responded to a series of difficult questions in a *disputatio* with his classmates, admonished Thomas' confreres with the prescient claim, "We call him the Dumb Ox, but the bellowing of that ox will resound throughout the whole world."

In 1252, Thomas returned to Paris to begin lecturing on the *Sentences* of Peter Lombard (*c.* 1096–1164). In some respects, Lombard's *Sentences* was the *Summa* of its day. But rather than a systematic presentation of arguments defending particular conclusions to various questions against objectors—as is the case with Thomas' *Summa*—Lombard's text collected the teachings of the early Christian Fathers, such as Augustine, John Chrysostom, and Pope Gregory the Great, organized around various theological topics. As was expected of him to progress to the next academic level, Thomas wrote an extensive commentary on Lombard's *Sentences*—akin to writing a doctoral dissertation today. In this earliest of Thomas' large-scale projects, he begins to use Aristotle as an authoritative resource, citing him twice as much as he cites Augustine. We will look at the rise of Aristotle's influence on Thomas and other Christian thinkers later on. During this time, Thomas also authored two shorter, but still intellectually powerful, treatises: *On Being and Essence* (*De ente et essentia*) and *On the Principles of Nature* (*De principiis naturae*). These writings are noteworthy not only for their content, but also for the evident influence of two Arabic thinkers impacting Thomas' thought: Avicenna (Ibn Sina) and Averroes (Ibn Rushd). As we will see further below, the Christian intellectual tradition owes a tremendous debt to these Muslim scholars for preserving and commenting upon the Aristotelian corpus, which was largely lost to the Latin world following the final destruction of the Alexandrian library in Egypt in the 4th century.

Although his commentary on Lombard's *Sentences* was not yet complete, in 1256 Thomas took up the duties of a "Master of Sacred Scripture"—a title commensurate today with being a newly minted Ph.D. These duties were *legere* (to read), *disputare* (to dispute or argue), and *praedicare* (to preach). The first involves reading and commenting on the Bible, and this would constitute Thomas' typical, everyday teaching activity. The second is a more active form of pedagogy that became one of the most distinctive characteristics of 13th-century academic life. Instead of passively listening to the master's lecture on a particular topic, students and other faculty members would pelt the master with argument after argument on a subject of the master's choosing. One of the master's advanced students—in effect, a graduate teaching assistant—would offer a preliminary response to each of these arguments. Then, the master would offer a definitive resolution to the question at hand. Transcriptions of these disputations would be later edited by the master into a publishable form. We have redacted accounts of several disputations in which Thomas engaged on matters of truth (*De veritate*), evil (*De malo*), spiritual creatures (*De spiritualibus creaturis*), virtues (*De virtutibus*), the soul (*De anima*), the power of God (*De potentia Dei*), and the Incarnation (*De unione Verbi incarnati*). In addition, during Advent and Lent each year, a public disputation would be held for the entire university community in which questions of whatever sort (*quaestiones quodlibetales*) could be hurled at the master by students and peers. Thomas no doubt found this form of teaching both more exciting and more illuminating for his students, as he modeled the structure of the *Summa* on the *disputatio* format. Thomas' third duty in his position at the University of Paris was to preach and, lest we commit the error of focusing solely on his academic scholarship, we must recall that the fundamental mission of the Dominican Order is to preach the Christian Gospel. Thomas did so on a regular basis and there are a number of extant sermons attributed to him. Furthermore, he composed a variety of specifically liturgical works, including prayers and hymns such as the widely popular *Adoro Te* and *Panis angelicus*, as well as a Mass and the Office for the Feast of Corpus Christi incorporated into the Liturgy of the Hours.

Thomas did not spend his entire career in Paris, although this is where he is most associated. As expected for a Dominican of his stature, Thomas attended the General Chapter meeting for the order at Valenciennes in June 1259. Following this date, there is uncertainty as to his whereabouts—whether he returned to Paris or was in Italy for the next two years. From 1261 to 1265, however, Thomas was assigned as a *lector*—reader and commentator on Sacred Scripture— at the Dominican convent in Orvieto. This time afforded Thomas the luxury of composing many works, including the second of his major systematic works—after his commentary on Lombard's *Sentences*— the *Summa contra Gentiles* (*Summary [of the Christian Faith] against Unbelievers*), which we will look at in detail later on, as well as an extensive commentary on the Book of Job. In 1265, Thomas was commissioned by his Dominican superiors to found a house of studies (*studium*) for the order at Santa Sabina in Rome. It was during these three years in Rome, inspired by the *carte blanche* he no doubt enjoyed in designing a curriculum of the new *studium* as he saw fit, that Thomas began composing the first part of the *Summa theologiae*.

Thomas returned to Paris in 1268. For the next four years, he lectured, participated in disputations, and wrote prodigiously. Reportedly, he dictated to three or even four secretaries simultaneously drafting texts as diverse as a commentary on one of Aristotle's works, a redaction of a recent disputation, a short polemical treatise on a controversial subject, a Scriptural commentary, or a section of the second part of the *Summa theologiae*. He was also embroiled in more pragmatic disputes concerning the status of the mendicant orders—Franciscans and Dominicans—as academic leaders above other faculty. Physical attacks were not uncommon; sometimes, Thomas and his fellow friars had to be protected by a detachment of royal archers. In 1272, in light of a dispute between the university and the Bishop of Paris, Thomas returned to Naples, where his Dominican vocation was rooted, and founded a new *studium*. He evidently chose Naples himself as the location of this new house of studies, as opposed to Rome or Orvieto, due to the city's "vitality" as a (at that time) Sicilian seaport where Christian, Jewish, and Muslim cultures intersected. Thomas, as we will see further below, was intellectually *cosmopolitan*. In Naples, he conducted courses on the Epistles of St. Paul and on the Psalms, while also composing the third part of the *Summa* and several other works.

Perhaps simply exhausted by his non-stop intellectual efforts, perhaps suffering a mild stroke, or perhaps experiencing a vision of the Divine Essence—or perhaps *both* the latter—Thomas suddenly stopped all scholarly activity after celebrating Mass on December 6, 1273. He said to his primary secretary (*socius*), Reginald of Piperno, "I cannot do any more. Everything I have written seems to me as straw in comparison with what I have seen." After a period of rest at his sister's home in San Severino, Thomas returned to Naples before being summoned to the Council of Lyons convened by Pope Gregory X. En route, Thomas struck his head on a tree branch and fell ill—perhaps from a hemorrhaged blood clot—near his niece's home and was taken there to recuperate. He later requested to be taken to the monastery at Fossanova. His health declining, he still continued to teach from his bedside, composing a commentary on the *Song of Songs* as a form of gratitude to the monks at Fossanova. Thomas died on March 7, 1274; he was about 49 years old. His body was moved around to various places that wanted to claim his spiritual patronage and now rests in Toulouse, France.

THOMAS IN CONTEXT

Thomas lived during an exciting time of intellectual and cultural interchange, though not always on peaceful terms. As we saw earlier,

Thomas systematically amalgamated a number of philosophical and theological views of Christian, Jewish, Muslim, and pagan origin. He was exposed to these various perspectives due to certain historical progressions that reached their apex in the 13th century. Perhaps the most significant is the Muslim occupation of various regions in Spain beginning in the 8th century and enduring—with many intervening battles trading territories back and forth—well into the 15th century. The latter centuries of this period witnessed the "rediscovery" of Aristotle by Latin scholars thanks to their interaction with Arabic scholars who had possession of Aristotle's works that had been lost to the Western European world for nearly a millennium. While the Latin Christians only had copies of part of Aristotle's logical works—known as the *organon*—Muslim philosophers and theologians had been writing commentaries on his major philosophical treatises, including the *Physics*, *Metaphysics*, *De anima*, and *Nicomachean Ethics*. Thomas, like many of his academic confreres, could not read Greek or Arabic. Fortunately, he was able to benefit from translations into Latin produced through cooperative interactions among religiously diverse scholars who, despite the bloody political battles raging around them, did not allow such differences to interfere with a joint pursuit of the truth. As Averroes (1126–1198) wrote in his essay "On the Harmony of Religions and Philosophy",

> And, if before us, somebody has enquired into [philosophical reasoning], we should derive help from what he has said. It is quite immaterial whether that man is our co-religionist or not; for the instrument by which purification is perfected is not made uncertain in its usefulness by its being in the hands of one of our own party, or of a foreigner, if it possesses the attributes of truth.

The other significant development flourishing in the 13th century was *scholasticism*. This term refers to the regulated style of teaching and learning that characterized the various universities that were founded in the immediately preceding centuries, structured around a combined liberal arts and theological curriculum—sometimes including also law or medicine—that has served as the model, even after theology lost its central place, for baccalaureate education into the 21st century. Less than two hundred years before Thomas' birth, still-extant universities had been founded at Bologna, Paris, Oxford, Cambridge, Salamanca, and elsewhere around Europe. Earlier medieval thinkers certainly did not labor in isolation, as evidenced by the famous exchange between Anselm of Canterbury and Gaunilo concerning the former's "ontological" argument for God's existence. Nevertheless, the creation of various schools—from smaller *studia*, such as the ones Thomas founded in Rome and Naples, to the large urban universities—facilitated a level of academic interlocution never before seen in the Western world—a scholarly revolution the likes of which would not be witnessed again until the invention of printed books in the 15th century. The scholastic university system also established a set of academic requirements to achieve the degree of *baccalaureus*, followed by the title of *magister* with the right to teach (*licentia docendi*).

If the spirit of scholasticism could be summed up in a single catchphrase, it would be "faith seeking understanding" (*fides quaerens intellectum*). While this attitude can be found among earlier Christian thinkers, such as Augustine, it was the definitive hallmark of intellectual exchange among the theological masters who flourished from the late 11th century onward, inspired by this prayer at the beginning of Anselm's *Proslogion*:

> I am not trying to scale your heights, Lord; my understanding is in no way equal to that. But I do long to understand your truth in some way, your truth which my heart believes and loves. For I do not seek to understand in order to believe; I believe in order to understand. For I also believe that [quoting Augustine] "Unless I believe, I shall not understand."

Scholastic philosophy has thus been criticized as violating the most sacred rule of philosophy, as it originated in the Western world with Socrates, which is to question everything and to avoid circular reasoning by not presuming the conclusion for which one is arguing. The negative perception of scholastic methodology was reinforced by the purported separation of mind and world, and the resulting *skepticism*, advanced by René Descartes (1596–1650). The 20th-century analytic philosopher Bertrand Russell thus proclaimed in his masterful, if opinionated, *A History of Western Philosophy*, that "there is little of the true philosophical spirit in Aquinas." It is one thing, however, to already believe in the truth of the conclusion for which one is arguing and quite another to utilize that belief as a premise in the logical structure of one's supporting argument. Thus, in Thomas' five arguments to demonstrate the existence of God, one never finds Thomas' belief in God's existence to play an invalidating role in the structure of the arguments themselves. God enters the picture only at the conclusion of each argument, and Thomas is well aware that the "God" he demonstrates to exist is not even necessarily the *Christian* God in whom his faith lies. Hence, he concludes each of the five arguments with some version of the statement, "and this everyone understands to be God" (Ia, q. 2, a. 3)—allowing for various nuanced conceptions of the divine nature.

Thomas and his scholastic colleagues understood well the distinction between truths that can be demonstrated through rational argument and truths that can be known only through faith. Nevertheless, both sets of truths have, in their view, the same source: God. Therefore, it would be impossible for any of them to contradict each other. The scholastic intellectual spirit is thus a far cry from contemporary debates that pit "religion" *against* "science" as if each gives us knowledge of truths that are incompatible with those delivered up by the other. To the contrary, Thomas and the other scholastics would view any alleged contradictions between the deliverances of faith and reason to be merely *apparent*; rather, one either has reasoned poorly or has a flawed understanding of the truths of faith. Hence, philosophy and theology mutually support and "fraternally correct" each other when practiced *virtuously*—requiring, as we will discuss when examining Thomas' treatise on virtue, both *intellectual* virtues that inform one's honest search for truth and *moral* virtues that allow one to humbly accept correction from others while charitably offering similar correction to those in error.

The primary starting-point for all Latin scholastic thought was, of course, the Bible. It is important to note, though, that Thomas and other scholastic theologians did not read Scripture in the *literal* sense that some Christians do today. They certainly took the words of Jesus literally, as when He took bread in His hands at the Last Supper and told His apostles, "This is my body," leading Thomas to develop a sophisticated metaphysical explanation for how something that has the look, smell, and taste of unleavened bread may nevertheless *be*—literally and not merely symbolically—the body of Christ. Other Scriptural texts, however, may not have such literal significance, but rather express theological truths in a *metaphorical* or *allegorical* fashion. For instance, Thomas understands terms that involve matter in their definition to only be ascribable to God metaphorically since God is incorporeal (Ia, q. 13, a. 3 *ad* 1). Hence, God does not literally have an "arm," even though Scripture refers to "the arm of God"; rather, this term is referring to the *function* of an arm "to do or to make," which is a power God possesses. We will see Thomas' sophisticated, non-literal understanding of Scripture at work in his treatise on "the work of the six days" in the Book of Genesis, where his interpretation of the creation story illuminates the theological truths communicated through the narrative without contradicting any conclusions properly arrived at through rational inquiry—setting Thomas' view in contrast to both secular atheists and biblical literalists.

Thomas, as noted earlier, spent most of his ordinary teaching time commenting on Sacred Scripture. But he was not merely offering his own opinion following a "cold reading" of the Word of God. Instead, like most intellectuals in any discipline, he "stood on the shoulders of giants" who had plumbed the depths of Scripture since the earliest days of Christianity. Scholastic theologians and philosophers accepted as *authorities* (*auctoritates*) various time-tested texts that were foundational to ever more refined and expanded intellectual exploration. These include the writings of the Greek and Latin Fathers of the Early Church, various neo-Platonic texts, and, by Thomas' time, the books of Aristotle.

The *Patristic tradition* includes a large number of theologians, many of them bishops or popes, who shaped Christian doctrine from the 1st through the 8th centuries—the term "Patristic" refers to their collective status as the "Fathers of the Early Church." Among the most influential for Thomas are the Greek Fathers John Chrysostom (*c.* 347–407) and Gregory of Nyssa (*c.* 330–*c.* 395), and the Latin Fathers Augustine (354–430), Jerome (*c.* 345–420), and Pope Gregory the Great (*c.* 540–604). Some of them participated in the initial *councils* held at locations such as Ephesus, Chalcedon, and Nicea, where fundamental tenets of Christian orthodoxy were defined. The Council of Chalcedon in 451, for example, defined Jesus Christ as *one person* possessing *two natures*: human and divine. This dogmatic pronouncement rendered heretical the contrasting *monophysite* view that Christ had only one nature. The Patristic writers were of both Greek and Latin origin, but all lived prior to the final schism between the Eastern and Western Christian churches in 1054. Thomas, however, did not betray a "Western" bias in citing various Church Fathers. During his time in Orvieto, Thomas assembled, at the request of Pope Urban IV, a collection of commentaries on all four Gospels from the Patristic scholars. This collection became known as "The Golden Chain" (*Catena aurea*), emphasizing the unbroken chain of truth emanating from the *Logos* himself—Christ, as described in the Prologue to the Gospel of John—through the four evangelists to the minds of the Greek and Latin Fathers. Thomas ended up citing 57 Greek Fathers and only 22 Latin Fathers. This project had a profound effect on Thomas' later scholarship as he cites Patristic sources in the *Summa* six times more often than he did in his earlier commentary on Lombard's *Sentences*.

The most authoritative of all the Early Church Fathers was Augustine of Hippo. In fact, an *Augustinian* approach to theology was predominant among the scholastics, and was not diminished—although some feared it might be—by the emergence of Aristotelianism. In fact, just the first 12 questions of the *Summa* cite Augustine 160 times, compared to only 55 times for Aristotle. Although Thomas is accurately credited with synthesizing many of the neo-Platonic elements found in Augustine's theology with Aristotelian philosophy, the aspects of Augustine's thought that most directly influenced Thomas fall in the realm of more strictly theological topics, such as the nature of grace and predestination, the Beatific Vision, the freedom without sin of the saved after death and the unfallen angels, and the Trinity. On other topics, however, such as his understanding of the human soul and how human nature can be understood to have been created in the "image and likeness of God" (*imago Dei*), Thomas' use of Aristotelian philosophical concepts is more prevalent; although whether this should be taken as a helpful alteration of Augustinian anthropology or an outright departure is subject to interpretive debate. During the latter part of Thomas' academic career, continuing after his death until his canonization in 1323, scholars who identified themselves as thoroughgoing "Augustinians"—typically Franciscans such as Bonaventure and John Pecham—understood some of Thomas' views to be erroneous departures from Augustine.

The rise of *Aristotelianism* in the Latin world was the source of significant controversy in the 13th and 14th centuries, often divided along the lines of the Dominican versus the Franciscan scholastic masters: the former embracing Aristotelian philosophy as an illuminative means of understanding the tenets of Christian faith handed down from Scripture through the Patristics; the latter viewing Aristotelianism skeptically as a departure from the neo-Platonic philosophy undergirding sound Patristic theology, especially Augustine's authoritative teaching. It is not the case, however, that there was a cleanly sharp divide between "Augustinians" and "Aristotelians," as various Dominican and Franciscan scholars had recourse to sources in both traditions; although no one attempted as thoroughgoing a *synthesis* of the two than Thomas.

While it did not effectively slow down Aristotelian scholarship, the University of Paris officially prohibited teaching and commenting on Aristotle's newly rediscovered works until 1250, and then only granted a limited license for certain scholars, including Thomas once he arrived there in 1252, to lecture on those works. Thomas was probably first exposed to Aristotle's writings during his initial studies in the Dominican house in Naples, where he may have taken a course covering Aristotle's natural philosophy and metaphysics. His exposure to Aristotle's ethics came through his discipleship with Albert in Cologne.

Thomas' approach to Aristotle's writings was not to offer a simple reconstruction of what Aristotle *literally* intended to say. Rather, his extensive commentaries on Aristotle's works reveal the general attitude of, what would Aristotle have said if he had possessed the gift of Christian faith? This leads Thomas, for example, to conclude that Aristotle's account of human happiness in the *Nicomachean Ethics* is incomplete without any consideration of humanity's ultimate contemplation of the divine essence and loving union with God—the completion of the *reditus* that starts with each person's creation. Thus, it is not, in Thomas' view, that anything Aristotle says about human happiness is mistaken; rather, it simply does not go far enough and, if Aristotle had possessed the gift of faith, he would have seen this for himself and arrived at Thomas' same conclusion. By the time he was composing the *Summa*, instead of making interpretive arguments on Aristotle's behalf, Thomas was utilizing his own "baptized" understanding of Aristotle's account of human happiness to support his conclusion that perfect happiness can come only from intellectual contemplation of the divine essence and loving union with God. As we make our way through the text of the *Summa*, various Aristotelian concepts that are central to the arguments Thomas formulates will be elucidated.

THE *SUMMA THEOLOGIAE* AMONG THOMAS' OTHER WRITINGS

Although the *Summa theologiae* is rightly considered Thomas' "masterwork," it represents only about one-fifth of his total authorial output. Following upon his encyclical *Aeterni patris* (1879), giving the papal *imprimatur* to Thomas as *the* Christian theologian *par excellence*, Pope Leo XIII commissioned a group of Latin paleographers and translators, who are also well-versed in Thomistic thought, to produce the definitive critical edition of the entire Thomistic corpus. The first volume was published in 1882 and, while the work of the "Leonine Commission" has progressed steadily ever since, only 30 out of 50 volumes have been published as of 2013—the nine volumes comprising the *Summa* were published from 1888 through 1906. In addition to the grand projects of the *Summa theologiae*, *Summa contra Gentiles*, and his commentary on Lombard's *Sentences*, Thomas published editions of his disputations on various subjects, biblical commentaries, commentaries on Aristotle and other philosophers, shorter treatises and polemical writings, letters in response to requests for expert opinion—such as his political essay *On Kingship to the King of Cyprus*—as well as liturgical works, sermons, and prayers. Many of these works have been discussed in passing throughout this introductory chapter; but, in setting the stage for the *Summa theologiae*, two other key works are pertinent to examine: the *Summa contra Gentiles* and the *Compendium theologiae*.

Like his drafting of the *Summa theologiae*, on which he worked steadily but not exclusively from around 1266 until he stopped writing in December 1273, Thomas composed the *Summa contra Gentiles* over a long period while also engaged in various other projects from around 1259 through 1264. His purpose in devoting so much time and energy to this four-volume work is clearly stated in the second chapter of the first volume: "I have set myself the task of making known, as far as my limited powers will allow, the truth that the Catholic faith professes, and of setting aside the errors that are opposed to it."

Reflecting Thomas' stated intention, some manuscript versions of the *Summa contra Gentiles* are entitled, *Liber de veritate catholicae fidei contra errores infidelium* (*Book on the Truth of the Catholic Faith against the Errors of Unbelievers*). There is some debate as to the exact purpose and intended audience of this work. The available options are 1) it is addressed directly to non-Christians, primarily Muslims and Jews in Spain, in order to present and defend the Catholic faith; 2) it is addressed to Christian missionaries in predominantly non-Christian regions in order to help them effectively evangelize; 3) it is not addressed to any particular audience, but seeks rather to elucidate and defend Catholic doctrine by use of Aristotelian philosophy. These options are not mutually exclusive and, perhaps in order to fulfill the first or second purpose, Thomas certainly accomplished the third.

The *Summa contra Gentiles* ranks as more of a clearly *philosophical* work than the later *Summa*; in fact, another title sometimes given to the *Summa contra Gentiles* in various manuscripts, presumably in order to create a clear contrast to the *Summa theologiae*, is *Summa philosophica*. This title is justified by Thomas' more laborious presentation, than in the later *Summa*, of various contrasting arguments concerning each question at hand and his greater reliance on *argument*, as opposed to Scriptural or Patristic *authority*, to support his conclusions. In many chapters, having just argued for a particular conclusion using one or more rational arguments that include no reference at all to theological sources, Thomas will quote Scripture in order to show that what he has just demonstrated by reason conforms to *revealed* truth as well.

Another work that fits within the category of Thomas' systematic treatises—albeit much shorter than its brethren—is the *Compendium theologiae*. For a long time, historical scholars believed that the *Compendium* was written toward the end of Thomas' life. This hypothesis is supported by the fact that only about a third of the *Compendium* was completed and by the characterization of the *Compendium* as a "Summa of the *Summa*." One can imagine Thomas' students, reading drafts of the *Summa theologiae*, as intended for "beginners," asking their master if he could distill the material down even further, eliminating the formal presentation of objections and replies and summarizing the central theological "take-home" lessons. This imagined scenario may not be too far off the mark, except that the *Summa contra Gentiles* is the longer work that Thomas felt compelled to reduce to its essential theological elements, presented in a clearer pedagogical fashion organized thematically around the three theological virtues of *faith*, *hope*, and *charity*. As mentioned, though, Thomas abandoned this work after writing only about a third of it: he completed the section on faith with 246 chapters, but wrote only the first ten chapters of the section on hope and nothing of the third section. Unlike the *Summa theologiae*, however, the *Compendium* was not left incomplete due to Thomas' death, but rather due to his apparent decision to adopt a different pedagogical approach more directly influenced by the structure of the scholastic *disputatio* which, as described earlier, was a regular form of teaching for Thomas.

So why did Thomas write the *Summa theologiae*? After all, by the time he started writing the *Summa*, he had already largely composed the *Summa contra Gentiles*, a large-scale systematic work that delves into various topics even more deeply and with more philosophical rigor than the *Summa*. That was the very problem with the other *Summa*: it was too dense. While a great instrument for presenting the strongest arguments in defense of Christian doctrine against challenges from non-believers, the *Summa contra Gentiles* did not serve quite as well as an instructional text for those who are just beginning their formal theological studies. Hence, even while completing the earlier *Summa*, he had already started work on the more accessible *Compendium theologiae*.

Thomas makes his intention clear in the Prologue to the *Summa theologiae*:

> Because the Master of Catholic Truth ought not only to teach the proficient, but also to instruct beginners (according to the Apostle: "As unto little ones in Christ, I gave you milk to drink, not meat" – 1 Corinthians 3:1–2), we purpose in this book to treat of whatever belongs to the Christian Religion, in such a way as may tend to the instruction of beginners.

There is some debate among Thomistic scholars concerning precisely who the "beginners" are that Thomas has in mind. As evident from the need for a guidebook such as this, the *Summa* is much too complex to be simply picked up and read by someone with absolutely no background in Christian theology or Aristotelian and neo-Platonic philosophy. So, recalling the order of education Thomas himself experienced, it is reasonable to conclude that he intended the *Summa* to supplant Lombard's *Sentences* as the next text that advanced theology students should approach after having completed their initial studies in the liberal arts, including biblical studies and philosophy. In the contemporary academic structure, Thomas would apparently intend the *Summa* to be the primary text for masters-level students in theology, who already have a well-rounded undergraduate education, in preparation for more in-depth doctoral research on a particular topic later on.

An equally reasonable conclusion is that Thomas did not plan the *Summa* for university education at all. Rather, his intended audience was "run-of-the-mill" Dominicans who may not be the most academically astute, but nevertheless needed to have sufficient theological understanding to effectively preach and give counsel during confession. This thesis is evidenced by the fact that the second half of the second part of the *Summa* (*secunda secundae*), which concerns primarily practical moral issues, is the largest section of the work, comprising 189 questions in comparison to the 119 questions of the first part (*prima pars*) and the 114 questions of the first half of the second part (*prima secundae*)—Thomas had only reached Question 90 of the third part (*tertia pars*) when he stopped writing altogether. On this interpretation, Thomas saw the *prima pars* and *prima secundae* as theoretical *prolegomena* grounding the philosophical and theological validity of the Church's practical moral teachings that would be the central focus of preachers and confessors.

Depending on which was indeed his intention for the *Summa*, Thomas would have been both gratified and annoyed at how the *Summa* was disseminated after his death. If he had in mind that the *Summa* would replace Lombard's *Sentences* as the standard graduate-level textbook for Dominican schools and universities, that did not occur. It would not be until the early 20th century, following upon Pope Leo XIII's exhortation in *Aeterni patris*, that the *Summa* would rise to be the centerpiece of theological education for Roman Catholic clerics. If

Thomas intended the *Summa* to be of more practical usefulness at the pulpit and in the confessional, then it was certainly successful in that regard as the *secunda secundae* was the most widely copied part of the *Summa*. Recall that manuscripts were still copied laboriously by hand at this point and thus were quite expensive; so it was rare that the entire *corpus* of the *Summa* would be copied or purchased as a single unit. According to one contemporary analysis of over six hundred manuscripts reproducing parts of the *Summa*, the *secunda secundae* accounts for 37 percent of the manuscripts, as opposed to only 20 percent for *prima pars*, 25 percent for *prima secundae*, and 18 percent for *tertia pars*. The *secunda secundae* also gained prominence by virtue of influencing—or being outright plagiarized—by myriad "manuals" for pastoral theology. In 1298, the Dominican John of Freiburg published his *Summa confessorum*, which was composed primarily of material derived or copied straight from the *secunda secundae*. Freiburg's *Summa* enjoyed tremendous success, being reprinted well into the 16th century and inspiring several more simplified manuals of Christian morality. What would have frustrated Thomas about the popularity of the *secunda secundae* is that it negated his central purpose in writing the *Summa* to provide sound *theoretical* grounding for practical moral theology. It is quite easy for a pastor to exhort the members of his flock with a list of moral "thou shalt's" and "thou shalt not's." It is more difficult, for those lacking the background provided in the *prima pars* and *prima secundae*, to explain *why* one ought to do or refrain from doing certain actions.

Thomas would also have been disappointed by isolated readings of the *secunda secundae*, or any part of the *Summa* for that matter, because there is a significant theological lesson to be drawn from the very organizational structure of the *Summa* as a whole. Thomas describes the macro-structure of the *Summa* in the prologue to Question 2 of the *prima pars*:

> Because the chief aim of sacred doctrine is to teach the knowledge of God, not only as He is in Himself, but also as He is the beginning of things and their last end, and especially of rational creatures . . . therefore, in our endeavor to expound this science, we shall treat: (1) Of God; (2) Of the rational creature's advance towards God; (3) Of Christ, Who as man, is our way to God.

These three subject areas correspond to the three major parts of the *Summa* with an organic progression from one part to the next, reflecting a neo-Platonic worldview Thomas receives through his reading of pseudo-Dionysius, known as *exitus-reditus* ("emanation" and "return").

Neo-Platonists, such as Plotinus and pseudo-Dionysius, conceived of God's essence as necessarily *emanating* into creation. This is due primarily to God being, in Platonic terms, the "Form of the Good" and goodness as being essentially "diffusive of itself." In other words, goodness cannot be wholly contained in just one being; rather, goodness will naturally seek to manifest itself in as many distinctive ways as possible. Thomas, as we will see later on, disagrees with the thesis that God *necessarily* creates a universe outside of Himself by an uncontrollable emanation of His being and goodness; on the contrary, creation is a *free* choice on God's part that warrants gratitude and worship on the part of created beings capable of recognizing the wondrous gift of their unmerited creation. He agrees with the neo-Platonists, however, that creation, in all its myriad forms, is inherently imbued with, and thereby manifests, God's goodness—albeit imperfectly.

Thomas thus begins the first part of the *Summa* by treating various questions related to the existence of God and the qualities of the divine essence (Questions 2–26), culminating in the relations among the three Persons of the divine Trinity: Father, Son, and Holy Spirit (Questions 27–43). He then discusses God's creation of other beings: first creation in general (Questions 44–46) and then different types of creatures (Questions 47–102), including angels (Questions 50–64) and human beings (Questions 75–102).

As rational creatures, angels and human beings have the capacity to know and love God. For reasons we will see later on, angels are created each with all the knowledge they will ever possess and, based on their knowledge of God, make a choice whether or not to love their creator. Those who choose not to love God include Satan and the rest of the "fallen" angels. Human beings, however, experience a finite lifetime in which we make, not just a single moral choice whether to love God, but many moral choices that move us either closer to or further away from a loving union with our creator. Our "return" to God, then, by means of our moral choices comprises the second part of the *Summa*. It begins with Thomas' analysis of human *happiness*, concluding with Augustine that our hearts are "restless" until they rest in the presence of God (Questions 1–5). He then delves into human *moral psychology* (Questions 6–48), importing Aristotle's thesis that moral development proceeds by means of the cultivation of various dispositions toward either willing what is good (virtues) or what is bad (vices) (Questions 49–89). He concludes the first half of the *secunda pars* with a consideration of the *moral law* human beings can rationally discern and ought to follow if we are to achieve our goal of happiness (Questions 90–108) and the *grace* that is necessary if human beings are to be able to will what is good (Questions 109–114).

In the second half of the *secunda pars*, Thomas focuses on specific virtues and vices that, respectively, assist or impede our moral progress toward happiness. He first treats the three *theological* virtues of faith, hope, and charity (Questions 1–46) and then the four *cardinal* virtues of prudence, justice, temperance, and fortitude (Questions 47–170). He concludes by showing how different states of life, especially vowed religious life, allow a human being to cultivate and live out these virtues (Questions 171–189). As already seen toward the end of *prima secundae* with his discussion of grace, Thomas holds that moral progress and the final attainment of happiness cannot be accomplished by human beings through our own natural abilities. Hence, the third part of the *Summa* focuses on the redemptive work of God as incarnate in the person of Jesus of Nazareth (Questions 1–59) and the various graces that flow from the *sacraments* of the Church (Questions 60–90), without which our final return to the source of our existence, satisfying all of our natural desires, could not occur. At this point, the *Summa* abruptly ends partway through Thomas' treatment of the sacrament of penance.

Aware of what his master was intending to discuss to complete the "return" to our divine source, Thomas' secretary, Reginald, compiled a "supplement" to the *tertia pars* out of Thomas' earlier commentary on Lombard's *Sentences*. The two main divisions of the *supplementum* is the completion of the discussion of the sacraments (Questions 1–68), followed by a treatise on life after death and the Resurrection (Questions 69–99). Although the supplemental text should be approached with caution as it represents Thomas' earliest treatment of these subjects—and hence one would be better served by consulting what Thomas says concerning them in Book IV (Chapters 56–97) of the *Summa contra Gentiles*—Reginald's work helpfully completes the circle of humanity's procession from God to our ultimate return to loving union with Him. We will continually emphasize this *exitus-reditus* structure as we make our way through various sub-parts of the *Summa*.

As noted in our earlier biosketch, Thomas was intensely productive in the latter part of his career—not that he was at all slothful in the early stages of his career either! He prudently selected various writing projects and teaching activities, however, to support his drafting of the *Summa*. For example, before beginning the discussion in the *prima pars* of God and creation, he engaged in a series of disputations on the power of God (*Quaestiones disputatae de potentia Dei*). Later, when working on his treatise on human nature in the *prima pars*, he engaged in another disputation on the nature of the human soul (*Quaestio disputata de anima*) and composed a commentary on Aristotle's *De anima*. Furthermore, Thomas' commentary on Aristotle's *Nicomachean Ethics* coincides with his work on the moral section of the *Summa*—the massive *secunda pars*—as well as his disputations on the virtues (*Quaestiones disputatae de virtutibus*) and on evil (*Quaestiones disputatae de malo*). Finally, in preparing to work out his Christological theory in the *tertia pars*, he held a disputation on the unity of Christ's being (*Quaestio disputata de unione Verbi incarnati*). Thomas worked hard, but he also worked smart!

THOMISM TODAY

"Thomism," as that term is generally understood today, did not immediately or uncontroversially develop, following Thomas' death in 1274, as a predominant form of Christian philosophical theology. As noted earlier, some of the Franciscan theological masters in Paris, who considered themselves to be more faithful adherents to authoritative Augustinian theology, criticized various theses held by Thomas and other Dominican Aristotelians. One of the most vocal, whose academic career in Paris coincided with Thomas' second regency there, was John Pecham (*c.* 1230–1292). In fact, one of Thomas' polemical treatises, *De aeternitate mundi*, was directed against Pecham and his confreres who "murmured" against Thomas to other colleagues and impressionable students—hence, the full title of the treatise, *De aeternitate mundi contra murmurantes*. This dispute between the two allows us to glimpse an expression of Thomas' humble nature, as he kept silent—despite being urged on by his students—to go head-to-head with Pecham during the latter's inception ceremony at the University of Paris. Pecham's inaugural address directly criticized Thomas' thesis regarding the question of whether the universe could be co-eternal with God, having no temporal beginning or end. Allowing Pecham to have his day, Thomas reserved his no-holds-barred critique for the written treatise.

De aeternitate mundi is one of two polemical treatises Thomas wrote in the last years of his life against the views of other scholars at the University of Paris. The second, *De unitate intellectus contra Averroistas parisiensis*, presents Thomas' most mature defense of the nature of the human intellect. Interpreting somewhat confusing passages on the subject in Book III of Aristotle's *De anima*, three basic theses were being debated among the scholastics. The first follows Avicenna's commentary that, while each individual human being has her own *passive* intellect that receives and retains knowledge of universal concepts and abstract ideas, there is a single *agent* intellect that "illuminates" such knowledge in each person's passive intellect. This view was popular among the Franciscans, who likened Avicenna's thesis to Augustine's theory of knowledge being illuminated directly by God.

The second thesis is that the entire intellect is singular and separate from the souls that animate the bodies of individual human beings. This view, advocated by secular masters such as Siger of Brabant (*c.* 1240–1280s), was derived from Averroes's commentary on *De anima*; hence, adherents of this view were known as "Latin Averroists" and it is directly to them that Thomas is addressing his *De unitate intellectus*. In this treatise, Thomas defends the third view that each individual human being has her own intellect as a faculty of the same soul that animates her body. Thomas lodges two primary complaints against the Averroist thesis. First, it ultimately denies the *personal immortality* of each human being, since it is due to the intellective faculty that the human soul is capable of existing and functioning after the death of its body. Second, it disrupts the *substantial unity* of each human being since the intellect would be a separate substance from the soul-body composite that defines the human essence; in short, the thing that lives and senses would not be the same as the thing that thinks. We will explore in detail later the philosophical foundations for Thomas' thesis and these arguments as he presents them in the *Summa*. For now, it suffices to point out this controversy in order to show that, although Thomas was clearly a widely read and influential theologian in his own lifetime, his views were not always accepted uncritically and his fame attracted detractors as well as adherents.

The controversy surrounding *De aeternitate mundi* was even more profound than the debate on the nature of the intellect and actually led to over a dozen propositions Thomas defended in various writings being formally condemned—along with over 200 other controversial propositions being defended by faculty at the University of Paris—by the Bishop of Paris, Stephen Tempier, in 1277. The debate centered on whether the universe was created with a temporal starting-point, allowing only God to exist eternally, or whether the universe is co-eternal with God. The latter thesis was held by Aristotle and Thomas defended its *reasonability*—meaning that it was philosophically defensible and could not be rationally disproven. This sufficed to get Thomas into hot water as this thesis appeared to threaten God's status as the universe's *creator*, as well as to directly contradict the account of creation in the Book of Genesis. Thomas, however, would not commit such obvious heresy and never actually held this thesis; he merely defended its reasonability. At the same time, he also defended the reasonability of the orthodox view that the universe had a temporal beginning. His ultimate conclusion was that neither thesis can be philosophically disproven, so either could be reasonably held, but the orthodox view is the true one according to revelation. As we noted earlier, Thomas had a nuanced understanding of the proper relationship between truth as discoverable by reason and as known by faith. Nevertheless, this nuance was lost on some of Thomas' intellectual adversaries who considered his view too permissive in potentially allowing for heresy. This and other academic debates led not only to the condemnations of 1277, but also inspired an Oxford Franciscan, William de la Mare, to publish a "*Correctorium*" of Thomas' writings that became required reading for Franciscan students. The Dominicans countered with a set of replies to what they called the "*Corruptorium*."

These disputes were pretty much settled by Thomas' canonization as a saint in 1323; however, this did not firmly establish Thomism as a formal school of thought among Christian intellectuals. As we saw earlier, Thomas' greatest influence after his death came in the proliferation of mostly the *Summa*'s *secunda pars*, both in disseminated copies of various portions thereof and in other manuals of moral teaching it inspired. Critics still abounded, though. One of Thomas' most ardent detractors was the Italian philosopher Pietro Pomponazzi (1462–1525), who was concerned that Aristotle was being primarily read and taught through a Thomistic lens, which led, in his view, to erroneous interpretations of Aristotle that were infected by neo-Platonic elements—recall that Thomas synthesized Aristotle's philosophical views with neo-Platonic views inherited through Augustine and pseudo-Dionysius. A primary focus of Pomponazzi's critique was Thomas' argument for the immortality of each individual human soul by virtue of its intellective faculty—defended, as we saw, in his *De unitate intellectus* and elsewhere. Pomponazzi did not favor the Avicennian or Averroistic readings either. Rather, he claimed that, while each individual human being has her own intellect as a faculty of her soul—as Thomas also argues—this does not entail her soul's immortality given its essential relationship to its body.

While Pomponazzi criticized Thomas' views from within the Aristotelian philosophical tradition, the centuries after Pomponazzi's death brought about wholesale changes in philosophical perspective from thinkers such as Descartes, the British idealists and empiricists—most notably, as a critic of Aristotelianism, David Hume (1711–1776)—German idealists, such as Georg Wilhelm Friedrich Hegel (1770–1831), and American pragmatists like Charles Sanders Peirce (1839–1914). Of course, there was also the drama of the Protestant Reformation and Roman Catholic Counterreformation, which led to increased diversification of theological perspectives in terms of both personal spirituality and academic scholarship—"scholasticism," in the formal sense of the term, was over.

In 1879, concerned with the growing influence of "modernism"—a catch-all term that included new socio-political theories such as Marxist socialism and nihilistic philosophy as found in the popular writings of Friedrich Nietzsche (1844–1900)—Pope Leo XIII issued an encyclical letter, *Aeterni patris*, in which he called for a "restoration" of Christian philosophy according to Thomistic thought. Leo's exhortation was affirmed by his successor, Pope Pius X, in his *Doctoris angelici* in

1914. This led Pius's successor, Pope Benedict XV, overseeing the revision of the Roman Catholic Church's Code of Canon Law in 1917, to include a requirement that those training for the priesthood or religious life should have at least two years of formal philosophical studies "according to the arguments, doctrine, and principles of St. Thomas which they are inviolately to hold." To fulfill this requirement, a number of "manuals" were published that provided a digest of Thomistic philosophy and theology for ready consumption by young seminarians and religious novices.

Unfortunately, these manuals often separated students from a direct encounter with Thomas' text itself, which opened the door for various distortions to creep in along with a lack of nuance in their understanding. Nevertheless, the resurgent focus on Thomistic thought inspired various intellectuals to a detailed reexamination of Thomas' writings, not only to understand his views within their historical context, but also to enter into the mind of Thomas more deeply so as to discern new ways of reformulating his views in light of different philosophical and theological traditions that arose in the centuries since his death. Hence, there emerged a variety of "Thomisms" that have helped to revitalize scholasticism, in altered fashion, both within and even outside Catholic intellectual circles. We will highlight just a few of the more influential varieties of 20th-century Thomism. French Thomists Étienne Gilson (1884–1978) and Jacques Maritain (1882–1973) are often identified as "Existential Thomists," though not because they read Thomas through the lens of French existentialist philosophers like Jean-Paul Sartre (1905–1980). Rather, this label refers to their emphasis on Thomas' rich conception of "being" (*esse*) as what primarily distinguishes Thomistic Aristotelianism from other commentators on Aristotle. The primacy of being in Thomistic metaphysics underwrites a peculiarly Christian philosophical approach that places God, as subsistent Being itself (*ipsum esse subsistens*), at the absolute center of all reality. God is understood as not only creating, but also *sustaining* everything that exists, as opposed to Aristotle's characterization of God in his *Metaphysics* as a remote "unmoved mover" who is not even aware of the rest of the universe. Aristotle's concept of God supports a theology of "deism" in which there is no personal relationship between God and the rest of the creation, as opposed to the personalistic "theism" of the Abrahamic religions that, thanks to the influence of neo-Platonism, allows for created beings to *participate* in the divine Being.

The *personalism* supported by Existential Thomism led, among the faculty of the Catholic University of Lublin in Poland, to develop a distinctive approach known as Phenomenological Thomism. This label refers to the aim of the Lublin Thomists to reframe Thomas' theology and philosophical anthropology—that is, his concept of human nature—in light of continental phenomenological philosophies from the likes of Edmund Husserl (1859–1938) and Max Scheler (1874–1928). The most famous student of this school of Thomism was Karol Wojtyla (1920–2005), who authored a seminal work of Thomistic phenomenology, *Person and Act* (1969), and later, as Pope John Paul II, reaffirmed Thomas as *the* philosopher *par excellence*, who successfully harmonized faith and reason, in his encyclical *Fides et ratio* (1998).

Pursuing such harmonization led the Lublin Thomists to read Thomas through the lens of modern phenomenological views. Other Thomists have also sought to harmonize Thomas' views with later philosophical theories. For example, the Transcendental Thomists, such as Bernard Lonergan (1904–1984) and Karl Rahner (1904–1984), sought to reconcile Thomas' theory of the human mind and his overall epistemology with the more radical subjectivism of Descartes—which is actually anticipated by Augustine—and the attempted synthesis of idealism and empiricism in the writings of Immanuel Kant (1724–1804). Most recently, Analytical Thomists see the scholastic philosophical approach, not only in Thomas' writings but also other medieval thinkers like Anselm, to cohere with the logically rigorous and linguistically focused approach of contemporary analytic philosophy, characterized by such thinkers as Bertrand Russell (1872–1970) and Ludwig Wittgenstein (1869–1951). The term "Analytical Thomism" was coined in a 1992 lecture at the University of Notre Dame by Scottish philosopher John Haldane (1954–); although this approach can be found in writings by Peter Geach (1916–2013) and Elizabeth Anscombe (1919–2001)—both students of Wittgenstein—going back to the 1950s.

There are active scholars writing from within all of these Thomistic schools today, thereby demonstrating that Thomism is indeed "the perennial philosophy," as defined by the Second Vatican Council, that will continue to have a significant influence on 21st-century philosophical and theological developments and his writings will remain a vital part of the philosophical canon. Whether one is ultimately influenced by, or ends up being critical of, Thomas' views, those approaching his texts, particularly the *Summa*, for the first time need to have a clear grasp of the theses he defended, the supporting arguments he constructed, and the concepts informing those arguments—hence, the *raison d'etre* of this guidebook.

SUGGESTIONS FOR FURTHER READING

The standard English edition of the *Summa* was translated by the Fathers of the English Dominican Province and published by Benziger Brothers in 1947–8. All quotations from the *Summa* throughout this guidebook will be taken from this translation. The 60-volume English-Latin edition is currently published by Cambridge University Press. For an excellent abbreviated edition, see *Summa theologiae: A Concise Translation*, ed. Timothy McDermott (Notre Dame, IN: Christian Classics, 1989).

Two authoritative biographies of Thomas Aquinas are Jean-Pierre Torrell, *Saint Thomas Aquinas – Vol. 1: The Person and His Work*, trans. Robert Royal (Washington, D.C.: Catholic University of America Press, 1996); and James A. Weisheipl, *Friar Thomas d'Aquino: His Life, Thought, and Work* (Garden City, NY: Doubleday, 1974). Other, more accessible, biographies include G. K. Chesterton, *Saint Thomas Aquinas: "The Dumb Ox"* (New York: Doubleday, 1956); Josef Pieper, *Guide to Thomas Aquinas*, trans. Richard and Clara Winston (San Francisco, CA: Ignatius Press, 1991); and Denys Turner, *Thomas Aquinas: A Portrait* (New Haven, CT: Yale University, Press, 2013).

Although sometimes questioned as the most valid way to understand the *Summa*'s conceptual structure, the influential neo-Platonic *exitus-reditus* framework in which the *Summa* is often read was initially proposed by Marie-Dominique Chenu in his *Toward Understanding Saint Thomas*, trans. Albert M. Landry and Dominic Hughes (Chicago: Henry Regnery, 1963). A dedicated textual analysis of the *Summa* is provided by Jean-Pierre Torrell, *Aquinas's Summa: Background, Structure, and Reception*, trans. Benedict M. Guevin (Washington, D.C.: Catholic University of America Press, 2005).

Other helpful guides to Thomas' philosophical views include Brian Davies and Eleonore Stump, eds., *The Oxford Handbook of Aquinas* (New York: Oxford University Press, 2012); Robert Pasnau and Christopher Shields, *The Philosophy of Aquinas* (Boulder, CO: Westview Press, 2004); Eleonore Stump, *Aquinas* (New York: Routledge, 2003); Norman Kretzmann and Eleonore Stump, eds., *The Cambridge Companion to Aquinas* (New York: Cambridge University Press, 1993); Brian Davies, *The Thought of Thomas Aquinas* (Oxford: Clarendon Press, 1992); and Étienne Gilson, *The Christian Philosophy of St. Thomas Aquinas* (New York: Random House, 1956).

Other helpful resources for delving specifically into the *Summa* include Stephen J. Loughlin, *Aquinas' Summa Theologiae* (New York: T&T Clark, 2010); and Brian Davies, ed., *Aquinas's Summa Theologiae: Critical Essays* (New York: Rowman & Littlefield, 2006).

For overview and analysis of the general approach and key themes characterizing scholasticism see Étienne Gilson, *The Spirit of Medieval Philosophy* (New York: Charles Scribner's Sons, 1936); Josef Pieper, *Scholasticism: Personalities and Problems of Medieval Philosophy* (New York: Pantheon Books, 1960); Norman Kretzmann, Anthony Kenny, and Jan Pinborg, eds., *The Cambridge History of Later Medieval Philosophy* (New York: Cambridge University Press, 1982); and A. S. McGrade, ed., *The Cambridge Companion to Medieval Philosophy* (New York: Cambridge University Press, 2003).

A collection of essays exploring the Augustinian themes in Thomas' theology can be found in Michael Dauphinais, Barry David, and Matthew Levering, eds., *Aquinas the Augustinian* (Washington, D.C.: Catholic University of America Press, 2007).

A thorough, but accessible, account of the "Aristotelian revolution" in scholasticism is Richard Rubenstein's *Aristotle's Children: How Christians, Muslims, and Jews Rediscovered Ancient Wisdom and Illuminated the Dark Ages* (San Diego, CA: Harcourt, 2003). The standard English translation of Aristotle's collected works is edited by Jonathan Barnes (Princeton, NJ: Princeton University Press, 1984).

The standard English translation of Thomas' *Summa contra Gentiles* is published in five volumes, with various translators, by the University of Notre Dame Press (1975). An excellent scholarly exegesis of the first two books of the *Summa contra Gentiles* is provided by Norman Kretzmann in his *The Metaphysics of Theism* (New York: Oxford

University Press, 1997) and *The Metaphysics of Creation* (New York: Oxford University Press, 1999)—Kretzmann was working on his exegesis of the third book when he passed away, but the first four chapters were published under the title "The Metaphysics of Providence" in the journal *Medieval Philosophy and Theology* 9:2 (2000).

The above quotation from Averroes's essay "On the Harmony of Religions and Philosophy" can be found in *The Philosophy and Theology of Averroes*, trans. Mohammed Jamil-al-Rahman (Baroda: A. G. Widgery, 1921).

The above quotation from Anselm's *Proslogion* can be found in the translation by Thomas Williams (Indianapolis, IN: Hackett, 1995).

The encyclicals of Popes Leo XIII (*Aeterni patris*) and John Paul II (*Fides et ratio*) are available on the Vatican's web-site: http://w2.vatican.va/content/leo-xiii/en/encyclicals/documents/hf_l-xiii_enc_04081879_aeterni-patris.html; and http://w2.vatican.va/content/john-paul-ii/en/encyclicals/documents/hf_jp-ii_enc_14091998_fides-et-ratio.html (accessed May 26, 2015).

For more on the history of Thomism, see Romanus Cessario, *A Short History of Thomism* (Washington, D.C.: Catholic University of America Press, 2005); John F. X. Knasas, *Being and Some Twentieth Century Thomists* (Bronx, NY: Fordham University Press, 2003); Gerald A. McCool, *The Neo-Thomists* (Milwaukee: Marquette University Press, 1994); McCool, *From Unity to Pluralism: The Internal Evolution of Thomism* (Bronx, NY: Fordham University Press, 1992); and Victor B. Brezik, *One Hundred Years of Thomism: Aeterni Patris and Afterwards* (Houston, TX: Center for Thomistic Studies, 1981).

Part II

THE *EXITUS/REDITUS* OF THE *SUMMA THEOLOGIAE*

Section 1

METAPHYSICAL STARTING-POINTS (*PRIMA PARS*)

2

GOD'S EXISTENCE AND ESSENCE

PREFACE—HOW TO READ THE *SUMMA*

Before embarking on our journey through Thomas Aquinas' *Summa theologiae*, a brief note is in order concerning *how* one ought to read the *Summa*. Since the present volume is a guidebook to the *Summa*, it will be presumed that you are reading it alongside your reading of a complete edition of the *Summa* itself; hence, quotations from the *Summa* will be sparse but specific questions and articles will be cited for easy cross-referencing. As discussed in the previous chapter, Thomas organized the *Summa* systematically and thus intended it to be read in its entirety; however, due to its voluminous nature, it is often encountered only in piecemeal fragments. Whether it helps readers to understand the logical ordering of the *Summa*'s questions, or facilitates selective reading of the most pertinent questions depending on one's topic of interest, each major part of the *Summa* is often presented as divided up into various "treatises." Hence, the first part (*prima pars*), comprising 119 questions altogether, is subdivided into treatises on God (Questions 1–43), creation (Questions 44–49), angels

(Questions 50–64), God's creative work as recorded in the Book of Genesis (Questions 65–74), human nature (Questions 75–102), and God's government of creation (Questions 103–119). Each major question is further divided into a series of sub-questions, or "articles." Thus, for example, Question 2 of the *prima pars* concerns "The Existence of God" and comprises three articles: 1) "Whether the existence of God is self-evident?"; 2) "Whether it can be demonstrated that God exists?"; and 3) "Whether God exists?"

Each article has four distinct components. First is a series of *objections* to the thesis Thomas holds, usually three or four of the strongest or most popular objections of the time, as compared to the more exhaustive list of objections Thomas raises and responds to in his *disputed questions*. The objections are followed by a direct assertion to the contrary (*sed contra*), which typically cites Scripture or an authoritative figure such as Aristotle, Augustine, or one of the Early Church Fathers. Thomas then lays out his detailed response (*respondeo*) that presents his argumentative support for the thesis asserted in the *sed contra*. Finally, Thomas replies to each of the previously presented objections. As we proceed through the *Summa*, we will primarily be focusing on the substantive arguments Thomas presents in the *respondeo* of various articles—cited forthwith in the form of Part, Question, Article, so that 'Ia, q. 2, a. 1' refers to the first article of the second question of the *prima pars* and 'Ia–IIae, q. 5, a. 3' refers to the third article of the fifth question of the *prima secundae*. Sometimes, an important objection or reply to an objection will be highlighted, which will be cited, e.g. as 'IIa–IIae, q. 30, a. 4 *obj*. 2,' referring to the second objection presented in the fourth article of the 30 question of the *secunda secundae*, or, in the case of the reply to this objection, 'IIa–IIae, q. 30, a. 4 *ad* 2.' Although rare, citations of the *sed contra* will utilize the initials '*s.c.*'—thus, 'IIIa, q. 14, a. 1 *s.c.*'. Finally, citations of any material from the "supplement" to the *Summa* that Thomas' secretary, Reginald, compiled from his earlier commentary on Peter Lombard's *Sentences* to round out the incomplete *tertia pars* will be preceded by 'Supp.' in place of 'IIIa.'

QUESTION 1—THE SUBJECT OF THE *SUMMA*

We are now ready to launch into the text of Thomas' *Summa*. In this initial chapter, we will focus on the initial 43 questions of the *prima pars* that form the treatise on God. There are three major topics covered in this treatise. The first is how it may be philosophically demonstrated that God exists (q. 2). After providing such a demonstration, Thomas proceeds to delineate the various qualities of the divine essence (qq. 3–13) and then focuses on God's operations of knowing and willing (qq. 14–26). The final set of questions concern the relations among the three persons of the divine Trinity (qq. 27–43).

There is one preliminary question that concerns the very subject of the *Summa* that sets the tone for Thomas' intellectual endeavor (q. 1). In this question, Thomas identifies the *Summa*'s mode of inquiry as "sacred doctrine" (*sacra doctrina*), which studies the truth God has revealed that goes beyond the limits of philosophical reasoning alone (a. 1) and the primary subject matter of which is God (a. 7). Thomas thereby makes clear from the outset that the *Summa* is first and foremost a *theological* work; interestingly, though, he does not identify the *Summa*'s mode of inquiry as "theology," but prefers "sacred doctrine" instead to distinguish his project from non-Christian theological investigations. Philosophical reasoning, however, plays a dual role in supporting the exploration of theological truths. First, there are some theological truths that are rationally *demonstrable*, such as the truth that God exists. Second, other theological truths that are not demonstrable by reason, but can be determined as true only through *faith* in the sources of divine revelation—Sacred Scripture and the Church's magisterial tradition—may nevertheless be shown to be rationally *coherent*. For example, while it is rationally demonstrable that God exists, it is not demonstrable that God exists as a Trinity of divine persons; however, belief in the Trinity is not *irrational* insofar as it can be shown that there is no internal incoherency in such a belief. Philosophy thus serves either to provide rational evidence for faith-based beliefs or to explain the rational coherency of such beliefs.

Thomas describes sacred doctrine as a *science* (a. 2), which may sound odd to modern ears accustomed to culture-war disputes of "faith vs. reason" or "religion vs. science." Ever since the Enlightenment and the development of the experimental methodology of the empirical sciences, the term "science" has typically been reserved for what, in Thomas' time, would have been referred to as the philosophy of nature. Although Thomas himself did not delve deeply into this realm of philosophical inquiry, his intellectual ancestor Aristotle certainly did, composing works on zoology, meteorology, physiology, and optics alongside his more abstract works on logic and metaphysics. The Latin term *scientia* refers to any form of knowledge and since God, as Thomas will argue later, is the source of all truth, then knowledge of God is the highest form of knowledge possible. Theology is thus not just *a* science, but the most noble and sublime of all the sciences (a. 5).

Thomas notes that the various sciences are ordered hierarchically: from the most empirically grounded that describe what is accessible to the senses, to those that postulate more general abstract theories to account for what is described in the lower sciences, to the most universal and ultimate explanation. Biology, as the science describing the structure and function of living organisms, depends upon the higher sciences of chemistry and physics, which describe how matter under different molecular and atomic forms interact with each other; these sciences, in turn, rely upon the science of reality itself—or "being *qua* being"—which Aristotle termed "metaphysics," leading to the science of the ultimate source of being, which is God. Hence, sacred doctrine is the highest science and furthermore "is wisdom above all human wisdom" precisely insofar as its practitioners study "the highest cause of the whole universe" (a. 6). As such, sacred doctrine is the most difficult of all the sciences to comprehend since only God knows His own essence directly and completely, which is why God reveals certain theological truths that would otherwise be incomprehensible to the limited human intellect. These revealed truths serve as "first principles" for any scientific inquiry, even if the inquirer is not explicitly relying on such truths or even denies their validity.

Hence, an atheistic cosmologist, investigating the nature and origin of the physical universe, presupposes in her investigation that there is indeed a physical universe—that is, she does not believe she is being deceived by a Cartesian "evil demon" or is unknowingly plugged into "The Matrix." If she were to investigate this presupposition, she would move from cosmological to metaphysical inquiry about the being (*esse*) of the universe. This investigation, according to Thomas, if conducted with proper and unbiased reasoning, would eventually lead her to the necessity of acknowledging the existence of a single source of the universe's being—a *creator*: God. Having established that the subject of the highest form of science is God

(a. 7) and arguing that no philosophical demonstration could contradict revealed theological truths since such truths are grounded in the very source of all truth (a. 8), Thomas is positioned to demonstrate that the subject of the highest science does indeed exist, in accord with what is revealed by Scripture.

Concerning Scriptural revelation itself, as noted in the previous chapter, Thomas is not a "Biblical literalist" in the way so-called "fundamentalist" Christians are today. He acknowledges that the Bible is shot-through with *metaphors* that allow the human intellect to better grasp divine truths (a. 9). It is not that Thomas thinks Scripture is devoid of certain historical facts that can be taken as literally true, but that any such historical truths must also be understood to have a threefold "spiritual sense" (a. 10). First, there is the *allegorical* prefiguring of the New Testament by events and persons comprising the Hebrew Testament; for example, the "suffering servant" described poetically by the prophet Isaiah (52:13–53:12) may be seen as a representation of Christ. Second, as a human being like us in all things but sin, Christ's actions serve as *moral* exemplars for how human beings ought to act. Third, what is recorded in Scripture *anagogically* signifies the eternal glory of God's Kingdom that we have not yet experienced, but for which believers live in hope.

QUESTION 2—ARGUMENTS FOR GOD'S EXISTENCE

Reading through Thomas' arguments for God's existence, a first question that may come to mind is why he felt the need to provide this demonstration. After all, the *Summa* is a work of *theology* and is addressed to avowed Dominicans. So could not the existence of God simply be presupposed? The primary purpose of the five arguments Thomas employs to demonstrate God's existence is to show that the subject of theological science exists, which in turn validates theology as based not only on revealed truth but also upon reason. Such validation is important because, even though God is the source of all truth and thus theology is the highest science, the limited powers of the human intellect allow for one to doubt this first principle.

As Thomas explains, God's existence is in itself a *self-evident* truth insofar as God's very essence is *to exist*. God's existence, however, is not necessarily known to be true by every human mind (a. 1).

Thomas rejects Augustine's theory of divine "illumination," whereby knowledge of God and other self-evident truths are directly infused in the human intellect and one can become aware of them through contemplative introspection (a. 1 *obj*. 1); although, not wholly divesting himself of Augustine's neo-Platonic influence, Thomas later characterizes the functioning of a human being's *agent intellect* as a "participation" in the light of the divine intellect (Ia, q. 79, a. 4) and also allows for God to infuse intellectual ideas directly into a human being's *separated* soul persisting between bodily death and resurrection (Ia, q. 89, a. 1).

Thomas also considers and rejects the so-called "ontological argument" presented by Anselm of Canterbury (*c*. 1033–1109). Anselm's argument begins with a purportedly self-evident definition of God as "that thing than which nothing greater can be conceived" (a. 1 *obj*. 2). Anselm then proceeds to show that such a being must exist not only conceptually, but also in reality; otherwise, anything that does exist in reality would be greater than the greatest conceivable being, which entails a contradiction. Thomas offers a threefold response invalidating Anselm's argument: 1) not everyone understands the term "God" to refer to the greatest conceivable being; 2) even those who understand the term "God" in this way do not necessarily understand that the being to which this term refers exists outside of the mind; and 3) in order to convince those who do not understand that the being to which the term "God" refers exists in reality, one must presume that there does exist in reality something the greater than which cannot be conceived, which begs the question at hand (a. 1 *ad* 2). To clarify this last contention, Thomas is claiming that the greatest being that exists in reality may not in fact be the greatest being of which one could conceive; the latter being could exist in the mind alone as merely the greatest *conceivable* being, period—only sensory *experience*, or an inference therefrom, can affirm whether any being that conceptually exists also exists in reality outside of one's mind.

Even if, however, the ontological argument is valid—and it certainly has its defenders today against the question-begging charge—Thomas is still correct that not everyone agrees that the term "God" refers to the greatest conceivable being. Not that Thomas denies that God is the greatest conceivable being, but rather Anselm's argument, even if valid, is not *convincing*. Since the human mind is incapable of grasping immediately and completely the divine essence, the existence of this essence in reality cannot be demonstrated simply and directly, as the existence of an effect can be demonstrated through knowledge of its cause. Instead, Thomas purports to demonstrate the existence of the cause of all things—God—by way of inference from various effects that are evident in the created universe (a. 2). Thus, each of Thomas' five arguments begins with a premise that is known to be true by every human mind—that is, some *empirically* known truth that is immediately evident to the senses and reason. Based on these five empirical truths, Thomas is able to rationally infer the existence of some ultimate foundation for each of these truths—a type of being that must exist if each of these truths is to hold. Thomas concludes each argument by stating that the type of being demonstrated by each argument is what everyone refers to by the name "God" (a. 3). It is important to note that the "God" demonstrated to exist by each of these arguments is not immediately shown to be the *personal* God of the Abrahamic faith traditions. Nevertheless, there are certain qualities that the God demonstrated by these five arguments must possess in order to function as the type of being each argument proves to exist. In subsequent questions, Thomas philosophically derives various qualities that define God's essence, contrary to the view of theologians who hold that God's essence cannot be described by human intellectual categories.

Thomas' first argument for God's existence begins with an empirical phenomenon that he takes to be the most directly evident to the human mind, requiring no degree of intellectual sophistication to understand: the fact of *motion*. By this term, Thomas means both *locomotion*—change in location—as well as any *change* whatsoever. The fact that things change is probably the most evident of things we see around us, but Thomas provides a deeper metaphysical description of change as a movement from a state of *potentiality* to a state of *actuality*. This is a key principle of Aristotelian physics and metaphysics we will encounter repeatedly throughout our exploration of the *Summa*. To explain this principle, Thomas uses the example of a piece of wood, which is potentially hot, and fire, which is actually hot. In order for a piece of wood to become hot, it must come into contact with the fire that is already hot. This principle applies to everything that is subject to change: "But nothing can be reduced from potentiality to actuality, except by something in a state of actuality" (a. 3). Consider the burning match used to light the wood on fire. It did not spontaneously combust, but was itself moved from a state of potentially burning to a state of actually burning by having been struck against a sufficiently rough surface to create a spark due to friction. In order for the spark to occur, the match and the struck surface must be actualized in certain specific ways—each must have certain qualities—such that an appropriate degree of friction will occur; striking a match against a smooth glass surface will not result in a spark. Furthermore, the match is not able to strike itself against the other surface, but must be moved by something else already in a state of actual motion: a hand.

The next central premise of the argument from motion is that there cannot be an *infinite series* of "moved movers." Thomas is not referring to an *accidentally ordered* series—e.g. a temporally ordered series stretching backwards in time, such as a series of biological generations like those reported in the Gospel of Luke 3:23–38. Rather, he is referring to an *essentially ordered* series of beings that must be actualized in relevant ways if an ordered progression from potentiality to actuality is going to occur leading to any observed change (Ia, q. 46, a. 2 *ad* 7). For instance, (a) my desire to be warm (b) actualizes my arm to move in such a way that (c) my hand strikes a match against a rough surface in order (d) to cause a spark that (e) ignites the match so that I may then (f) burn a piece of wood. Events (b) through (f) are accidentally ordered to one another, such that one of them may occur without the subsequent one following—e.g. (c) may occur without (d) following if, say, the match were damp—or one of them may occur without its antecedent—e.g. (d) may occur by means other than (c), such as striking two stones against each other. Events (b) through (f), however, are essentially ordered to (a): were (a) absent, none of the other events would occur—in other words, everything depends upon my persistent desire to be warm. If, for example, I initially desired to be warm and thereby struck and ignited the match, but then someone hands me a coat before I set the wood aflame, my desire to be warm by means of lighting a fire may cease. There will thus be no event (f) since that event would only follow from (e) if (a) were still actualized, which it no longer is once I have a warm coat. In sum, in an essentially ordered series, if one of the essential elements is removed from the chain, the entire process will be disrupted: without my desire to be warm both *initiating* and causally *sustaining* the chain of events from (b) through (f), those events will not occur.

Thomas contends that there cannot be an infinite series of essentially ordered events as there cannot be an *actually* infinite multitude of any real beings (Ia, q. 7, a. 4). For example, there can be an infinite series of positive integers insofar as numbers are, in themselves, conceptual beings; however, one cannot *actually count* all of the positive integers for such activity would never be completed—there will always be another potential number to which one could actually count. In order actually to count all of the positive integers, there would have to be a *last* number to which one could count and complete the series. This does not present a problem, however, since numbers are only accidentally ordered—as evidenced by the fact that one can start or stop counting at any random number or denote arbitrary limits for any ordered series of numbers (1 to 100; 153 to 1,917; 597,113 to 1,285,312). For an essentially ordered series, however—such as an actual series of moved movers—there must be a *first* mover that is not moved by anything else. Rather, its very nature is to be actual in whatever ways would be necessary to actualize all other motion in the universe. Thomas thus concludes that there is such an "unmoved mover" and the term "God" is properly applied to this being. Later, he will show that God alone, as the first mover, must be *purely actual* and not potential in any way (Ia, q. 9).

The second argument for God's existence is structurally quite similar to the first. The main difference is that the observed phenomenon that starts off the argument is not motion (or change) itself but the *causal* relationship that underlies the movement from potentiality to actuality. Here, we should note the different types of "causes" that Thomas employs in his explanatory framework. In both *Physics* (Book II, Ch. 3) and *Metaphysics* (Book V, Ch. 2), Aristotle defines four causes of any being. The *material* cause is the matter that composes it, that out of which it is produced—e.g. the marble out of which a statue is made. The *formal* cause is the shape or other qualities that define it as the type of thing it is; in scholastic terms, the formal cause answers the question, *quid est?* (What is it?)—e.g. the figure of David into which a hunk of marble may be shaped. The *efficient* cause is the agent or activity that instantiates the form in the matter, that which produces the thing—e.g. Michelangelo shaping a hunk of marble into the figure of David. The *final* cause is the end or purpose for which the thing is produced—e.g. to be a piece of art, to be a source of income for Michelangelo, to bring Michelangelo fame, etc. In his second argument for God's existence, Thomas is utilizing the notion of efficient causation in reference to the agent that actualizes the potential of something else, thereby effecting a change in the latter.

Just as nothing can move itself from a state of potentiality into actuality, but must be so moved by something else that is already actual in the relevant fashion, nothing can be its own efficient cause but must be caused efficiently by something else. It would be inherently contradictory for something to be its own cause, because then it would have to pre-exist itself. An effect does not exist until it is caused, but a cause must exist in order to bring about its effect. Thomas recognizes that there may be complex levels of causation, even when focusing just on efficient causation, and thus a series of "caused causes" that all contribute to any particular effect. For example, soil, water, and sunlight all act upon a seed to cause it to grow into a tree; take away any one of these causal agents and the seed will not grow. In the earlier case of (f) the wood being set aflame, (e) the lit match, (d) the spark resulting from friction, (c) the hand moving the match across the rough surface to generate the spark, and (b) the arm moving the hand, all function as caused causes in an *ordered series*. All of these events, however, are only *accidentally* ordered since any one of them could occur without either its antecedent—if some other cause were present—or its consequent—if something interfered with the causal relationship. There is, however, an *essentially ordered* cause of this series: (a) one's desire to be warm—absent this desire, none of the other events in the causal chain would follow. Once again, there cannot be an actually infinite series of essentially ordered causes; and so there must be some first "uncaused cause." Although not explicitly argued for here, Thomas implicitly identifies the uncaused cause with the unmoved mover of the first argument and states that the term "God" applies to both.

Thomas' third argument begins with the observation that things in the world come into being and then later pass away, which means they have the *possibility to be or not to be*. Contemporary metaphysicians refer to this possibility as *contingent existence*; although Thomas restricts his use of "contingency" to *physical* things subject to generation and corruption, as distinct from "necessary" beings not subject to physical generation or corruption, but nevertheless could possibly not exist—such as incorporeal angels whose nature is purely intellectual, as we will discuss in the next chapter.

The book you are holding contingently exists insofar as it did not exist in 2010 and it can pass out of existence if it were committed to the flames. It is also contingent in that it need not have ever existed at all; if I had not written this book and the publisher put it into print, it never would have existed. It is evident, according to Thomas, that everything that exists in the universe is contingent; perhaps even the universe itself is contingent. Although it is difficult to conceptualize absolute *nothingness*, it is not an incoherent concept. Nevertheless, the fact that everything in the universe is contingent does not logically entail that the universe itself is; such reasoning would commit the *fallacy of composition*—claiming that something is true of a whole just because it is true of each of its parts.

To avoid this fallacy, Thomas argues that, given an infinite amount of time, all possible sets of contingent beings will be realized. For example, at the present time both you and the book you are holding exist, but you may have existed at a time when this book did not—assuming you were born before it was published—and the book may exist at a time when you do not if it is still around after your death. One of the possible sets is the *null*-set in which no contingent beings exist. Thomas then makes a problematic assertion that, given the possibility of the null-set at some point in the past, nothing would exist now since there would have been no actual being to cause any other contingent being to exist; no being can self-generate *ex nihilo* ("out of nothing"). This assertion is problematic in two ways. First, it does not appear to avoid the fallacy of composition as it is not logically necessary that the null-set ever exist; it could be the case that there is at least one contingent being at any given time. Second, it rests on the contestable premise of time stretching infinitely into the past. As discussed in the previous chapter, the possibility of a universe without a temporal beginning is philosophically reasonable, according to Thomas, but so is a universe that is not temporally infinite and the latter is what Thomas actually believes as a matter of faith.

Regardless of these issues, Thomas concludes that if the only beings that exist are contingent, and that there was a time in the past at which no contingent beings existed, then nothing would now exist, which is clearly false. He also considers the existence of necessary beings—that is, beings not subject to physical generation and corruption, such as incorporeal angels—that may possibly not exist and thus derive the necessity of their existence from another being; repeating a fundamental premise of the previous two arguments, Thomas concludes that there cannot be an actually infinite regress in the chain of causation of such necessary beings. Therefore, there must be an *absolutely necessary* being—a being that neither comes into existence nor passes away, that *must* exist at all times—so that the null-set could never have been the case. This argument is Thomas' version of the so-called "cosmological argument" that purports to respond to the question, "Why is there something rather than nothing?" Since no contingent being could, either alone or collectively, sufficiently answer this question, there must be a necessary being responsible for causing the existence of potentially existing contingent beings—either directly or by virtue of causing one contingent being that causes another contingent being and so on. Thomas thus implicitly links the necessary being demonstrated by his third argument with the uncaused cause and unmoved mover of his other two arguments. At this point, one may wonder whether each of these arguments, if sound, leads to the conclusion that there is only *one* necessary being, uncaused cause, or unmoved mover. The short answer is, no, these arguments alone do not entail that there is only one being to which the term "God" is applicable; Thomas' argument for there being only one God will come later (Ia, q. 11).

The empirical foundation of Thomas' fourth argument is the evident *gradations* of various qualities found among different types of beings. Consider the following predications of the term "good": My daughter is a good student; Vanilla ice cream tastes good; Pope Francis is a good person. It is clear that the term "good" is not being used in the exact same fashion in each of these cases; it is being used *analogously*. Analogous use of a term means that it does not have the exact same—*univocal*—meaning in each case, as the term "human" does when it is predicated of both Socrates and myself. It does not, however, have a completely different—*equivocal*—meaning in each case, as the term "bank" does when it refers to a building where money is stored securely versus the side of a river or the sharp turn of an airplane. Rather, there is some quality possessed by my daughter in her capacity as a student, by vanilla ice cream when I taste it, and by Pope Francis that is accurately termed "good" in each case. It is clear, though, that this quality is not possessed to the same degree in all three cases. For my daughter to be a good student is *better* than for ice cream to taste good; it is preferable for my daughter to be a good student than for ice cream to be delicious—I wouldn't trade my daughter's academic excellence for a tasty ice cream cone. On the other hand, Pope Francis's nature as a good person is superior to both academic excellence and deliciousness; it is preferable for my daughter to be a morally admirable person like Pope Francis than to be the smartest person in the room.

What goes for goodness goes for other qualities such as being, truth, nobility, and beauty. All of these qualities are classified, by Thomas and his neo-Platonic predecessors, as *transcendentals*—meaning that they transcend Aristotle's categories of different types of beings and qualities to refer to qualities that *all* beings possess in commensurate degrees. Thus, all beings are good to whatever degree that they exist. Beings *exist* to varying degrees based on the different *intrinsic potentialities* they possess due to their respective natures. For example, a living organism has more intrinsic potentialities, which allow it to sustain its own existence, grow, and reproduce, than an inert rock has. A sentient animal has more intrinsic potentialities, which allow it to be consciously aware of its environment and to move itself, than a plant. Finally, a human being, as a *rational* animal, has more intrinsic potentialities than other animals, as we will discuss further later on. Hence, the existence of an animal is greater than that of a plant, and that of a human being has more value than that of another animal; this does not entail that humans may treat animals in any way they see fit, but it does allow humans to utilize animals in ways that are necessary to sustain their own existence and flourishing.

Given the evident gradations of different types of beings, Thomas argues that there must be some *highest exemplar* that instantiates each of the transcendental qualities to their maximal degree so that not only comparisons of the different gradations may be intelligible, but also the very existence of such qualities in their varied degrees is possible: every being possesses existence, truth, beauty, goodness, and nobility to the extent that it exemplifies the most perfect being who possesses all of these qualities maximally and is the cause of such qualities in all other beings. Such a perfect being, echoing Anselm's *Monologion*, is that to which the term "God" is properly applied. God thus serves as the *extrinsic formal cause*, as well as the efficient cause, of everything that exists. An "extrinsic formal cause" is the ideal form that pre-exists the particular form that is instantiated in a material substance. For example, before carving marble into the statue of David, Michelangelo had an idea in his mind for how the statue should appear that guided his carving of the marble to instantiate that form: the idea in Michelangelo's mind is the extrinsic formal cause of the statue; once carved, the marble now possesses *intrinsically* the form of David. As we will see in more detail when discussing the nature of creation and God's creative activity, everything that exists instantiates forms that first exist as ideal *exemplars* in the divine mind; the transcendental qualities, however, are not merely divine ideas, but are definitive qualities of the divine essence possessed to a perfect degree.

Thomas' fifth argument for God's existence begins with the evident *ordering* of beings in the universe toward their own flourishing and the collective functioning of the universe as a whole. Here, the operative notion is that of *final causality*—that is, everything acts for the sake of some end. Some beings are consciously aware of the ends toward which they act, as a lion is aware of the gazelle it is hunting in order to satisfy its hunger—although the lion may not be consciously thinking about the *connection* between its hunger and its desire to eat the gazelle. Human beings, on the other hand, are not only aware of the ends toward which they act, but are capable of *deliberating* about those ends and *choosing* among alternatives that are judged to contribute toward their flourishing—we will discuss this further in reference to Ia–IIae, qq. 1–5. But even non-conscious entities, such as plants and rocks, act for the sake of naturally instilled ends: plants take in nutrients, sunlight, and water in order to grow and a rock succumbs to the gravitational attraction between itself and the Earth's iron core caused by their respective masses when it falls to the ground—the law of gravity describes a feature of the universe's structure that allows for ordered physical activities that would otherwise be chaotic.

Thomas draws an analogy that, just as an arrow does not direct itself toward its target but is guided there by the aiming of an archer, the universe and its constituent entities do not direct themselves toward their respective ends, but rather follow a causal ordering established by divine intelligence. Even human beings, despite having the ability to deliberate and choose which ends to pursue, are guided by a divinely instilled intrinsic desire for "happiness," and deliberation, if properly executed, should lead to certain objective conclusions about what will lead to happiness in accord with human nature—more on this when we discuss the *secunda pars*.

It is important to note that Thomas is not employing the so-called "argument from design" critiqued by David Hume in his *Dialogues Concerning Natural Religion*. The argument the character Cleanthes defends in that dialogue is an argument *by* analogy; whereas Thomas only utilizes the archer analogy for illustrative purposes, while the foundation of his argument is the concept of final causality. Neither is Thomas' argument the same as the "intelligent design" thesis defended primarily by contemporary Evangelical Christians against the Darwinian account of biological evolution through natural selection. Thomas' view, in fact, is compatible with an evolutionary account insofar as every living being is naturally driven to sustain and reproduce itself, and those which are more successful in pursuing that end than others succeed in replicating their genome; as different species evolve over time, other naturally desired ends emerge, such as an animal's desire for *pleasure* in addition to merely surviving and reproducing, higher mammalian species' desire for *social relationships*, and human beings' desire for *knowledge*. Of course, all of these emergent natural desires can be accounted for within an evolutionary account by their contributing to survival and reproductive advantage, but that does not belie their existence as naturally instilled *ends* toward which each type of living being directly acts. Even if an evolutionary explanatory framework weakens Thomas' fifth argument as a *demonstration* of God's existence, the two frameworks are at least *compatible* explanations at two levels of scientific inquiry—one physical and the other metaphysical/theological.

It is worth noting the two objections to which Thomas responds in this article, for both are echoed by contemporary theorists who deny God's existence. The first raises what is known as the "problem of evil," which, in this form, finds God's infinite goodness incompatible with the evident evil in the world (a. 3 *obj*. 1). A complete response to this problem comprises various points Thomas makes throughout the

Summa, culminating in his treatment of the incarnation and Christ's redemptive sacrifice in the *tertia pars*. In his reply here, Thomas cites approvingly Augustine's thesis that God *permits* evil to occur only as a means for His goodness and power to become manifest in actively bringing a greater good out of such evil (a. 3 *ad* 1). Of course, such "greater good" may not always be apparent to the limited human intellect: Did the Holocaust and humanity's collective remembrance of it prevent an even greater genocide from occurring in the future? Thomas' brief reply characterizes God as a sort of *consequentialist*; but this conclusion would be too hasty without the full picture of Thomas' account of God's response to evil.

The other objection Thomas considers applies the notion of *ontological parsimony*—later labeled as "Ockham's Razor" in honor of a 14th-century Franciscan scholar. The objection asserts that one ought not to postulate the existence of God if the natural world can be sufficiently explained by natural principles and the operations of the human will (a. 3 *obj.* 2). Placing his reply after the article's *respondeo*, in which he lays out his five arguments for God's existence, Thomas is able to appeal to his previous demonstrations that the principles of nature that govern motion (change), causal relationships, and the ordering of natural activities toward specific ends are not self-explanatory, but require the postulation of an intelligent being that is both first mover and first cause in order to sufficiently explain these observed natural phenomena. Furthermore, the contingent existence of natural beings, including human beings and their volitions, requires the postulation of a being whose existence is necessary (a. 3 *ad* 2).

QUESTIONS 3–26—THE DIVINE PERFECTIONS

Having thus established that the subject of theological science exists, Thomas next considers what such scientific inquiry can tell us about the nature of this subject. This is a tricky endeavor insofar as God, unlike the created beings inhabiting the natural world, does not have a nature that is definable within the limited categories that the human intellect utilizes to differentiate genera and species of being in the world. Rather, God's nature is simply *to exist*; Thomas thus asserts that the biblical name YAHWEH given by God to Moses (Exodus 3:14)— translated by Thomas as "He Who Is"—is the most proper name of

God (q. 13, a. 11). This does not preclude predicating other qualities of the divine nature beyond existence. There are basically three ways in which to proceed. One approach is the *apophatic*—or "negative way" (*via negativa*)—in which one discerns what God is *not* based on what one already knows about God through the conclusions of the previous five arguments for God's existence. For example, Thomas argues that, because God is both the First Mover and the First Being who causes all other beings to exist by virtue of moving them from a state of potentiality to actuality, God can only be in a state of *pure actuality* with no admixture of potentiality. Hence, Thomas concludes, God *cannot* be a body (q. 3, a. 1). The second approach predicates certain qualities to God *positively* on the basis of what has already been demonstrated about God's relationship to creation. For example, since God is the First Cause of all other beings—not just as a remote *initiator* of their existence, but as an immanent *sustainer* thereof—God must be *omnipresent*: that is, God is in all things everywhere by virtue of His creative power (q. 8). Note that this is quite different from *pantheism*, in which God's being is reduced to mere immanence within, or even to being a product of, the totality of created beings—think of "Eywa" in James Cameron's *Avatar* or the "Force" in George Lucas *Star Wars*. Rather, while God is immanently present to all created beings as their first efficient cause, He remains essentially transcendent as existing outside of the natural world. The third approach, which we will discuss further when we reach Question 13, is by discerning *analogous* qualities that God possesses as creator of other beings that possess such qualities, which is a logical consequence of Thomas' fourth argument concluding that God possesses perfectly the transcendental qualities of being, goodness, truth, beauty, and unity.

As noted, Thomas begins in Question 3 by arguing that God cannot be a body, since material existence entails potentiality (a. 1), which leads directly to the conclusion that God is not composed of matter and form (a. 2). Since there is no composition in God's being, Thomas concludes that God is *identical* with His essence or nature (a. 3). To understand this last claim, consider an individual human being. No individual human being is identical to *humanity*, the formal essence in which all human beings share. Rather, humanity becomes *individuated* into the distinct material *supposits* by virtue of various hunks of "designated matter," which occupy three-dimensional space and which each instantiates the human essence, resulting in the form/ matter composites that are you, me, President Obama, etc. The divine essence, on the other hand, is not individuated in terms of distinct material supposits. Thus, Thomas concludes, while no human being is identical with the human essence, God is identical with His essence. Hence, whatever qualities are predicated of the divine essence are *identified* with God's being. For instance, instead of stating "God is good," as if goodness were some sort of property that God possesses in the same manner that Pope Francis has goodness, it is most properly stated that "God is goodness itself" and that Pope Francis is good insofar as he *exemplifies*—albeit to a limited degree—God's absolute goodness (q. 6). Denying that God is composed of matter and form, or is distinct from His essence or any of the qualities that define the divine essence, Thomas concludes, quoting Augustine, that "God is truly and absolutely simple" (q. 3, a. 7 *s.c.*).

Thomas, as seen above, argues that God cannot be a body or be composed of matter and form insofar as God is purely actual insofar as God is the "unmoved mover" and the "uncaused cause." This directly entails that God is *perfect*, meaning that there is nothing lacking in God's nature (q. 4). If God lacked some quality or activity, then God would not be fully actual. One might think at this point, what about *evil*? Doesn't God lack evil and so there is potentiality in God's nature? It is important to keep in mind Thomas' view that evil does not, strictly speaking, exist. Rather, evil is a *privation* of goodness, just as blindness is a privation of sight or darkness a privation of light (q. 48, a. 1). Thus, in Questions 5 and 6, Thomas relates goodness and being, and concludes that God, insofar as He perfectly exists, is also perfectly good. God would not be more perfect or more fully actualized if He possessed evil in addition to goodness; for evil subtracts from one's perfection and puts one in a state of *potentially* being good as opposed to being *actually* good to the maximal degree.

If God is perfect and fully actual, then it follows that God's being, power, knowledge, goodness, etc., are *infinite*; for any limits on God's existence or essential qualities would entail potentiality to be or have more and thus a lack of perfection (q. 7). Furthermore, God's infinity entails the conclusion mentioned earlier that God is present in all things everywhere (q. 8). There is no limit on where or when God exists or acts.

Two other qualities that follow directly from God's perfection are *immutability* and *eternity*. If God is fully actual and lacks nothing, then there is no potential for God to actualize, which is the very definition of "change" as noted in the first argument for God's existence. Something only changes in order to gain some quality that it currently lacks, but God lacks nothing; hence, God does not change (q. 9). If God does not change, then God exists outside of *time*; for time, as defined by Aristotle in Book IV of his *Physics*, is the measure of change. Thomas thus concludes that God is eternal, adopting Boethius' definition of eternity as "the simultaneously-whole and perfect possession of interminable life" (q. 10, a. 1).

We must be careful here to determine precisely what this definition means. It does not mean to enjoy *everlasting* existence, which is to exist *throughout* the temporal continuum. If there will be no end to the existence of the created universe, then it will last forever; however, time clearly passes within the created universe and so the universe's potentially limitless existence is not eternal. Also, since the universe's future existence has not yet occurred, it doesn't possess its entire existence perfectly as a simultaneous-whole. Of course, as temporal beings, it is difficult to conceptualize the nature of eternal existence, but we can gain a rough idea by considering God's eternal perspective on the temporal world. According to Thomas, God's infinite knowledge (*omniscience*) comprises God's own essence and everything that exists insofar as it is causally and formally dependent on God's essence (q. 14). In describing God's knowledge, Thomas asserts that it is not *discursive* insofar as discursive reasoning involves *successive* movement from one premise to another to another, etc., leading to a conclusion. God, however, "sees all things together, and not successively" (a. 7). He later concludes that God knows "future contingent things" since "all things that are in time are present to God from eternity" (a. 13); future events are contingent *relative to us* since we are temporal beings who have yet to experience or act in the future, but God knows all events from an *atemporal* perspective in which the terms "past," "present," and "future" are not truly applicable.

Properly speaking, there is no "future" from God's point of view, only from ours; all events are simultaneously *present* to God. This does not mean that God perceives a disordered jumble of events all at once; God perceives all temporal events in their proper ordering of "before" and "after." God knows that His speaking to Moses from the burning bush occurs before the battle of Jericho and that the resurrection of the dead occurs after the battle of Jericho. Nevertheless, it would not be proper to refer to God acting by the use of *tensed* verbs, such that God *spoke* to Moses or *will* raise the dead. From God's perspective, He *is* speaking to Moses, bringing down the walls of Jericho, sustaining your existence while reading this book, and raising you from the dead. To understand roughly what the eternal perspective is like, consider reading a page in a comic book in which your eyes take in all of the panels in one glance instead of looking at each panel successively. You know that the panels are ordered such that the action that occurs in the top-left panel is prior to the action in the bottom-right panel, but you're able to comprehend all of the action in one perceptual moment.

The final quality of the divine essence that Thomas concludes through the *via negativa* is God's *unity*, which entails a lack of division that would contradict God's simplicity. Furthermore, Thomas argues that there can be only *one* God due to "the infinity of His perfection"; for, if there were more than one God, then the two would have to be differentiated by virtue of one possessing a quality that the other lacked, which would violate the essential divine quality of absolute perfection. Finally, alluding back to his fifth argument for God's existence, Thomas infers that the created universe's order implies a single intelligence ordering each type of being to its natural end for the sake of universal harmony (q. 11, a. 3).

In Questions 12 and 13, Thomas considers whether God, as defined by the previous questions, is knowable by the human intellect and how it is that one can speak *positively* of the qualities of the divine essence and not simply reason from what God is *not*. Thomas' first thesis is that the human intellect can know the divine essence, which follows from our natural desire to know the ultimate cause of things (q. 12, a. 1). Although, the intellect cannot know the divine essence by means of its own natural powers, but requires *grace* to enlighten it with such knowledge since the natural mode of human knowing is through sense-perception and God is not a sensible material body (a. 2); Thomas thus preserves a functional space for Augustine's concept of "divine illumination." This conclusion invokes an important principle in scholastic epistemology: whatever is known is known according to the mode of the knower. Consider the sun, which as the source of light is the most eminently visible object in the solar system. The sun's light, however, can only be received in a limited fashion due to the structure of the retina. Furthermore, to stare directly at the sun would overpower the retina and destroy one's capacity to receive any of the sun's light, at least temporarily. Finally, some people have better functioning eyes than others, and so visibility will differ, not with respect to the sun itself, but with respect to the individual sensory capacity of those who see by its light.

Analogously, Thomas states that the divine essence is eminently knowable, but actual knowledge of God will be relative to the various intellectual capacities of different persons. By acknowledging that different individuals have varying intellectual capacities to know God, Thomas is not distinguishing, say, Albert Einstein from someone who is cognitively impaired. Rather, having established that grace is required to grant knowledge of the divine essence to the human intellect, individuals will merit such grace and its attendant knowledge to different degrees based on their relative perfection according to the virtue of *charity*. For charity is the virtue of *love* for God that yields the *desire* to know God: the more intense one's love for God, the more intense one's desire to know God, the more grace one will receive to know the divine essence (a. 6).

Although Thomas reasons that the human intellect cannot know God's essence without divine grace, and that such knowledge can be had by the intellect only when it is separated from its natural mode of knowing through its material body (a. 11), limited knowledge of the divine essence can be naturally attained by reasoning from God's effects in the created world (a. 12)—as Thomas has been doing for the past several questions—both apophatically and by means of affirmative predication (q. 13, a. 12). Care must be taken, however, in predicating qualities to God insofar as how such qualities exist in the divine essence differ significantly from how they are found in any created essence.

This leads us to Thomas' famous doctrine of *analogy*. Thomas explains that when we predicate some quality to God, such as goodness or wisdom, we ought not to think merely in terms of God's being the *most good* or the *most wise* being; for such implies that goodness and wisdom exist separately from God, which Thomas has shown earlier is not the case. Rather, God *is* goodness and truth in themselves. Thus, for God to be good is simply to be Himself and to be wise is to know Himself. Thomas thereby contends that one cannot speak of God's goodness and wisdom and that of, say, Pope Saint John Paul II in a *univocal* fashion. Nor, however, should these terms be taken to be completely *equivocal* between God and creatures; as Thomas' fourth argument demonstrates, God is the formal exemplar cause of such qualities in creation as well as being—per the second argument—their first efficient cause: "Thus, whatever is said of God and creatures, is said according to the relation of a creature to God as its principle and cause, wherein all perfections of things pre-exist excellently" (q. 13, a. 5). Thomas concludes that there is an *analogical* relationship between the concepts of goodness and wisdom as predicated of God and as predicated of creatures. To understand what it means for St. John Paul II to be good and wise is to understand *somewhat* what it means for God to be perfectly good and wise; but even the vision of the divine essence with which St. John Paul II has now presumably been graced does not entail perfect comprehension of God's goodness or wisdom as these infinite qualities cannot be fully grasped by the limited human intellect (q. 12, a. 7)—one can only pour so much liquid into a finite container.

In discussing God's knowledge, Thomas invokes a concept common to both Platonic and Aristotelian metaphysics: that of "form." As Thomas explains in Question 15, forms are the *types* that categorize various species of being, as well as the *principle* inherent in each individual being whereby it can be known as belonging to a specific type. For example, there is a *form of humanity* that exists, according to Thomas, in the mind of God as an exemplar—similar to a blueprint for a house that exists in the mind of a builder—that is also instantiated in each individual human being—just as the form of the house in the builder's mind becomes instantiated in the actual brick-and-mortar of a particular house once built. The intellectual capacity to receive cognitively the forms of various types of beings—a process that will be explained later—leads to the apprehension of *truth* and, insofar as the received forms exist perfectly in the mind of God as the exemplar causes of all types of beings, God not only has perfect knowledge but in fact *is truth itself* (q. 16, a. 5). Insofar as created beings may fall short of exemplifying the perfect form in the mind of God, or may not be accurately or fully comprehended by a human being's senses or intellect, *falsity* enters into the picture (q. 17).

Questions 18 through 25 concern God's *activity*. Thomas first notes that the term "life" is properly attributed to God insofar as "a thing is said to live in so far as it operates of itself and not as moved by another" (q. 18, a. 3). God, as the purely actual "unmoved mover," perfectly exemplifies this concept. Other intellectual beings—angels and human beings—who have *free will*, exemplify life in an analogous fashion; while other types of living beings—non-rational animals and plants—move themselves by virtue of their *natural inclination* toward nutrition, warmth, and whatever else they may require to survive, thrive, and reproduce.

God's being alive entails that God has a *will*, which follows from God possessing an intellect; for one's intellect comprehends the nature of beings, which includes each being's relative degree of goodness and to be good is to be desirable (q. 19, a. 1). Thus, whatever one's intellect comprehends it desires to the degree that it perceives the subject as good—we will study this operation in detail in the later treatises on human nature and activity. God, of course, perfectly comprehends every being, including Himself as the supreme good; hence, God desires His own self and every other being insofar as it has a measure of goodness according to its specific nature (a. 2)—recall that, at the conclusion of each day of creation in the Book of Genesis, God declares that whatever has been created is good.

A key question concerning God's will is whether, whatever God wills, He does so *necessarily* (a. 3). We can link Thomas' discussion of this issue in Question 19 with that of God's *power* in Question 25. Thomas distinguishes between two types of necessity: *absolute* necessity and necessity *by supposition*. The first type of necessity refers to logical truths that cannot be false due to the relations between subjects and predicates—e.g. that human beings are animals, that a bachelor is an unmarried male, that circles are not squares, and that numbers are either odd or even. Owing to the simplicity and perfection of the divine nature, God wills things in relation to Himself by absolute necessity—such as His goodness.

The other type of necessity is premised upon certain contingencies being supposed and would not be the case if those contingencies did not obtain. For example, if it is the case that Socrates is sitting, then he must necessarily sit so long as he is sitting. In other words, so long as Socrates is sitting, it is impossible that he be standing; though it is possible for him to stand and thus no longer be sitting. This type of necessity applies to God's willing in reference to anything outside of Himself. Thomas concludes that it is not absolutely necessary for God to create anything outside of Himself—nothing about the definition of God entails that He create. Having created a universe outside of Himself, however, creation becomes necessary by supposition due to the fact that God's nature includes immutability and thus His will cannot change (q. 19, a. 7).

This conclusion raises the question of whether God's will is *free* (q. 19, a. 10). Thomas maintains God's freedom insofar as absolute necessity applies only to God's willing anything concerning His own self. It would involve a logical contradiction, for instance, if God were to will His own non-existence or anything contrary to His perfect goodness. Despite affirming that God is *omnipotent* (q. 25, a. 3), even a being of infinite power cannot do that which is *logically impossible*—not even God could square a circle or make $2 + 2 = 47$. God's freedom thus consists in the power to will whatever is logically possible, which includes whether or not to create a universe outside of Himself. Again, once God wills to create, the act of creation becomes necessary by supposition; counterfactually, though, if God had not willed to create, then there necessarily would not have been a universe. Thomas utilizes this same reasoning to conclude that not even God could make the *past* not to have been (q. 25, a. 4). While it is not absolutely necessary that any particular past event occurred, once it did occur and is thereby known from God's eternal perspective, its occurrence is necessary by supposition. This distinction in types of necessity also allows Thomas to conclude that while, absolutely speaking, God could have willed otherwise than He does, once God wills X, X is necessary by supposition and God's immutable will cannot will not-X (q. 25, a. 5). Analogously, once Socrates sits, he cannot simultaneously be standing; although he could have not sat.

Another pertinent question in this context is whether God wills *evil* (q. 19, a. 9). As noted earlier, Thomas follows Augustine in claiming that God "permits" evil to occur only if a greater good could be brought about (q. 2, a. 3 *ad* 1). This is very different from stating that God "causes" or "wills" evil to occur. It would be logically impossible for God, who is identified as *goodness itself* (q. 6), to will anything that is not good and evil is a privation of goodness. Hence, even in His omnipotence, God cannot will what is evil. Yet, God can permit evil to occur insofar as it is *unavoidably concomitant* with the good God wills; this is a theological application of the principle of "double-effect" that we will discuss in the context of various moral prohibitions outlined in the *secunda pars*, such as whether one may licitly kill someone in self-defense (IIa–IIae, q. 64, a. 7). God wills the existence of rational beings who have free will, which in itself is good, knowing that they will misuse their freedom to cause evil. The possibility of evil is unavoidably concomitant with the creation of beings with free will; although it was not absolutely necessary that evil actually occur. From His eternal perspective, however, God knows that evil will occur through misuse of free will and, Thomas reasons, allows such evil to occur because He also knows and actively brings about greater good. Presumably, if God were to have seen from His eternal perspective that no greater good could possibly be brought about in light of the evil committed in the created universe, then God would not have created in the first place.

Thomas notes that we use the term "evil" to refer not only to *immoral* acts, as we have been discussing, but to any privation of goodness, such as the death of a stag when it is killed by a lion or the destruction of a prairie town by a tornado. Such evils result, not from the wills of free rational beings, but from God's intelligent ordering of the universe referenced in Thomas' fifth argument for God's existence. Again, though, such evils are not *directly* willed by God, but rather are *tolerated* as unavoidably concomitant consequences of other proportionally related goods: the stag's death is concomitant with the proportionate good of the lion's nutrition, and the devastation of the prairie town is concomitant with weather patterns that produce destructive tornadoes as well as the wind, warmth, and moisture that allow living organisms to thrive. Thomas holds that God directly wills the evil of *punishment* for moral wrongdoing, but only insofar as it is concomitant with the good of *justice* and, even then, God may forego punishment on account of His *mercy* (q. 21).

QUESTIONS 27–43—THE TRINITY

No discussion of the nature of God, within the Christian context, would be complete without an analysis of the concept of the *Trinity*: the peculiarly Christian dogma that God is both *one* and yet *three* in the persons of the Father, the Son, and the Holy Spirit. This brief elucidation cannot do the slightest justice to the voluminous Patristic and conciliar writings that shaped the formation of this fundamental dogma that Thomas inherits as part of the deposit of the Christian faith. As an essential thesis of Christian dogma, Thomas makes clear that he considers belief in the Trinity to a matter of *revealed* theology that is assented to by those with the gift of *faith*. Knowledge of the Trinity is not attainable by means of natural reason alone (q. 32, a. 1). This is due to the fact that knowledge of God, insofar as it is accomplished in the preceding questions of the *prima pars*, can only be rationally derived from some sort of empirical datum human beings experience in the natural world. While, as Thomas clearly argues, such reasoning leads to the conclusion that there is a single, perfect God who is the world's creator, nothing that we rationally derive from empirical experience entails the conclusion that God exists as *three distinct persons*. On the other hand, reason does not preclude belief in the Trinity and, in fact, could be utilized to show the internal *coherency* of belief in the Trinity and the *congruency* of this belief with our empirical experiences and rational derivations therefrom (q. 32, a. 1 *ad* 2).

How, then, does philosophical reasoning help us to unpack the Trinitarian dogma? The first question is whether it makes sense to hold that there is *procession* in the divine nature (q. 27). The term "procession" refers to an activity that issues in another internal (intransitive) or external (transitive) activity (q. 27, a. 1). As an example of the former, thinking about my daughter processes intransitively into my feeling unconditional love for her; for the latter, my expressed desire to drink a beer processes transitively into the bartender at my favorite Scottish pub pouring me a robust ale. As seen from these examples, procession—whether transitive or intransitive—can occur from either intellectual or volitional activity, and such activity on God's part yields the various interpersonal relationships that define the Trinity: God the Father, God the Son, and God the Holy Spirit each exists insofar as they stand in certain *relations* to each other (q. 28).

The relationship of the Father and the Son proceeds from God's *intellectual* activity, as testified by St. John's description of Christ as "the Word" (*Logos*) in the prologue to his Gospel; and Thomas affirms that "the Word" is the proper name for the Son (q. 34, aa. 1–2). As *word*, the Son proceeds intransitively from—is *begotten* of—the Father, just as, when one vocalizes the word "tree," that word proceeds immediately from one's intellectual concept of "tree." The concept serves as the *foundation* for the vocalized word; Thomas thus describes the Father as the *principle* from which the Son proceeds (q. 33, a. 1).

To see how these two divine persons could yet be *one*, think of the duality you may experience in yourself as you attempt to convince yourself whether you should work or play at a particular moment. Such two-mindedness is, of course, foreign to God insofar as God does not engage in discursive reasoning or need to "make up His mind" about anything. Nevertheless, the human phenomenal experience of mental duality allows us to comprehend, at least somewhat, the claim that God's intellective activity processes into the creation of a distinct person. Again, if we are careful not to equate the two cases, we can reasonably understand how the procession of the Son from the Father is no more a threat to divine unity than your "talking to yourself" is no threat to your own unity.

The other procession within the divine essence is *volitional* and results from the *interpersonal love* between the Father and the Son (q. 27, a. 3). Recall that God is the *supreme good* (q. 6, a. 2) and is thus eminently lovable. It thereby follows not only that all volitional creatures should love God, but that God loves His own self. This self-love on God's part—mutually expressed between the Father and the Son—processes into the Holy Spirit (q. 37). The procession of the Spirit differs from the Son's relation to the Father insofar as the former proceeds from God's volition. Unlike the intellectual procession of the Son, the Spirit is not immediately begotten by the Father. For, while a word follows from—and thereby *possesses*—the intellectual concept that is its principle, volition is *aimed toward* its principle insofar as it does not possess it but rather *desires* it. Furthermore, insofar as the Spirit is the personification of the love *between* the Father and the Son, it has *both* of the other divine persons as its *principle* (q. 36, a. 4); whereas the Son differs insofar as His principle is the Father alone.

Thomas thus affirms that there are *three*, and no more than three, persons in the divine essence based on the two processions (q. 27, a. 5) and four essential *relations* that have been delineated: Paternity, Filiation, Spiration, and Procession (q. 28, a. 4). The Father's *paternity* is defined by His serving as the principle from which the Son is immediately begotten as the Word; and the Son's *filiation* is defined by His being the Word begotten by the Father (q. 33, a. 3). *Spiration* is the relation of the Father to the Son in love entailing the *procession* of the Spirit from both of them, "which name expresses a certain vital movement and impulse, accordingly as anyone is described as moved or impelled by love to perform an action" (q. 27, a. 5; cf. q. 36, aa. 2–4).

Each member of the Trinity—Father, Son, and Holy Spirit—is defined as a *person* (q. 29). Thomas adopts the definition of "person" from the 6th-century philosopher and theologian Boethius: "an individual substance of a rational nature" (a. 1). He must qualify Boethius' definition, though, due to the analogical relationship between known persons in the natural world—namely, human beings—and the divine persons of the Trinity. First, the divine persons are not "substances" in the natural sense of being composites of matter and form. Rather, they are each *subsistent beings* (a. 2), which means that they exist on their own without inhering in another being. It is not as if there is one being—God—who possesses three *qualities* that we term "Father," "Son," and "Holy Spirit"; instead, each divine person exists and can be referred to individually despite being essentially related to the other persons of the Trinity. One can refer, for example, to the Word without necessarily referencing the Father or the Holy Spirit; even though the Word exists only insofar as both the Father and the Holy Spirit exists. Conversely, one cannot refer to the whiteness of a piece of paper without referencing the paper itself insofar as the paper's whiteness does not *subsist* on its own but only as a quality of the paper.

In the natural world, substances are *individualized*, according to Thomas, by virtue of "designated matter": I exist as an individual distinct from all other substances insofar as the matter composing my body comprises a three-dimensional region not shared by the chair in which I am currently sitting. God, however, is not a material substance and so the divine persons cannot be individualized from each other by this criterion. Rather, Thomas emphasizes the *incommunicability* of the divine persons (a. 3 *ad* 4). Persons are incommunicable in the sense that the being of each cannot be shared by any other person: it is impossible for two persons to compose the same being. Hence, Thomas contends that there is a "real distinction" between each of the divine persons (q. 30, a. 1), despite each standing in an "essential relation" to the others (q. 29, a. 4).

Finally, as noted earlier, God does not have a "nature," properly speaking, insofar as this term denotes a being capable of categorization into a species under a genus—and God's being transcends any such categories—nor is God "rational" in the same way that human beings are by virtue of our capacity to engage in discursive reasoning—God's knowledge is infinite, eternal, and fully actual. Yet, God clearly has an intellect as is required for Him to order everything in the created universe to determinate ends—as demonstrated by Thomas' fifth argument for God's existence. Hence, understood in analogical terms, each member of the Trinity qualifies as "an individual substance of a rational nature," or, more precisely, *an incommunicable subsistent intellectual being*. Thomas thereby concludes that the term "person" is properly applied to each member of the Trinity in "a more excellent way" than it is applied to other intellectual beings—namely, angels and human beings (q. 29, a. 3). He further asserts that personhood is properly attributed to God insofar as it represents a being of "high dignity," equating such dignity with possessing intelligence and concomitant freedom of volition, which God possesses preeminently (a. 3 *ad* 2).

This concludes our brief excursion toward a deeper understanding of God's existence and nature, as understood and rationally defended by Thomas. Although the immediate demonstration of Thomas' famous five arguments is of the so-called "God of the philosophers," characterized as an *impersonal* entity responsible for creating the universe and nothing more—a view known since the modern era as "deism"—he subsequently derives various *personal* qualities that define the divine nature, including knowledge, goodness, and volition—even *love* (q. 20). Thomas' philosophical defense of the coherence of belief in the Trinity opens the door for him to later—in the *tertia pars*—expound upon Christ's loving activity in His salvific sacrifice that allows humanity to receive the grace needed to complete our individual and collective *reditus* toward the source of our existence. Before we move on to discuss the *reditus*, however, we must first complete Thomas' exposition of the *exitus* of the created universe from God in Chapter 3, culminating in his detailed treatment of human nature in Chapter 4.

SUGGESTIONS FOR FURTHER READING

For a detailed commentary on Questions 1–13 of the *prima pars*, see Brian J. Shanley, *The Treatise on Divine Nature* (Indianapolis, IN: Hackett, 2006). See also Rudi te Velde, *Aquinas on God: The "Divine Science" of the Summa Theologiae* (Burlington, VT: Ashgate Publishing, 2006).

An explication of *sacra doctrina* as a form of *scientia*, linked with Thomas' later discussion of the theological virtue of *faith*, can be found in John I. Jenkins, *Knowledge and Faith in Thomas Aquinas* (New York: Cambridge University Press, 1997).

For further elucidation and analysis of Thomas' five arguments for God's existence, see John Wippel, "The Five Ways" in his *The Metaphysical Thought of Thomas Aquinas* (Washington, D.C.: Catholic University of America Press, 2000), Ch. 12; and Anthony Kenny, *The Five Ways: St. Thomas Aquinas' Proofs of God's Existence* (New York: Routledge, 1969).

For a careful treatment of Thomas' concepts of *accidentally* and *essentially* ordered series in his first two arguments for God's existence, see Gaven Kerr, "Essentially Ordered Series Reconsidered" *American Catholic Philosophical Quarterly* 86:4 (2012): 541–555.

For more details on the Thomas' understanding of the transcendentals, especially the convertibility of "being" and "goodness," see the essays by Jan A. Aertsen and Paul Vincent Spade in *Aquinas's Moral Theory: Essays in Honor of Norman Kretzmann*, eds. Scott MacDonald and Eleonore Stump (Ithaca, NY: Cornell University Press, 1999). A more general discussion of the subject from both Thomistic and other medieval perspectives can be found in *Being and Goodness: The Concept of the Good in Metaphysics and Philosophical Theology*, ed. Scott MacDonald (Ithaca, NY: Cornell University Press, 1991).

Thomas' indebtedness to neo-Platonic influences has been carefully documented by Wayne J. Hankey, "Aquinas, Plato, and Neoplatonism" in *The Oxford Handbook of Aquinas*, eds. Brian Davies and Eleonore

Stump (New York: Oxford University Press, 2012), 55–64; and Fran O'Rourke, *Pseudo-Dionysius and the Metaphysics of Aquinas* (Notre Dame, IN: University of Notre Dame Press, 2005).

An in-depth elucidation of Thomas' understanding and use of analogical predication is provided by Ralph McInerny, *Aquinas and Analogy* (Washington, D.C.: Catholic University of America Press, 1996).

For a more fully developed Thomistic response to the problem of evil, see Eleonore Stump, *Wandering in Darkness: Narrative and the Problem of Suffering* (New York: Oxford University Press, 2010).

For more detailed discussion of God's simplicity, eternity, and knowledge, see Eleonore Stump, *Aquinas* (New York, NY: Routledge, 2003), Chs. 3–5.

Additional resources for exploring Thomas' account of the divine Trinity include Giles Emery, *The Trinitarian Theology of St. Thomas Aquinas*, trans. Francesca Aran Murphy (New York: Oxford University Press, 2007); and Timothy L. Smith, *Thomas Aquinas' Trinitarian Theology* (Washington, D.C.: Catholic University of America Press, 2003).

3

CREATION

We have seen Thomas' arguments demonstrating the existence of a single, infinite, eternal, omnipotent, omniscient, omnibenevolent—in short, *perfect*—Being who functions as the ultimate efficient, formal, and final cause of every other being. The next step in the *Summa* is to explicate how this Being exercises His infinite power in creating all other beings out of nothingness (*ex nihilo*) and establishing the providential ordering of all created beings into a harmonious whole. We will then explore Thomas' treatment of the first type of created intellectual beings—angels—before moving on in the next chapter to his more in-depth treatment of another type of created intellectual beings—humans.

QUESTIONS 44–49—CREATION *EX NIHILO* AND THE ORIGIN OF THE UNIVERSE

In Question 44, Thomas outlines several implications concerning the relationship between God and every other being in the universe based on what he concluded in the previous treatise concerning God's existence and nature. The first implication is that every being that exists outside of God is necessarily created by God insofar as "God is the essentially self-subsisting Being" and enjoys perfect unity, such that every being that is not God must somehow "participate" in God's being (a. 1); although each individual being still has its own act of existence. Thomas extends this conclusion to cover not only all *actually* existing beings, but even what merely has the *potential* to be formed into a being—termed "prime matter" (a. 2). This term refers to the substratum composing every material substance in which a specific form inheres, thereby resulting in a particular being of a certain species.

For instance, a human being is composed of a certain type of form—an "intellective soul"—informing matter that constitutes a living animal body of the human species. Upon the death of a human being, her soul no longer informs her material body and we term the material remains a "corpse." Death involves, in Aristotelian terms, a *substantial change* in which one substance—a human person—ceases to exist and another substance—a corpse—comes into existence; the picture is actually a bit more nuanced but we will return to this topic later. Clearly, a human person is not *the same thing* as the corpse that remains after her death; yet, it is just as clear that there is some sort of *material continuity* between what was at one moment a living body and is now relatively inert matter. What persists through such a substantial change, that which was first actually a living body while potentially a corpse and is now actually a corpse while potentially a living body—if resurrected according to Christian belief—is what Thomas means by "prime matter."

It is important to keep in mind that prime matter is not the same as whatever fundamental particles or energy-states of matter physics has, or may in the future, discover to be the underlying substrate of all material things in the universe; for even such micro-level particles or energy-states exist as *informed* matter—"matter" understood here broadly to include specific types of *energy*. An up-quark is not the same type of particle as a down-quark; hence, each is matter with a distinct type of form. Rather, prime matter is something common to both types of quarks that is potentially one or the other depending on which type of form inheres in it. In short, prime matter is absolutely *formless*, possessing no essential qualities other than *the potential to receive form*.

Thomas' radical thesis about prime matter is that it too was created by God. Many ancient philosophers understood prime matter to be a primordial component of an eternally existing universe and that divine creative activity consisted only in giving form—in a variety of types—to this initially formless substratum. Prime matter would thus be analogous to the unformed clay that a sculptor shapes into the form of a statue; the sculptor does not create the clay itself, but rather forms a statue out of it. Thomas disagrees and argues that God creates prime matter as well; without God's creative activity, there would be *absolutely nothing* that exists outside of Himself. Part of the reason is that Thomas does not conceptualize prime matter as ever existing without a form of some sort. This is where the analogy of prime matter with unformed clay breaks down insofar as the latter does have *a* form—with certain qualities of shape, color, texture, etc.—it just does not have the form of a statue until the artist shapes it. Prime matter, on the other hand, has no intrinsic qualities of its own; as noted earlier, even the most elementary particles or energy-states discovered by physics are instances of *informed matter*. Unlike the artist who shapes clay into a statue or a group of assembly-line workers who manufacture an automobile out of various mechanical and structural parts, God alone *creates* in the proper sense of the term as referring to bringing *being* out of *not-being* (q. 45, aa. 1 and 5). Natural causal agents within the universe can pseudo-create new things by bringing about *formal changes* within a given material substrate, but lack the power to bring about matter itself (a. 2).

Thomas directly links his discussion of creation with his previous discussion of the Trinity by describing how, given his account of the procession and relations of three divine Persons, each contributes to God's unified creative activity (a. 6). Consider again the analogy of a sculptor molding clay into a statue. Before putting her hands to the clay, the sculptor has an *idea* in her mind—an exemplar or formal cause—of how the eventual statue ought to look; of course, she may modify this idea as she works the clay, but the point is that she moves her hands in direct response to some idea in her mind that she *desires* to instantiate within the clay. There is both an intellectual and a volitional component to the sculptor's activity. As we saw in the previous chapter's discussion of the Trinity, Thomas conceives of the Son as the Word (*Logos*)—that is, He is the Wisdom of God;

while the Holy Spirit is the Love of God. Thus, God the Father exercises His Power in creative activity according to His Wisdom out of Love for Himself and for the beings He creates (a. 6 *ad* 2). The result is not only that beings outside of God are willfully created, but also that they are *providentially* created in an intentionally harmonious order according to God's Wisdom and Love. Thomas thus concludes that every created being shows "a trace of the Trinity," but especially rational beings—angels and humans—who possess both intellect and will (a. 7).

In Question 46, Thomas lays out his highly controversial position—as discussed in Chapter 1—that it cannot be rationally demonstrated that the universe had a temporal beginning and does not share in God's eternal existence. On the one hand, it makes sense to hold that the universe is co-eternal with God insofar as God's will is purely actual and thus whatever God wills He wills eternally. So, if God wills the universe's creation, He wills it eternally and so it is reasonable to conclude that the universe is eternally created and sustained. This conclusion does not necessarily follow, however, for two reasons. First, Thomas had previously argued that creation is not a *necessary* act on God's part; God has the freedom, in an absolute sense, to create or not to create (q. 19, a. 3). Of course, since God clearly has created, then God's immutable will entails that creation is necessary *by supposition*—just as, if it is the case that you are sitting right now, it cannot be the case that you are also standing right now and so you are necessarily sitting on the supposition that you are in fact sitting right now. Second, even though whatever God wills is willed eternally, it does not follow that the *effects* of God's will eternally occur. God wills, for example, to speak with Moses from a burning bush, to be born of a virgin Jewish girl, and to cure a nun from Parkinson's disease through the intercession of Pope St. John Paul II. All of these events—taking them as factual historical occurrences, as Thomas would, for the sake of discussion—occur at temporally distinct moments; yet, they are simultaneously willed by God in a single eternal volitional act. Analogously, I may will that my daughter receive all of my property upon my death, but the effect of that volition does not occur at the time of my willing it; rather, it is delayed until after my death and the reading of my written will. Hence, it is reasonable to hold that God eternally wills the universe's creation and yet the universe has a temporal beginning, just as other eternal divine volitions may yield temporally indexed effects. Thomas thereby concludes that belief in the universe's temporal beginning is ultimately based on faith, in accord with what Thomas takes to be the optimal interpretation of Genesis 1:1, but is nevertheless a rationally defensible position to hold. It is worth emphasizing that Thomas considers it crucial to subject such an important, foundational belief to a high level of critical scrutiny; otherwise, merely accepting a faith-based belief that cannot be rationally defended would prompt ridicule from non-believers.

Thomas next treats the issue of why there are diverse types of beings in the created universe. He is responding to the Islamic theologian Avicenna's thesis that, if God is "supremely one," then, as the efficient, formal, and final cause of the universe, the latter should be similarly unified (q. 47, a. 1 *objs*. 1–3). Thomas responds that God freely willed to create beings outside of Himself as a manifestation of His essential goodness; however, God's goodness being infinitely perfect, no one creature could perfectly exemplify it. Hence, there must be a variety of different types of beings that each represents divine goodness in its own specific fashion as part of a well-ordered— i.e. *harmonious*—whole (aa. 1 and 3). An important corollary of this discussion is that created beings are not only of diverse genera and species, but also that the different types of beings are *qualitatively* diverse—that is, each species not only represents divine goodness in a distinct manner from other species, but also manifests it to a different *degree* (a. 2). Furthermore, contrary to Avicenna's thesis that God *necessarily emanates* His Being into the created universe, Thomas holds that God *freely wills* to create beings outside of Himself. Created beings thus manifest God's *wisdom*, the diversity of species reflecting the diversity of ideas in the divine mind.

Thomas follows Aristotle in "carving nature at its joints" by identifying broad categories that distinguish various types of beings with respect to their causal properties and other increasingly complex qualities. So, Thomas concludes, compound substances are "more perfect" than their constituent elements, living organisms more than non-living substances, sentient animals more than merely living plants, rational animals—humans—more than merely sentient dogs and cats, and purely intellectual beings—angels—more than materially constituted humans. These qualitative distinctions allow, for example, animals to consume plants for nutrition and for humans, when necessary, to use animals for food, labor, or experimental purposes. Nevertheless, it must be kept in mind that each type of being has its own degree of *intrinsic goodness* manifesting God's supreme goodness. Thus, humanity's "dominion" over other animal species given in Genesis 1:26–28 does not authorize treating animals as one would treat a plant or a mineral, and the legitimate use of animals should be aimed at the survival and well-being of human beings according to our objectively ordered nature—as we will discuss further in Chapter 11. Thus, while Thomas would presumably have no issue with the humane use of animals for testing potentially life-saving medical treatments; harmful testing of cosmetic products on animals would not be justifiable.

If creation is a manifestation of God's supreme goodness, whence comes the all-too-evident *evil* in the universe? We saw in the previous chapter how Thomas views evil not as a *being* in itself, but rather as a *privation* of being and goodness that ought to be according to the natural order providentially willed by God (q. 48, a. 1). For example, by nature human beings ought to have the power of sight, but some human beings lack this power; blindness is not a different power those individuals possess, but rather a lack of the power of sight they ought naturally to have. In another example, I ought to be naturally inclined toward helping a fellow human being in need or who is suffering; if I lack empathy and compassionate desire to help someone in need when I have the capacity to do so, then I have a moral defect analogous to the physical defect of blindness. Again, evil is not something that exists in itself, but is rather a *defect* that is found in created things (a. 2).

It is important to emphasize here that evil is a "defect" insofar as it is a lack of being or goodness that *ought* to be according to the natural order. Due to the fact no created being can exist perfectly or be perfectly good in an absolute sense—only God could be so—there will always be some degree of being and goodness lacking in every finite creature. In other words, for God to create a universe with no imperfections is for God to create a perfect universe. But a perfect universe would stand in potency to nothing; it would be pure act, in which case it could not be created. Thus, a perfect universe is *logically impossible* and thus not open to God's omnipotence—not due to any limitation on God's power, but because it is something that cannot be done.

Natural limitations of being and goodness do not constitute "evils"—just as it is not "evil" that human beings lack the echo-location capacity of bats or wings to fly like birds (a. 3). Thomas then makes a key point that evil does not corrupt the "whole good" of a being (a. 4). Insofar as evil is a lack of being and goodness, an *absolutely* evil being could not exist. Even the most corrupt human being— e.g. Adolf Hitler—or angel—e.g. Satan—possesses some minimal degree of goodness insofar as they exist at all. Thomas thus rejects the Gnostic thesis that there is both a Supreme Good—God—and a Supreme Evil that is the cause of all evil in the universe (q. 49, a. 3). This is an important foundational thesis for Thomas' theology of sin and redemption that we will discuss later in the *tertia pars*.

The privative nature of evil has the seemingly paradoxical conse-quence that goodness is the *cause* of evil insofar as evil must be caused by something that exists and whatever exists is good (q. 49, a. 1). Thomas' nuanced view, however, is that goodness is the cause of evil in only an *accidental* sense. Basically, whenever a causal agent acts, it acts for the sake of some good—either by unconscious natural inclination (as when a rock falls to the ground), or by conscious but determined natural inclination (as when a non-rational animal pur-sues food), or by conscious will (as is the case for humans and other persons). Sometimes, due to a defect present in the agent or in the activity the agent performs, evil results as an effect of the agent's pursuit of some good. In the case of non-rational agents, such defects do not involve any moral culpability and the resultant evils are called "natural." In the case of rational agents, such defects may involve moral culpability and the resultant evils are called "sin"—as we will discuss in the context of the *secunda pars*. Some natural evils occur, though, not as a result of a defect in the causal agent, but merely as a concomitant side-effect of the agent's proper activity; Thomas cites the example of a fire consuming combustible material as it sustains and spreads itself.

Setting aside sin—i.e. moral evil caused by rational agents mis-using their free will—it would appear that God could at least be held responsible for the existence of *natural* evils insofar as everything is traceable back to God as the First Cause (a. 2 *obj.* 2). Thomas responds that natural defects are an unavoidable consequence of a finite universe that cannot perfectly manifest God's infinite goodness; nevertheless, God's goodness is manifest, not in the being of each individual creature, but in the providential *order* of creation as a whole. Thus, the death of a gazelle that is hunted down and eaten by a mountain lion is a privation of life—and thus a natural evil—with respect to the gazelle; but its death is a concomitant side-effect of the mountain lion's natural pursuit of the good of nutrition to sustain its own life. The predator-prey relationship within the animal kingdom is good insofar as it reflects a harmonious ordering of beings within the universe. Evidence of this ordering can be witnessed when the predator-prey relationship is interrupted—say, by humans killing or capturing all the mountain lions in a region—and the gazelle population increases exponentially to levels that cannot be sustained by the available food sources on which gazelles rely for survival and they starve. All this being said, one may still be inclined to hold God accountable for creating a universe in which the death of gazelles through either predation or starvation—and the associated physical suffering they experience—is an unavoidable necessity for the sake of "harmony." Could not an omnipotent God who can do whatever is logically possible have created a universe with a more harmonious order? Perhaps God did, but that initial order—as depicted in the Genesis story of the "Garden of Eden"—was despoiled by human sinfulness and, in the restoration of the "Kingdom of God," it will be the case that mountain lions and gazelles will peacefully co-exist as prophesied in Isaiah 11:6–9. Further discussion will have to await our exploration of Thomas' theology of sin and salvation in the *tertia pars*.

QUESTIONS 65–74—THE "SIX DAYS" OF CREATION

A vociferous debate among Christians, and between some sects of Christianity with the secular scientific world, concerns the account of God's creation of the universe given in the first chapter of the Book of Genesis, in which God's creative activity is described as occurring over the course of "six days." Lest one think that controversial understandings of this key biblical text is limited to contemporary cosmological and evolutionary accounts of the origins of the universe and intelligent life on this planet, there were various non-literal interpretations of the Genesis creation story from the earliest centuries of Christianity. Thomas' account of the "six days" of creation includes four key propositions we will examine: 1) the creation of the material universe is *good*; 2) creation of the material universe was effected by God *alone*; 3) God's creative activity was *complete* by the end of the sixth day; and 4) the "six days" of creation can be understood *metaphorically*.

The first two articles of Question 65 establish the proposition that the creation of the material universe and the various corporeal creatures that populate it is in accord with God's goodness. Thomas here is objecting to two opposing theories. First, there is the view of the heretical Manichees and other so-called "Gnostics," who held that only spiritual beings are good and come from God, while material beings are evil and come from another source. Second, there is the view of the 3rd-century theologian Origen, who contended that God created material beings as a form of *punishment* for the sin of spiritual beings—similar to Plato's view, absent the juridical component, that human persons are purely intellectual beings who are entrapped in physical bodies.

Relying on his initial arguments for God's existence and his conclusions that God alone is "self-subsistent Being" (q. 3, a. 4) and thus all created beings come from God (q. 44, a. 1), Thomas refutes the Manichees by re-affirming that every being, in whatever form, must be created by God (q. 65, a. 1). Origen's view acknowledges Thomas' first conclusion, but then gives a punitive rationale for why God would create material beings. Thomas refutes this view by appeal to both Scripture and reason. Scripturally, Origen's thesis runs afoul of the proclamation at the end of each of the "six days" that God reviewed all He had made and "saw that it was good." Rationally, Thomas appeals to the evident order in the universe among the various types of material beings, on which he had previously based not only one of his arguments for God's existence (q. 2, a. 3), but also a further conclusion that the *diversity* of created beings reflects God's infinite goodness (q. 47, a. 1).

Thomas' second key proposition regarding creation is affirmed in the latter two articles of Question 65. Here, he refutes the view others have promulgated that the material universe was created through the agency of the *angels*, who, as we will discuss below, are purely spiritual substances. Thomas' metaphysics of causation does allow for God, as the First Cause, to work through various *secondary* causes to produce particular effects—just as a general wins a battle, not by charging the enemy himself, but by commanding his troops to do so in accord with the general's strategic plan. This exemplifies Thomas' conception of an *essentially ordered* causal series, in which the posterior causes in the series are inherently dependent on some ultimate prior cause—e.g. without the general's strategic plan, no orders would be issued to his troops and, without such orders, the troops would not implement the plan. So it is not absolutely impossible that God produces various effects by means of the activity of angels, humans, or any other secondary causal agent. *Creation*, however, can be effected only by God directly insofar as it involves bringing a being out of nothing (*ex nihilo*); secondary causes can only bring about effects that involve *changing* an already existing being (q. 65, a. 3). A sculptor, for example, is able to change a hunk of marble into a statue, but cannot create the marble itself; even the latest breakthroughs in "synthetic biology" involve, not creating life out of nothing, but rather manipulating already extant matter to take on the properties of a living being.

Question 66 begins the discussion of God's creative activity. Thomas first has to resolve the issue of what there was "in the beginning." As we saw earlier, one view of the material universe is that formless matter—termed "prime matter"—existed prior to any particular types of material beings being created, and in fact may even be "co-eternal" with God. This view renders God akin to the sculptor who shapes already extant marble into a statue but does not create the marble itself. Thomas argues to the contrary that prime matter does not temporally precede the creation of informed material beings. Rather, matter exists only insofar as it is informed and thus all of the matter in the universe came to be as constitutive of various types of informed material beings (q. 66, a. 1). The only proper way to speak of prime matter as having any sort of "priority" with respect to informed material beings is due to the fact that such beings can exist only insofar as they exist materially; in other words, just as "formless matter" does not exist on its own, "matter-less form" (in the case of essentially material beings) does not exist on its own. Hence, prime matter is *ontologically* prior to informed material beings since the latter is dependent upon the former to exist; nevertheless, prime matter is itself ontologically dependent upon its being informed.

The other issue Thomas has to resolve in this question is the creation of *time*. As discussed in Chapter 1, Thomas defends the controversial thesis that it is reasonable to hold that the universe is co-eternal with God; although it is equally reasonable to hold that it has a temporal beginning, which Thomas ultimately affirms in accord with Scripture. What constitutes, then, the *beginning* of time? Thomas follows Aristotle in defining time as the *measure of change*. Hence, in order for time to exist, there must be change that can be measured, which entails "duration." God exists atemporally insofar as He does not change, but creation involves a change from there being nothing to there being something: once something other than God comes into existence and is able to cause further changes, time ensues (q. 66, a. 4).

In Questions 67 through 73, Thomas works his way through each of the six days of creation plus the seventh day on which God "rests." The various articles these questions comprise mostly address interpretive issues and puzzles raised by various theological commentators and are largely not issues with which contemporary theologians or philosophers of religion are concerned. One key point Thomas asserts in this context is that creation was *complete* after the "six days" and that God does not create anything new *ex nihilo*: everything seemingly "new" that comes into existence after the initial creation of the universe existed previously in some fashion (q. 73, a. 1 *ad* 3). On the face of it, this claim appears to run headlong into evident difficulties. First of all, new individual beings seem to be created all the time, as, for example, living organisms produce offspring. This is not a case of "creation," however, as biological offspring are not produced out of nothing, but rather "pre-exist" *in a sense* in the causal principles in their progenitors that allow for them to be produced. To clarify, Thomas is not claiming that tiny puppies or tiny human children already exist in the loins of their parents—we will discuss Thomas' view of human reproduction in the next chapter. Rather, he is claiming that everything causally necessary for a puppy to be produced already exists in the biological constitution of its parents and requires only activation for the puppy to move from a state of *potentially* existing to *actual* existence. One may metaphorically think of Michelangelo's famous claim that the statues he carved already existed within the hunks of marble that were delivered to his studio from the Carrera mines; all he had to do was to chip away the extraneous bits.

If Thomas' response satisfactorily accounts for the pre-existence of individuals, what about the emergence of novel *species*? Post-Darwin, any satisfactory origin story must account for the process of biological evolution. Here, although evolutionary biologists often deride Aristotelianism as having been supplanted by Darwinism, the real counterpoint to Darwin is *Plato*, who held that material individuals are reflections of transcendental, unchanging exemplar forms of each species. The Aristotelian concept of species, however, does not entail that specific forms are fixed and eternal, but rather allows for novel species to emerge through the mixing of forms of other species. Thomas explicitly acknowledges that new animal species may come into existence, but such species still "pre-exist" *in a sense* in the preceding causes that actualize them; for example, the species of mule exists potentially by virtue of the existence of the species of horse and donkey, and becomes actualized once a horse and donkey successfully mate (q. 73, a. 1 *ad* 3).

The final key point to emphasize regarding Thomas' account of creation is that he, along with earlier Christian thinkers, does not interpret the concept of the "six days" in a *strictly literal* sense, as do contemporary fundamentalist Christians. In Question 74, Article 2, he adjudicates a debate between Augustine and other Patristic writers regarding whether there were seven—including the day of God's "rest"—*physical* days of creation, or whether—Augustine's view—there was a singular moment ("day") of creation that was revealed to those who witnessed creation—namely, the angels—in a sevenfold fashion appropriate to their degree of intellectual comprehension. Treating this subject with care, Thomas does not arrive at a definitive conclusion but seems to favor Augustine's view, which supports a non-literal reading of the creation story in Genesis 1. This reading makes sense given Thomas' account of God's eternal nature, which entails His presence and activity with respect to every moment of creation to sustain *its* existence and activity. It thus does not make sense for creation to have unfolded over a number of days and then be completed. Creation is ongoing; although there is a set of ontologically prior necessary conditions that must be established in order for the rest of creation to come into being. Even if Thomas ultimately had rejected Augustine's view, the fact that he does not rule it out as contradicting Scripture—something of which one doubts Thomas would ever dare accuse Augustine!—demonstrates his general attitude toward Scriptural exegesis as being quite different from certain contemporary Christians, who go to great lengths to justify a literal reading of the biblical creation story as necessarily involving six physical days.

QUESTIONS 103–105 AND 115–116—DIVINE GOVERNANCE AND ORDER WITHIN THE UNIVERSE

For thematic reasons, since the next chapter will focus on Thomas' treatise on human nature (Questions 75–102), we will skip that large set of questions here and jump to the very end of the *prima pars*, wherein Thomas discusses how created beings—including humans, hence its placement after the treatise on human nature—participate in God's *governance* of the universe. Thomas finds it evident that there is some sort of providential ordering of things in the universe since natural substances operate in a harmonious fashion toward actualizing various optimal ends as opposed to mere chaos ensuing (q. 103, a. 1). Furthermore, while each individual natural substance acts for the sake of one or more particular ends that are suitable to its nature, the universe as a whole is moving toward a transcendent end insofar as its existence is from a cause outside of itself—namely, God (a. 2). Thomas thus affirms that there is a *single* governor of the universe (a. 3); although, the effects of God's eternal governmental action are *manifold* (a. 4). Insofar as God is the First Cause and subsistent Being itself, Thomas concludes that everything in the created universe is subject to God's providential governance (a. 5)—although God does not immediately cause everything in the universe but works through secondary causes (a. 6)—and thus nothing can occur outside of God's ordering of the universe (a. 7).

At this point, one may question how *evil* could occur insofar as that would seem to be a disruption of the universe's harmonious order and, relatedly, whether human beings can be *free* if, like everything else in the universe, we are subject to divine governance. We will examine Thomas' highly nuanced discussion of human freedom in later chapters; suffice it to say, for the moment, that free actions are a part of God's providential order insofar as God a) wills there to be free rational beings, b) has perfect knowledge of all the choices such beings make, and c) orders the universe in light of the knowledge of the choices rational beings make. Thus, Thomas asserts, when a human being wills evil, it is in accord with divine governance—not because God *intends* that a human being will evil—but, knowing that a human being wills evil, God intends that he suffers a just punishment (q. 103, a. 8 *ad* 1).

In subsequent questions, Thomas elucidates the *ontological dependence* of every created being upon God, who is subsistent Being itself and thereby both *creates* and *sustains* every other being that exists (q. 104, a. 1); again, though, God's sustaining activity may function by means of secondary causes (a. 2). The dependence of all created beings on God's sustaining activity thus leaves open the possibility that God may *annihilate* any being simply by ceasing to sustain it (a. 3). God, however, does not actually annihilate anything as such would not be in accord with God's providential governance (a. 4). This seemingly minor point is important to highlight as it shows how one of God's essential qualities—namely, His power—may be limited by another of God's essential qualities—namely, His wisdom: while God has, absolutely speaking, the power to annihilate any created being and nothing outside of Himself can limit this power, God's internal nature can so limit this power since it is not in accord with God's wise ordering of the universe to violate the natural course of beings to persist until, in the case of *contingently* existing beings composed of form and matter, they are corrupted by natural causes.

This last point also informs Thomas' definition of a "miracle," such as the various miracles reported in Scripture—e.g. the parting of the Red Sea in the Book of Exodus (Ch. 14) or Christ's multiplication of the loaves and fishes to feed five thousand followers (Matthew 14:15–21). On the one hand, each of these events must be part of God's providential ordering of the universe insofar as He eternally knows and wills that they occur in accord with His essential goodness; on the other hand, each of these events is a departure from the natural ordering of secondary causes that God effects as a particular manifestation of His power in accord with His goodness (q. 105, a. 6). Thus, for instance, God establishes the natural order of water to flow in a continuous manner by means of gravitational and other forces controlling its movement through a channel; in a certain instance, though, God contravenes this natural activity in order to bring about a particular good that could not be manifested otherwise: allowing the Israelites to escape the Egyptians while simultaneously demonstrating His power to both parties. It is not that the natural ordering is faulty or lacking in goodness, but it must be contravened in a particular case as a means of realizing a higher good in accord with God's overall plan for salvation history. Thus, both the natural ordering of how water should flow and the contravention of that flow to allow the Israelites to escape are eternally willed by God, and thereby both constitute aspects of His providential plan for creation.

So much for God's *direct* activity within the created universe, what about the activity of *secondary* causal agents? We will discuss the particular questions concerning the activity of angels and demons below and the activity of human beings throughout the remainder of our journey through the *Summa*. Here, we will briefly discuss Thomas' consideration of the activity of non-intelligent corporeal substances in Questions 115 and 116. First, Thomas affirms that created bodies can act: natural substances have natural *potencies* proper to their respective natures and are not absolutely inert (q. 115, aa. 1 and 2). He then discusses whether "heavenly bodies"—namely, the sun, moon, planets, and stars—can cause changes on earth (a. 3). While Thomas' cosmological understanding is excessively outmoded, the fact that he allows for such bodies to function as secondary causes coheres with our understanding of how gravity and radiation from extraterrestrial sources have causal effects on everything from tidal waves to cellphone receptivity.

One important exception, though, is human action that follows from our free will since, as we will see in the next chapter, the human intellect and will do not function through bodily organs that could be affected by external physical causal agents (q. 115, a. 4). Thomas thus disagrees with astrologers who see the position and movement of various celestial bodies to have a direct impact on human *fate* (q. 116, a. 1). Thomas conceives of "fate" as the ordering of secondary causes to effects as eternally known by God (q. 116, a. 2). This definition of fate has two important consequences. First, there are no *absolutely* random or chance occurrences insofar as every event is eternally known by God and is part of His providential governance of the universe. Randomness or chance refers either to our ignorance of the relation between a secondary cause and its ordered effect, or to an effect that lacks an immediate secondary cause but is nonetheless still causally dependent upon God's knowledge and will. Thus, according to Thomas, seemingly "random" effects at the quantum-level would be either a function of an *epistemic* lacuna resulting in their unpredictability, or a true lack of secondary causation—and thus lack of predictability from any known causes—but such effects would still be known and willed by God as the First Cause. The other key consequence is that the human will, in one sense, is not subject to fate insofar as it moves itself without the need of any secondary causes; although, in another sense, it is since whatever one wills is known eternally by God and thus constitutive of His providential governance of the universe.

QUESTIONS 50–64 AND 106–114—ON ANGELS AND DEMONS

Having discussed creation in general, we can now turn to Thomas' treatment of particular types of beings. The first type—angels and their fallen kindred, demons—either fulfill or fail to fulfill their *reditus* to God upon the moment of their creation, as we will discuss here. The second type—human beings—have a corporeal lifetime to attempt the moral journey back to their creator and ultimate good, discussion of which will consume the remainder of the *Summa*.

There are two reasons why Thomas postulates the existence of angels. First, their existence is reported throughout Scripture—for example, the Annunciation of the conception of Christ to Mary by the angel Gabriel (Luke 1:26–38). Second, in the ontological hierarchy of different types of beings reflecting God's perfect being and goodness, there is a significant gap between the highest of material beings—namely, human beings as "rational animals"—and God. It thus makes sense that there would be a distinctive genus of beings who exist as *pure intellects*, without a corporeal nature (q. 50, a. 1). Interestingly, because they do not have material bodies and designated matter is what individuates specific forms, "angel" does not denote a *species* comprising various individuals—as the term "human" does—but rather a *genus* comprising various species: each angel is its own species (a. 4). Nevertheless, angels are able to communicate and relate to each other analogously to how individual human minds do (qq. 106 and 107) and even communicate with individual human minds (q. 111), especially in the case of the protective activity of "guardian" angels (q. 113) or the temptation of demons (q. 114). It may occur to those familiar with Scripture that angels are reported as appearing to human beings in *bodily form* in ways that go beyond mere hallucination. Thomas affirms that angels may "assume" bodies—or demons "possess" bodies—moving them efficiently just as Plato conceived of the human soul to move its body (q. 51, a. 2); as we will see in the next chapter, Thomas disagrees with Plato's view of the human soul and conceives of it as the *formal*—not efficient—cause of its body.

Angels are thus like humans insofar as both have intellective minds capable of understanding the nature of reality, being reflexively aware of themselves, freely willing their own activity, and, most importantly, knowing and loving God (qq. 54–60). Angels are unlike humans, however, insofar as they do not gain knowledge *discursively* by means of sensation and reasoning (q. 58, a. 3). Rather, they are given all the knowledge they will ever have through direct infusion by God (a. 2)—a consequence of which is that they are not susceptible to falsehood (a. 5). Upon the infusion of knowledge, each angel has a choice to make: whether to will to be in loving union with God (q. 62) or to reject God out of *pride* (q. 63). According to Thomas, Satan and the other demons have the same *generic* nature as Gabriel and the other angels—although they each differ *specifically*, which allows them to exist in different hierarchical degrees—but their initial volition upon their creation was not a loving orientation toward God but a selfish orientation toward their own power. Due to the fact that the angels and demons are created with all the knowledge they will ever have by virtue of not having bodies that would allow them to gain further knowledge via sense-perception—nor would they presumably have anything new to learn if they did have bodies that would add to the knowledge they are given initially—their wills are everlastingly *confirmed* in a state of either loving union with God (q. 62, a. 8), or prideful rejection of Him (q. 64, a. 2).

SUGGESTIONS FOR FURTHER READING

There is not a lot of scholarly treatment, even among Christian philosophers and theologians, of Thomas' "angelology." A good, accessible resource is Peter J. Kreeft, *Angels (and Demons): What Do We Really Know about Them?* (San Francisco, CA: Ignatius Press, 1995).

4

HUMAN NATURE

PREFACE

The final major section of the *prima pars* focuses on the nature of human beings, completing the exposition of the *exitus* of created beings from God. There are four primary subtopics that Thomas discusses in this section. First is the *ontological* structure of human beings as composite unities of an immaterial soul and a material body, which places humans at the top of the hierarchy of material beings, but distinct from angels—discussed in the previous chapter—insofar as the latter exist as pure intellects without bodies. Second is what would be termed today Thomas' *philosophy of mind*, explaining how the human mind processes both sensory and intellectual information. Following his discussion of the mind's intellectual capacities, Thomas next elucidates the mind's *volitional* capacities and explains how the human will differs from the non-rational, instinctual appetites of other animals. Finally, Thomas returns to his exploration of the beginning of the Book of Genesis to explain the pre-Fallen existence of the first human beings, as well as the method by which the human species propagates itself from those first "parents."

All of these topics are essential pre-requisites for humanity's *reditus* to God discussed throughout the remainder of the *Summa*. In order to know what is objectively "good" for human beings, an understanding of our ontological make-up is in order. To understand how human beings make moral decisions and cultivate our moral characters, one must have a clear idea of the interrelated functioning of the intellect and will, as well as a defensible thesis of why the latter can be construed as "free" so as to underwrite the *moral responsibility* of human agents for our consciously willed actions. Finally, if he is to provide a coherent account of the theological roles of original sin and divine grace, Thomas must explain the origins of the human race and how natural procreation allows for the "stain" of original sin—requiring Christ's redemptive sacrifice discussed in the *tertia pars*—to have been passed on through the generations.

QUESTION 75—IMMATERIALITY OF THE HUMAN SOUL

In Socrates' death scene recorded at the end of Plato's *Phaedo*, he makes clear to his disciples that they may do whatever they like with his body after he succumbs to the fatal effects of the hemlock he drinks as *he* will have already departed. This scene depicts Plato's *dualist* view that a human being is essentially an immaterial soul—a mind—that is "entrapped" in a physical body until freed by death. Opposing Plato's view of the human essence is that of many contemporary metaphysicians and scientists who hold that a human being is nothing "over and above" one's physical body with its functioning brain; in other words, the mind is nothing other than the brain and a human being is nothing other than an animal capable of rational thought by virtue of having such a sophisticated brain. Thomas follows Aristotle in holding a middle-position, known as *hylomorphism*, in which a human being is defined as a *composite unity* of an immaterial soul informing a material body. The first two questions of Thomas' treatise on human nature in the *Summa* define, first, the nature of the human soul (q. 75) and then the union of soul and body to compose an individual human being (q. 76).

The first thing that needs to be clarified is what Thomas means by the term "soul." Due to the influence of Plato, Descartes, and other dualist philosophers and theologians, "soul" has become synonymous to modern ears with "mind" or "spirit." In one sense, this is true for Thomas as well insofar as the mind is one of the human soul's *powers*; but the soul is more than just the mind and there are other types of soul in addition to that of human beings. Furthermore, what is typically meant by the modern term "mind" does not correspond precisely with what Thomas terms the "intellect."

Thomas closely follows Aristotle in defining the soul as "the first principle of life in those things which live" (q. 75, a. 1). This definition characterizes the soul as a type of *substantial form*, informing matter to compose a certain type of being—namely, a *living* being. Human beings are, of course, alive; but there are also many other species of living beings: bacteria, plants, mice, cats, etc. While Aristotle utilizes the term "soul" (in Greek, *psuchē*; in Latin, *anima*) to refer to the special type of form that defines the essence of living versus non-living substances, he further differentiates three types of souls. *Vegetative*—sometimes termed *nutritive*—souls are had by basic living entities capable of nutrition, growth, reproduction, and the other activities that biologists and microbiologists find common to both amoebae and oak trees. *Sensitive* souls inform the bodies of non-rational animals that are not only alive, but are also capable of sensing their environment and responding to it. Finally, *intellective*—sometimes termed *rational*—souls endow at least one species of animal—*Homo sapiens*—with the capacities for not only life and sentience, but also rational thought, self-awareness, and free will. As far as Thomas, or for that matter anyone today, knows for sure, only human beings possess the definitive capacities of a rationally ensouled animal; however, further research with dolphins and members of the Great Ape species, not to mention the possibility of intelligent extraterrestrial life, may yield the discovery of additional sub-species of "rational animals" or "intellective beings."

In sum, a soul—including the intellective soul of a human being—is a special type of substantial form endowing the matter it informs with certain capacities essential to the existence of a living, sentient, or rational being. The intellective soul is distinctive, however, insofar as it is capable of *subsisting* in the absence of its body (q. 75, a. 2). Like any other substantial form, the souls of plants or non-rational animals are naturally annihilated upon the death of their bodies, when basic vegetative functions irreversibly cease and all that is left is non-living matter (q. 75, a. 3). This is due to the fact that all of the essential vegetative and sensitive functions of plants and non-rational animals are executed by means of physical organs: there is no photosynthesis without leaves and chlorophyll, and no seeing or hearing without eyes or ears. For human beings, these same types of functions also depend upon one's physical body: no respiration without lungs, and no smelling or touching without a nose or skin. The *intellective* and *volitional* capacities of human beings, however, do not function through bodily organs. Despite our temptation to think of the brain as the "seat of the soul," and the overwhelming evidence of "neural correlates" of conscious mental activity, Thomas argues that a human being's intellective and volitional activity cannot be reduced to the brain's neural activity: while neural happenings occur simultaneously whenever one thinks or wills, the act of thinking or willing is not identical to such neural happenings, and the latter is ontologically dependent on the former.

Thomas' arguments for this astonishing conclusion are based upon the nature of what the human intellect is capable of understanding. First, he notes that the human intellect can potentially "have knowledge of all corporeal things" (q. 75, a. 2). While there are certainly limits to the human intellect—we cannot, for example, have complete knowledge of the divine essence—the natural world is completely open to us and each of us can come to understand the nature of anything that exists in the physical universe. Thomas then claims that, if the intellect were itself material, then its material nature would impede its capacity to potentially know the nature of any other material object. A full explanation of why this is the case will have to await our discussion of Thomas' account of the intellectual cognitive process later in this chapter. For now, in order to justify his claim, Thomas draws an analogy to a sick man whose tongue is infected with a "bitter humor" and thereby cannot sense anything sweet—if you want to conduct a similar experiment, just try drinking orange juice immediately after having eaten sugary candy. Thomas also utilizes the analogy of viewing a liquid inside a colored vase: golden-hued lager appears amber when inside a brown-glassed bottle.

Thomas provides a second argument for the intellective soul's immateriality by noting that what the intellect understands are not *individual* objects—*this* dog, *that* book over there on the desk—but the *universal nature* of dogs and books. This means that the intellect must *abstract* what it understands from the particular material conditions of individual objects it perceives through sensation—again, this complex cognitive process will be explained in detail below. Thomas' point here is that, if the intellect were itself material, then it would be able to understand only individual material objects and not their essential natures: a particular dog, Fido, is a material object, but Fido's *canine* nature—his "dogness" so to speak—is immaterial and common to both Fido and all other dogs. Therefore, since what the intellect understands is something immaterial, the intellect itself must be immaterial (q. 75, a. 5).

Due to the intellective soul's immaterial nature, Thomas draws the further conclusion that it is *incorruptible* (q. 75, a. 6). To understand his reasoning here, we must first clarify what Thomas means by the term "corruption." For a substance to corrupt is for its matter to cease being informed by its substantial form, insofar as the matter no longer supports the form's definitive powers and other qualities. For instance, a wooden log consumed by fire is corrupted insofar as it loses its structural qualities as a unified hunk of "wood" and is converted into a distinct and disaggregated substance: a pile of ash. Technically speaking, then, only *substances* can corrupt by virtue of losing their substantial forms; such forms do not merely separate from the matter they previously informed, but are naturally annihilated insofar as their powers and other qualities cannot exist without matter—the hardness of a wooden log cannot exist immaterially. The only exception is the intellective soul insofar as it has powers of intellective thought and autonomous volition that, as argued in previous articles, are immaterial and thereby do not require bodily organs in order to function. Hence, while a human being suffers corruption at the moment of death when her soul ceases to inform her material body—and her previously living animal body becomes a "corpse"—her soul is not annihilated in the process, but continues to exist and function as a thinking and willing thing. We will return below to discuss Thomas' nuanced discussion of the "separated soul's" nature and activity, as well as the ultimate post-mortem destiny of human beings.

Given Thomas' assertion that a human intellective soul can persist beyond its body's death, one might be inclined to conceive of him as a "dualist" akin to Plato. While it is appropriate to label Thomas as a sort of dualist, we must distinguish his brand of "hylomorphic dualism" from Plato's view. Thomas fundamentally disagrees with Plato's thesis that a human being *is* her soul, meaning that one is *identical* to her soul and is merely causally related to her body—akin to how a driver is connected to her car by being in the driver's seat. Thomas unequivocally asserts the contrary thesis that a human being is *not* identical to her soul (q. 75, a. 4). Identifying a human being with her soul would render one more akin in nature to an *angel*; as we saw in the previous chapter, angels are defined by Thomas as pure intellects without bodies. The essential nature of human beings, however, is to exist as composed of *both* an intellective soul and a material body of which it is the substantial form. Thus, even a subsistent human soul existing without its body would be quite different in nature from an angel (q. 75, a. 7).

QUESTION 76—UNION OF BODY AND SOUL

This is one of the most important questions in the entire *Summa* for, following upon his arguments for the immaterial and incorruptible nature of the human intellective soul in the preceding question, Thomas must now account for how such a soul is united to a living human body to compose an individual human being. Thomas' hylomorphic anthropology will inform not only his view of human cognitive operations, but also his theories of human moral psychology, what constitutes human happiness, and the ultimate disposition of human beings after death.

As noted above, Thomas' hylomorphic view is equivalent to neither Platonic dualism nor contemporary reductive materialism; although, in a sense, his view is both dualist and materialist insofar as he holds that there are *two* metaphysical components of a human being, one of which is *matter*. Contemporary metaphysicians, whether defending or critiquing dualism, typically refer to the "mind–body" or "soul–body" relationship, implying that there is an organized, living, individual hunk of matter—the body—and something else—the mind or soul—that is somehow related to it. According to Thomas, though, an organized, living, individual body can exist only insofar as it is informed by a soul, as defined above in Question 75. The putative "soul–body" relationship is thus more accurately characterized as a "form–matter" relationship; specifically, for a human being, an intellective soul informs matter to compose an individual living body capable of sentience and supportive of rational operations. In short, a human body only exists as a living, sentient animal by virtue of being informed by an intellective soul that is itself capable of rational thought and volition. When a human body informed by an intellective soul comes into existence, so does a human being—a "rational animal."

How does Thomas argue for hylomorphism over the competing Platonic view? Recall Plato's thesis that a human being just *is* her intellect (soul), which is causally connected to a body, such that the former moves the latter just as you drive your car. To refute this thesis, Thomas first notes that the primary activity of the intellective soul is to *know* and the primary activity of a human body is to *live*. He then contends that it is the numerically same soul that both knows and by which a human body lives. This is a controversial view, however, as some of Thomas' contemporaries held that there could be multiple souls involved: one soul informing the human body as a living, sentient animal, and the other soul being the intellect that causally interacts with the body. Thomas retorts that such dualists must account for the *phenomenological* evidence that a human being is conscious of both her own intellectual thinking and her sense-perceptions—the latter being cognitive functions realized by the body's sense-organs and brain (q. 76, a. 1).

To appreciate the strength of this evidence, consider what occurs when the motion-sensor in my house detects the movement of an intruder and sounds an extremely loud alert that wakes me from deep sleep, I promptly come to the rational realization that there is an intruder in my house and react appropriately. I am self-conscious of both my hearing of the painful alarm noise and my rational realization of its meaning. But I am not directly conscious of the sensing of the intruder's movement that tripped the alarm; that sensory activity was accomplished by the motion-sensor and I have no direct awareness of its activity, only of the noise it generates as a result. If Platonic dualism is correct, then my body's sensory activity would be akin to that of the motion-sensor, alerting my intellect to sensory data which it can utilize in its reasoning process. But I wouldn't be self-conscious of the sensation itself, which contradicts our first-person experience.

The definitive activity of human beings is intellectual understanding and a human being is a living, sentient animal. Thus, to avoid disrupting a human being's ontological *unity*, the same substantial form by which a human body exists as a living, sentient animal must be the same as the form by which a human being intellectually understands—namely, the intellective soul (q. 76, a. 1). Thomas must reconcile this conclusion with his earlier arguments in Question 75 that the intellective soul is *immaterial* insofar as the intellect does not function by means of any bodily organs. Here, it is important to disavow the modern identification of the soul with "the mind" and recall that, for Thomas, the immaterial intellect is but a *power*—or rather a *set* of powers—of the soul (q. 76, a. 1 *ad* 1). The intellective soul informs a human body and its vegetative and sensitive powers operate through bodily organs, just not its intellective powers.

In addition to Platonic dualism, another popular view among Thomas' contemporaries was that there is but a single, universal intellect, whose knowledge "illuminates" the individual minds of angels and human beings. The Christian forerunner of this thesis of *divine illumination* was Augustine, but Thomas' interlocutors were fellow scholars at the University of Paris influenced by the Islamic Aristotelian commentator, Averroes—the so-called "Latin Averroists." Thomas shows that this thesis is untenable regardless of whether one adheres to Platonic dualism or Aristotelian hylomorphism (q. 76, a. 2). The latter argument is key insofar as the Averroist view also claimed to be an interpretation of an ambiguous passage from Aristotle's *De anima*. From the Platonic perspective, since a human being is identical to his intellect, it follows that, if there were only one intellect for all human beings, then Socrates would be identical with Plato, which is absurd. From the Aristotelian perspective, Thomas argues that if the intellect is a power of the soul that is also the form of a human being—as established in the previous article—then there cannot be one intellect for a human being since that would entail we all share the same form, and thus the same being, resulting in the same absurdity as in the case of Platonism.

Finally, Thomas argues that, no matter how one accounts for the union of intellect with a particular human being, the Averroist view suffers the entailment that every human being is *the same thinker*—akin to one person sitting in a large monitoring room receiving sensory data from billions of cameras simultaneously and formulating intellectual thoughts based on that data. While this analogous picture is coherent in itself since, on a much smaller scale, a security guard can monitor data from multiple cameras simultaneously and formulate thoughts based on said data, the cameras themselves are not conscious and the guard does not cause each of them to believe that it is thinking by transmitting his thoughts back to the camera. But that's exactly what would be occurring if there were one intellect doing all of the thinking that each of us perceives ourselves to be doing.

As noted earlier, some of Thomas' contemporaries held that the intellective soul was not necessarily the substantial form of the human body since, given the diverse powers related to life and sensation, there may be a diverse number of souls—vegetative, sensitive, and intellective—all composing a human being. Thomas cites three problems with this thesis (q. 76, a. 3). First, echoing his central complaint against Platonic dualism, it would destroy the *substantial unity* of a human being as *unum simpliciter* ("one unqualifiedly") (q. 76, a. 1). There are various ways in which something may be considered a *unity*. For example, a heap of stones is a unity in terms of the constituent stones being spatially continuous; a house is a unity in terms of its constituent parts being functionally organized in a certain fashion; and a mover and that which it moves are a unity in terms of their agent/patient relationship. None of these types of unity, though, count as *substantial* unity—they are not *unum simpliciter*. Examples of things that are *unum simpliciter*, according to Thomas, are elemental substances, certain mixtures of elemental substances, immaterial substances, and living organisms. The notion that a human being is an aggregate of a mover and that which it moves is analogous to the aggregate of a sailor and the ship he pilots. One would not say that a sailor and his ship compose one substance; analogously, one would not say that a human being's soul—the mover—and his body—the moved—compose one substance. One could say that a sailor and his ship, as well as one's body and soul on the Platonic account, are unified in a certain respect or compose an aggregate sum, but such unity would not be *unum simpliciter*. The same would be true if there were more than one soul composing a human being: one soul being that by which a human being is alive, another by which he is an animal, and another by which he is rational. Each soul would be a substantial form composing three distinct substances and thus could not be unified as a single substance.

Second, Thomas makes an argument based on the logic of *essential predication*—namely, that certain terms are predicated of a being insofar as they are definitive of the kind of being it is. In the case of human beings, our essential definition is "rational animal." Hence, the term "animal" is essentially predicated of human beings. But this would not be the case if a human being were not informed by a soul with both rational and sensitive powers—the latter being definitive of animality. Finally, Thomas notes that the various powers of the human soul *causally interact* with each other; specifically, a sensitive power can obstruct the intellective power—as when, for example, one attempts to think rationally while intoxicated or feverish.

Thomas concludes that there must be one substantial form—one soul—that has all of the definitive powers of the three types of soul Aristotle defines: vegetative, sensitive, and intellective. He adopts an illustration Aristotle utilizes from geometry involving more complex figures containing less complex figures "virtually"—e.g. within a hexagon, there is virtually a rectangle, and within the rectangle there is virtually a triangle (see Figure 1).

Thomas' conclusion also counters the view that there is another substantial form that is the principle of a human body's basic existence and structure, rendering it suitable for intellective ensoulment (q. 76, a. 4). This view continued to have ardent defenders after Thomas' death—most notably John Duns Scotus, Henry of Ghent, and William of Ockham.

Having established that there is a single substantial form—the intellective soul—informing matter to compose a living and sentient human body, Thomas shows how it is "proper" that the intellective

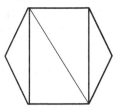

Figure 1 The tripartite soul.

soul be united to this type of body. He first notes a general Aristotelian metaphysical principle: "Since the form is not for the matter, but rather the matter for the form, we must gather from the form the reason why the matter is such as it is; and not conversely" (q. 76, a. 5). While a complete explanation will have to await our discussion of Thomas' account of the interplay between sense-perception and intellective cognition, suffice it for now to note that the intellect requires the human body's sense-organs and cognitive operations that we share with other highly evolved animals to provide sense-data—in the form of what Thomas terms "phantasms"—for the intellect to derive conceptual understanding. For this reason, as we will see later on, even though an intellective soul can persist and continue thinking and willing without its body, its cognitive functioning will be *diminished* until it is reunited with its body—with all of its physical organs of life and sensation—at the Resurrection.

The final key point worth emphasizing in this question is Thomas' assertion that the *whole* intellective soul exists in *each part* of the body it informs (q. 76, a. 8). Given that uninformed *prime* matter cannot exist, Thomas' denial that there is more than one substantial form of a human body, and the soul's *simple* nature—it cannot be divided into parts except conceptually, as Thomas divides up the soul into diverse powers—it follows that a soul must be present, in its entirety, in every part of its body. Thomas illustrates this point with an analogy to the whiteness that colors a surface area; each part of the surface is *as white* as every other part, meaning that the whiteness is wholly present at each part of the surface. Analogously, each part of the human body is *as human* as every other part unless it ceases to be informed by one's soul: when Luke Skywalker's hand is cut off by Darth Vader, it is no longer informed by his soul and thus is no longer "a human hand," properly speaking. This does not mean, however, that a human being can see with her big toe or breathe with her liver; the soul's *powers* can exist in distinct parts of the body that are suitable for their operation.

QUESTIONS 77–78—THE DEFINING CAPACITIES OF HUMAN NATURE

In the first two questions of his treatise on human nature, Thomas describes the hylomorphic view of humanity's ontological constitution—

that is, the nature and relationship of the two metaphysical components of each human being: an intellective soul informing a material human body. With this anthropological structure in mind, Thomas now moves on to a detailed analysis of the various *capacities*—or *powers* (Latin: *potentiae*)—that are attributable to either the intellective soul alone or the soul-body composite. In one sense, all of a human being's capacities belong to her soul insofar as it is the substantial form of her body, such that her body would not exist as a living and sentient animal if it were not informed by her soul (q. 77, a. 5 *ad* 1); however, many of the soul's capacities—namely, all those associated with life and sensation—would exist as mere *potentialities* and not be actualizable without the requisite material organs of the human body. Thus, some capacities—namely, the intellect and will—can be actualized within the soul alone, and some only within the soul-body composite (q. 77, a. 5). Thomas states, though, that all of a human being's capacities and activities are most properly attributed to *the person* herself.

Thomas first makes the claim—widely accepted in his time—that a soul is something distinct from its powers (q. 77, a. 1). Thomas would thus deny the claim—popular among contemporary materialists—that "soul" does not refer to anything that is really distinct from the body, but is rather merely a shorthand term for the set of capacities found in a living, sensing, and thinking human body. On the contrary, as affirmed in the previous questions, "soul" refers to the principle by which matter exists in the form of a body endowed with capacities for life and sensation, supportive of rational thought and volition; this formal principle is ontologically prior to its capacities, which are also dependent—in the case of the vegetative and sensitive capacities—on a body with the proper material organs for their actualization.

Thomas then notes that, while a soul is ontologically *simple* insofar as it is an immaterial form with no divisible *parts*, it can be conceptually understood as having diverse capacities: there are many different types of operations a soul—either on its own or by means of the body it informs—can perform (q. 77, a. 2). The enumeration of the soul's capacities is not arbitrary, but based on distinguishing criteria. Hence, there is not a capacity to walk distinct from a capacity to run or to stand still; rather, there is a general capacity for *locomotion*, which may be actualized in the form of walking or running, or not at all when one is standing still. The primary criteria by which the soul's capacities are distinguished are each capacity's *activity* and *object* (q. 77, a. 3). With respect to the first criterion, Thomas distinguishes between *active* and *passive* activities. As the terms imply, the former refers to the soul's capacity to *perform* some activity, such as to move, to think, to grow, etc.; the latter refers to the soul's capacity to be the *recipient* of some activity, such as when light stimulates the eye and visual cortex such that one sees, or heat is transduced through the skin and nervous system such that one feels that something is hot.

Each of these broad categories of capacities may then be subdivided by the distinct objects of each capacity. In the case of active capacities, the object is the *end* toward which the activity is directed; for example, growth is directed toward the body realizing its appropriate size, and locomotion is directed toward a human being's or other animal's appetites being satisfied—we will take up Thomas' discussion of *appetite* later in this chapter. In the case of passive capacities, the object is that which acts upon the soul and the capacities are diversified according to the diverse types of such objects; for example, color is the object of sight, and sound is the object of hearing.

With these criteria and subdivisions of the soul's capacities in mind, Thomas further describes the evident *order* among the soul's capacities (q. 77, aa. 4 and 7). This order is reflected in various relationships among the types of capacities. For instance, one capacity may *control* another—as the will controls the body's locomotive capacity, and the intellect in general can exercise varying degrees of control over the soul's sensitive capacities. Another way of ordering the soul's capacities is in terms of their ontological dependence upon each other, reflected in the order in which they come into existence in a developing human organism—as we will see in the last section of this chapter, Thomas conceives of human beings as first coming into existence as merely vegetative entities, then developing into sentient animals, and finally developing a sufficiently sophisticated degree of sentience to support rational thought. Reason is thus dependent—in a qualified way—on sensation, which is in turn dependent on an animal—human or otherwise—being alive.

In Question 75 (aa. 2 and 6), Thomas argued that an intellective soul is a *subsistent* form that does not suffer corruption upon the death of the body it informs. This conclusion follows from such a soul possessing certain capacities—namely, for intellectual understanding and autonomous volition—that do not depend upon or function through any material organs of the human body. Thomas thus characterizes a human being's intellectual and volitional capacities as being in her soul as their *subject* (q. 77, a. 5) and so those capacities will remain, and remain active, in the soul after death. The soul's vegetative and sensitive capacities, however, do not remain in the soul in the same way; although they persist in a certain way. Such capacities, since they are actualized through bodily organs, must await the soul's reunion with its resurrected body in order to be actualizable again. Nevertheless, a human being's resurrected body only exists as a living, sentient human body, and as *her* body, by virtue of being re-informed by *her* soul. Thus, the vegetative and sensitive capacities that will be actualized through the organs of one's resurrected body must persist in what Thomas terms a "virtual" sense (q. 77, a. 8).

To understand Thomas' nuance here, consider someone who has had both of his legs amputated and so cannot actualize his natural capacity for self-movement: locomotion—of course, he could move himself by means of a wheelchair, but let's set that option aside for the moment. Before losing his legs, he could walk as well as stand still and, when in the latter state, retained his capacity to walk. Now, having lost his legs, he no longer possesses the immediately exercisable capacity to walk. If, however, artificial legs were attached to his body or a fictional "miracle drug" allowed his legs to be regenerated, he would regain the immediately exercisable capacity to walk. This possibility shows that, even when he lacked the capacity to walk in the immediate sense, he retained a *virtual* capacity to walk again if provided with new legs.

To contemporary ears the term "virtual" implies something not entirely real, as in the "virtual reality" of computer-game environments or the "virtual world" of the fictional Matrix. In Thomas' lexicon, however, it is derived from the Latin term *virtus*, which means "power" just as the Latin term *potentia* does—we will see in Chapter 7 how Thomas relates *virtus* to the dispositions that define one's moral character. So, while an amputee lacks the *potentia* to walk until he receives new legs, he retains the *virtus* to walk again. This can be verified empirically by the fact that his nervous system and the motor cortex of his brain have the ability to functionally assimilate and control the movement of his new legs; graft artificial legs onto a tree and it still will not go anywhere. Analogously, then, while a separated intellective soul—persisting between bodily death and resurrection—cannot see, hear, grow, breathe, etc., and lacks the respective *potentiae* for such activities, it retains the *virtus* to inform matter to constitute a resurrected living animal body with the appropriate organs to engage in these activities.

Employing his criteria for differentiating the human soul's capacities (q. 77, a. 3), Thomas delineates five broad genera of capacities that define the human essence: vegetative, sensitive, appetitive, locomotive, and intellective (q. 78, a. 1). Each genus comprises distinct sets of capacities: for instance, the vegetative capacities include nutrition, growth, and reproduction (a. 2); and the sensitive capacities include the five external senses—sight, hearing, touch, taste, and smell (a. 3)— as well as four *internal* senses that we will discuss below (a. 4). Some of these more specific categories may be further divided into sub-specific capacities: for example, there is both an intellective appetite—termed the *will*—and a sensitive appetite (q. 80, a. 2), the latter divisible into a *concupiscible* and an *irascible* appetite (q. 81, a. 2). In the following sections, we will discuss in detail the soul's intellective and appetitive capacities.

Before moving on, though, we need to elucidate what Thomas is referring to by *internal* sensitive capacities. The five external senses are well-familiar and it is evident that these sensory capacities, in some fashion, are shared by humans and many other animal species; some animal species may have only a subset of these capacities, or may have certain sensory capacities human beings lack—e.g. the echo-location capacity of bats. The four internal senses Thomas defines are less immediately familiar, but a brief review will reveal their evident presence in the cognitive architecture of humans and other animals. The first is what Thomas terms the *common sense*. This is not the common sense that your parents wanted you to develop as a child and that philosophers are often accused of lacking. Rather, this term refers to the capacity to take in the various types of sense-data arriving through the external senses and putting that information together into a coherent, unified sensory experience. At this moment, for example, I am looking at my computer screen, hearing Chris Isaak's voice stream off the internet, feeling the chill of the air conditioner, tasting the coffee I just drank, and smelling the residual chemicals used by the cleaning staff. I perceive each datum through a discrete sensory organ and each is first processed by a discrete part of my brain; however, I do not *experience* these data discretely, but all at once in a single conscious experience. Furthermore, I am able to recognize that two discrete sensory experiences provide information about the same object—e.g. when I feel the hardness of my desk while simultaneously seeing its brown color, smelling the wood of which it is made, and hearing the sound it makes when I rap my fist on it, I know that all of these sensory experiences are related to *this desk*. The common sense is what allows me to distinguish the various types of sense-data I am receiving while also relating them to one and the same source, or to different sources as the case may be, all within a unified conscious experience (q. 78, a. 4 *ad* 2).

The data provided to the common sense via the five external senses results in the reception of the *sensible forms* of individual material objects. These forms are received and stored in the next internal capacity of the sensitive soul: the *imagination* (Latin: *phantasia*). Thomas terms the sense-data recorded in the imagination "phantasms" (Latin: *phantasmata*). Although one may think of the imagination storing sensory *images*, phantasms should not be understood as merely visual representations of perceived objects in the mind. Rather, phantasms are "likenesses" of perceived objects that contain all of the information about them as perceived by one's external senses. For instance, when thinking of his grandmother, a person may recall not only a visual representation of her, but also the sound of her voice singing a lullaby and the particular scent of her home. The purpose of phantasms is to be available for the intellect to use in abstracting the *intelligible form* of perceived things—a process that will be explained in the next section. Hence, phantasms are something between the immediate mental impression of an object perceived by sensation and the intellectual understanding of that object's nature as abstracted from any individuating characteristics. And since phantasms are not mere colocations of bits of sensory data, but, thanks to the common sense, are cohesive in the same way as the physical objects in the world they represent, there is a *formal isomorphism* between a phantasm and the object from which it is derived. This allows for Thomas to hold a version of *epistemic realism*, the primary thesis of which is that there is a causal relationship between objects in the world and phantasms created in the mind such that one can avoid the extreme *skepticism* of the ancient Pyrrhonians before Thomas or of Descartes after him.

Once a particular object has been perceived by the senses and a phantasm of it produced in the imagination, there is an immediate cognitive *estimation* of whether the object is something desirable that one should go after—e.g. food, water, shelter, a mate, etc.—or something that is a threat one should avoid—e.g. a predator, an obstacle, a competitor, etc. This type of cognitive apprehension is common to both human beings and other animal species; although humans are able to engage in an even higher level of cognitive assessment and are able to freely choose how to respond to perceived goods or threats, while other animals react instinctively based on their estimation of perceived objects. The sensible forms one receives, combined with the cognitive assessment of whether these forms represent something that ought to be pursued or avoided, is stored in the fourth internal sensory capacity: *memory*. Hence, when a human being or other animal perceives another object of the same type, it can more immediately identify and react to it based on its past perception and estimation of similar objects, which explains why a domesticated dog will typically run to its owner with tail wagging—unless it has been the subject of abuse—but bark aggressively at a stranger. Having delineated the sensory capacities human beings share with other animal species, Thomas now shifts focus to the peculiarly human capacities of *intellect* and *will*.

QUESTIONS 79, 84–89—HOW AND WHAT THE HUMAN INTELLECT KNOWS

In Question 79, Thomas distinguishes the various capacities of the human intellect. Later, in Questions 84–89, he details the cognitive operations in which the intellect engages. In between—Questions 80–83—Thomas discusses the nature of the other distinctive capacity of the human soul, the will, saving a more detailed discussion of the will's operations for the first treatise of the *secunda pars*.

As noted earlier, Thomas' hylomorphic definition of the term "soul" differs from the Platonic identification of the soul with the intellect alone, as well as post-Cartesian uses of the term to refer to the "mind" or "consciousness." Thomas differs from the latter insofar as he recognizes that non-rational animals are also conscious and capable of a certain degree of cognitive activity, which he terms the "estimative capacity"; they can thereby be said to have minds, just not intellects. The intellect, Thomas concludes, should be understood as an *essential capacity* of the human soul (q. 79, a. 1). It is not, however, a simple, singular capacity, but comprises various sub-capacities. This does not mean that each person has more than one intellect, but rather that the *one* intellect engages in various types of operations; Thomas re-affirms his objection to the Latin Averroist and other alternative theories that conceive of the intellect as a single, universal mind that actualizes—"illuminates"—knowledge within each human being (q. 79, aa. 4 and 5).

One point of agreement between Thomas and his Aristotelian inter-locutors is that there is a distinction between the so-called "agent" and "possible" intellects (q. 79, aa. 2 and 3). Where they disagree is in terms of whether these labels refer to two *aspects* of a singular intellect that is a capacity of each individual human soul—Thomas' view—or whether there is an *ontological* distinction between the two types of intellect such that each human being has her own possible intellect but there is only one, universal agent intellect—the Averroist view. Thomas first discusses the possible intellect as the *tabula rasa* that is potentially able to receive any "intelligible form." This term refers to the universal *nature*, or *essence*, in which the individual members of a specific type of being all share insofar as it is under-standable by the intellect. All human beings, for instance, share in the nature labeled "humanity"; it is the form of *humanity*, not the form of an individual human being, which is received by the possible intellect.

Thomas, following Aristotle, describes the possible intellect as "at first like a clean tablet on which nothing is written" (q. 79, a. 2). This is a clear repudiation of Plato's theory of *innate ideas* expressed in his dialogue *Meno*, in which Socrates guides an uneducated slave boy to arrive at certain geometric conclusions through a series of questions. This exercise not only exemplifies the Socratic pedagogical method, but is the basis for Plato's contention that human souls must pre-exist their bodies, existing in the realm of pure ideas and thus possessing knowledge of such ideas prior to being born; the trauma of embodi-ment causes the soul to forget the knowledge it previously possessed until it is educed by means of guiding questions—analogous to the psychotherapeutic process of educing repressed memories of past traumas.

In characterizing the possible intellect as empty of innate ideas, however, Thomas does not deny that the intellect has a *cognitive architecture* that allows it to comprehend the intelligible forms it eventually receives. Such architecture is analogous to Noam Chomsky's thesis that human beings are born with an innate language-learning mechanism allowing us to intuitively organize the sounds we hear as infants into a coherent structure and derive the rules governing that structure so we can eventually understand and speak meaningful language. In short, we are not born knowing English, Spanish, Romanian, etc., but with the capacity to *learn* language; analogously, we are not born with knowledge of geometry, physics, logic, or ethics, but we are born with what is necessary to *attain* such knowledge potentially (q. 84, a. 3).

As with Aristotle, Thomas disagrees with Plato's view that the universal forms of beings exist eternally in a separate realm—except as ideas in the mind of God (q. 85, a. 5)—and that material individuals are mere "shadows" imperfectly representing the ideal forms. Rather, universal forms exist *within* each individual subject of its kind: each individual human being possesses humanity, but humanity cannot be identified with any individual human being since it is universally shared by all human beings. To understand humanity as such, the intellect must *abstract* the intelligible universal form from its sense-perception of individual human beings. All natural human knowledge, according to Thomas, begins with *sensation*. Thomas can thus rightly be labeled an "empiricist"; although his form of empiricism differs from the reductive skepticism of David Hume or the limited methodology of the modern "scientific method"—see the discussion of Question 1 of the *prima pars* in Chapter 2. Thomas contends that empirical science—that is, knowledge of the natures of material objects—would be impossible if universal forms existed wholly separate from particular objects perceived through sensation (q. 84, a. 1).

The abstraction of intelligible forms is accomplished by the agent—or "active"—intellect (q. 79, a. 3). Again, one should not think that human beings have two types of intellect; rather, we each have one intellect that functions both actively, in abstracting the intelligible forms of perceived objects from the phantasms produced in the imagination, and passively, in receiving and retaining the abstracted forms for use in further cognitive activities, such as reasoning. To summarize the basic intellectual cognitive process:

1   The senses perceive an individual material object, meaning that the object's "sensible form" is received by the imagination: I perceive a particular person in front of me.
2   The imagination produces a "phantasm" representing the perceived object in terms of its received sensible qualities: I form a mental representation of this person.
3   The agent intellect abstracts the "intelligible form" from the phantasm and deposits it in the possible intellect, meaning that the intellect sifts the universal qualities definitive of the object's essential nature from its particular sensible qualities: I understand this person to be *human*.
4   The intellect retains the received form and is able to utilize it in further reasoning processes, as discussed below: I deduce that this person is mortal because she is human.

It is thus evident for Thomas that intellective cognition is impossible for human beings, in our natural condition, without turning to phantasms of objects perceived through sensation (q. 84, aa. 6 and 7), as evidenced by the fact that intellectual activity is *hindered* when one's senses are damaged or corrupted (q. 84, a. 8)—as in cases, for instance, of someone who is severely intoxicated, neurologically impaired, or in a persistent vegetative state.

Thomas states that the intellect *retains* abstracted intelligible forms (q. 79, a. 6); but the capacity of "intellective memory" does not refer to some sort of "storehouse" of intelligible forms that have been abstracted from one's previous sense-perceptions. Rather, it refers to a *disposition* (Latin: *habitus*) on the part of the possible intellect to actualize previously comprehended forms (q. 79, a. 7). Contemporary neurological evidence indicates that sensory-level memory functions in a similar fashion: it is not as if every memory of a past experience is neuro-chemically "stored" as a discrete entity, but rather the brain has a disposition toward re-actualizing previous neural patterns that generate a *simulacrum* of a previous sensory experience. This *dispositional* aspect of the brain fits with Thomas' understanding of the soul as the form of the body insofar as such neural activity could not occur unless the matter composing one's brain were formed in a specific way such that it is disposed toward performing just such activity.

In the final step of the intellectual cognitive process, the intellect utilizes the received intelligible forms to derive additional knowledge through *reasoning*. Thomas thus states that "reason" is not a distinct capacity from the intellect, but rather is something that the intellect *does* after the initial reception of intelligible forms (q. 79, a. 8). In Question 85, Thomas delineates the three primary operations of the intellect when confronted with a particular object delivered through sensation (q. 85, a. 5). First, as described already, the intellect apprehends the object's intelligible form—otherwise known as its fundamental "whatness" (Latin: *quiddity*)—which is the essential nature common to all individual members of the object's species. The intellect's apprehension of the intelligible form involves abstracting it from the phantasm formed by the imagination by means of conceptually stripping away all of the particular conditions of *this* object that is sensed. A pithy way of expressing the difference between sensation and intellection is as "seeing" versus "seeing *as*": perceiving *this person* versus understanding this person *as human*. It is important to emphasize that Thomas is drawing a *conceptual* distinction here; as *phenomenally* experienced, all human "seeing" intrinsically involves "seeing as." That is, one does not first perceive a dog and *then* understand what she is seeing *as* a dog. Rather, one *immediately* perceives a dog *as* a dog, which then allows her subsequently to form the propositional attitude: "What I am seeing is a dog."

As we noted earlier, non-rational animals are capable of sensing individual objects, estimating their status as something either desirable or threatening, and storing a cognitive representation of the sensed object along with the associated estimation of it as something desirable or threatening. While this allows a dog to differentiate his owner who loves and feeds him from a potentially dangerous stranger, and to react accordingly, what a dog cannot do is comprehend the abstract concept "humanity" as the specific nature in which both his owner and the stranger share. Rational animals—i.e. humans—can comprehend such abstract universal concepts, but this is only the first step in the process of intellective cognition.

Next, the intellect is able to "compound and divide" the various concepts it has comprehended, facilitating both a deeper understanding of the nature of cognized objects and an ability to create *fictional* objects. In the first case, the intellect can divide the species "humanity" into its component conceptual parts: "rational" and "animal," understanding one to refer to a wider genus to which human beings belong and the other the specific difference distinguishing human beings from other animal species. This also allows the intellect to comprehend which characteristics—essential properties, accidental features, dispositions, relations, etc.—various species may have in common as well as what differentiates them. In this process, the intellect "affirms or denies" various characteristics as components of a perceived object's intelligible species and formulates *propositions* in the grammatical form of sentences with a subject and predicate: Horses are four-legged; Liquids are convertible into gases and vice versa; Music must have a melody. The intellect can also utilize characteristics of known species to create novel fictional species of beings, as when certain characteristics of a horse and a bird are combined to form the mythical, chimeric Pegasus, or the concepts of a human boy and magical power are combined to create Harry Potter.

Finally, the intellect can take the various intelligible species it has comprehended, along with their component concepts and the propositions it has formed, and put them together in syllogistic form to draw novel conclusions—*reasoning*. Hence, for example, once the intellect comprehends the species "human" and that one of its essential conceptual components is "mortality," the following syllogism can be easily formulated:

1   All human beings are mortal.
2   Socrates is a human being.
3   Therefore, Socrates is mortal.

One does not have to directly perceive Socrates' mortality—that is, actually see him die—in order to know that he is mortal; one only needs to perceive that Socrates is human and intellectually understand that being human entails being mortal.

Reasoning can take various forms, depending on the *object* and *purpose* for which it is employed; Thomas is clear, though, that these are not distinct rational capacities, but rather the intellect simply reasoning in various fashions. First, Thomas distinguishes between so-called "higher" and "lower" reason (q. 79, a. 9). The former refers to reasoning about *eternal* objects, such as God, mathematics, or the principles of logic, and may be more accurately labeled "contemplation," the goal of which is to attain "wisdom." The latter category refers to reasoning aimed at *temporal* objects and would thus include the empirical scientific fields that seek to draw general conclusions about objects populating the created universe, as opposed to the eternal truths that underlie the universe itself or its Creator. Hence, for example, the fields of chemistry, biology, and psychology would fall into the category of "lower" reasoning; while theoretical physics, geometry, and theology would fall into the "higher" category.

All of these modes of reasoning would be forms of what Thomas terms "speculative" reasoning—that is, reasoning aimed at discovering what *is* the case. But reason also operates in a "practical" mode aimed at determining what one *ought* to do—in other words, *moral* reasoning (q. 79, a. 11). A detailed analysis of how reason operates practically is, of course, the primary emphasis of the *secunda pars*. Here, Thomas notes a key feature of human beings' cognitive architecture required for moral reasoning to be possible: *synderesis*. To understand what Thomas means by this technical term, let us first recall a point made earlier that the human intellect has an innate *structure* that allows it to acquire knowledge. This structure comprises a set of "first principles" of which one may not be consciously aware, but nevertheless utilizes as background premises in everyday reasoning. In speculative reasoning—that is, any scientific, mathematical, or metaphysical inquiry—one operates on the *principle of non-contradiction*: The same thing cannot both be and not-be at the same time in the same respect. In a simple case of reasoning, if I see that it is sunny and cloudless outside my window right now, I know that it cannot be also raining outside my window right now. In a more complex case of reasoning, physicists were initially confused by experiments showing that light apparently travels in both particle (photons) and wave form, because they believed that the categories of "particle" and "wave" were *mutually exclusive* categories—particles were, by definition, not-waves and vice versa. Hence, nothing could be both a particle and a wave on pain of violating the principle of non-contradiction.

The revolution in physics resulting from these experiments was the recognition that "particle" and "wave" were not mutually exclusive categories, since the only alternative would be to deny the principle of non-contradiction and the intellect cannot rationally embrace such a denial.

Just as there are first principles of speculative reasoning, Thomas affirms the existence of first principles of practical reasoning, the most fundamental of which is "good is to be done and pursued, and evil is to be avoided" (Ia–IIae, q. 94, a. 2). Again, it is not that humans are born with conscious knowledge of these first principles; rather, such principles constitute the subconscious architecture of our reasoning process. Thomas thus defines "synderesis," not as a distinct intellectual capacity, but as a fundamental *disposition* of the intellect to reason practically in accord with first principles. When a human being actively uses first principles to arrive at a moral conclusion about how she, or others, ought to act in a particular situation, Thomas terms this conscious application of first principles "conscience" (q. 79, a. 13).

Every human being, insofar as each is composed of a body informed by an intellective soul, is born with the same set of fundamental capacities and dispositions toward knowing and applying both first principles and intelligible forms abstracted from sense-perception. It is evident, however, that two individual persons could have exactly similar sensory experiences of some object, and yet qualitatively differ in their intellectual understanding of said object—some persons, in short, are evidently more intellectually capable than others. This does not mean, however, that some persons receive an *inferior* intellective soul compared to others—as implied by Plato's delineation of various classes of citizens in his *Republic*. Rather, each person's soul, as her body's substantial form, is *adapted* to the functional capacities of her body, such that a functionally deficient body would not be able to facilitate the actualization of all of its soul's capacities to their optimal degree (q. 85, a. 7). The result is that some human beings are more "fully actualized" than others, not that the former is any more human than the latter.

Thomas holds that the intellective soul is able to know itself. However, contrary to the Cartesian understanding of self-consciousness—wherein one's own mind is the only thing of which one is indubitably aware—Thomas contends that the intellective soul does not know itself *directly* (q. 87, a.1). Rather, the soul knows itself by means of its activity of intellectual abstraction; in short, in coming to know something external to itself, the soul also comes to know itself. Self-consciousness, then, is a sort of by-product—or *epiphenomenon*—of the process of intellectual cognition. This difference between the Thomistic and Cartesian views reveals in stark contrast the former's moderate realist epistemology versus the latter's skepticism.

The final key question concerning the functioning of the human intellect regards how it functions when separated from its body during the temporal period between death and resurrection (q. 89). Thomas established in Question 75 that the intellective soul is immaterial, does not function through a bodily organ, and thereby does not corrupt when its body does upon death. He also holds, as we will discuss in the context of the "supplement" to the *tertia pars*, that there is a period of time between death and the resurrection of one's body in which the soul exists and functions intellectively on its own. How can this be the case, though, when Thomas has made clear that the soul depends upon sensation to derive intellectual knowledge and requires phantasms produced by the imagination even when it is recalling knowledge already acquired (q. 84, a. 7)? Aristotle, interestingly, would agree with Thomas in postulating that the intellective soul could persist beyond bodily death *if* it were capable of an immaterial activity without any dependence on bodily organs; nevertheless, he ultimately denied that the intellective soul could be immortal insofar as the intellect cannot actively think without utilizing phantasms.

Thomas concludes that a separated intellective soul can, by virtue of its own intrinsic capacities, reflect upon intellective knowledge it had already gained in its pre-mortem life and thereby gain insight and new knowledge by reaching conclusions through discursive reasoning (q. 89, aa. 5 and 6). In addition, with divine assistance, it can cognize new intelligible forms directly infused in it by God (q. 89, a. 1 *ad* 3) and, upon being granted knowledge of the divine nature, will itself to love God as the source of perfect happiness (q. 82, a. 2). While these activities secure the persistence of one's soul as a thinking and willing thing beyond bodily death, Thomas nevertheless argues that resurrection is necessary insofar as a separated soul does not alone possess the complete nature of the human species. The human essence includes both an intellective soul and a material body the soul informs in order to exercise its vegetative and sensitive capacities in addition to its intellective and volitional capacities. Thomas thus conceives of a separated soul, due to its essentially being the substantial form of a particular human body, to have a natural "longing" for reunion with its body (q. 76, a. 1 *ad* 6)—we will discuss Thomas' account of bodily resurrection in Chapter 10.

An interesting—perhaps disturbing to some—consequence of Thomas' cognitive theory is that the separated souls of the deceased cannot directly know what is occurring in the lives of their loved ones who are still alive. He quotes Augustine, "the souls of the dead have not concern in the affairs of the living" (q. 89, a. 8). Thomas notes, however, that not all of the Early Church Fathers agreed with Augustine and postulates a nuanced account that could accommodate the various sides of this debate. He notes that it is possible for the dead to have a *general concern* for the welfare of the living even if separated souls cannot have direct cognitive awareness of their still-living loved ones' joys or sorrows—just as the living may have a general concern for the welfare of the dead while incapable of knowing their exact state (q. 89, a. 8 *ad* 1). He also reasons that, even if the deceased—at least those who are in "blessed" union with God—were to be aware of the particular sufferings endured by their loved ones, they would not be saddened as they can now understand the positive value of such suffering in accord with God's *justice*.

QUESTIONS 80–83—FREEDOM OF THE HUMAN WILL

The other primary capacity that the intellective soul possesses as a subject, not requiring any bodily organ to actualize it, is what Thomas terms "the will" (Latin: *voluntas*). The will, as a definitive capacity of the intellective soul, is a member of more expansive genera of capacities that non-rational animals, living organisms, and even inanimate substances possess. Thomas notes that every natural substance has at least one *natural inclination* according to its form (q. 80, a. 1). A clear example, for Thomas, is fire, which exhibits a natural inclination to rise—as we see flames shooting upward—as well as to propagate—as we witness fire spreading as it consumes combustible material. This does not at all imply that fire is *conscious* of its activity or has the ability to *control* itself; hence, there is something both true, but also seriously misleading, in a scene from the film *Backdraft* (dir. Ron Howard, 1991) in which Robert de Niro's character exhorts his protégé that a firefighter must understand how fire behaves, "To know that this flame will spread this way across the door and up across the ceiling, not because of the physics of flammable liquids, but because it *wants* to." Living, but non-sentient, organisms also have a *natural appetite* oriented toward their own continued existence and that of their species. The most basic functions of something that is alive involve resisting entropy—e.g. by absorbing nutrients and secreting waste—growing, and reproducing. Thus, while a plant is not conscious of the sunlight streaming in from a nearby window, it will naturally grow in the window's direction.

Animals, insofar as they are more complex organisms as well as being sentient, have *sensory appetites* over and above the natural inclinations of their particular organs. An animal's eye, for instance, is naturally inclined toward taking in light in order that the animal may see; and it will still be inclined to do so even if it is detrimental to the animal as a whole or otherwise goes against the animal's more global appetite—as evidenced when one is trying to fall asleep in a bright room and their eyelids keep opening (q. 80, a. 1 *ad* 3). Finally, human beings—as *rational* animals—have an *intellectual appetite* distinct from their sensory appetite (q. 80, a. 2).

Thomas identifies two distinct, global sensory appetites that all animals possess: the *concupiscible* and the *irascible* (q. 81, a. 2). The former refers to an animal's *desire* for whatever it cognitively apprehends—by means of its estimative capacity—to be *good* for it: whatever is pleasurable or necessary to sustain its own existence, propagate its species, or otherwise perfect itself according to its nature, primary examples of which are food, water, shelter, and sex. The concupiscible appetite also motivates an animal to flee from whatever it apprehends to be *harmful*, often attended by feelings of aversion, unpleasantness, or fear. Animals, of course, are not simply programmed automata, and so each one's cognitive estimation and subsequent appetitive inclination may not always result in its doing what is optimal for it; hence, a particular cat, concupiscibly oriented toward a particular type of food he enjoys, may turn his nose up when presented with a healthier, but unfamiliar and perhaps unpleasant smelling, alternative. The irascible appetite functions as a helpmate to the concupiscible by driving an animal to resist obstacles to the fulfillment of its desires; hence, two alley-cats may brawl over a scrap of food or a potential mate, meowing threateningly and scratching at each other.

Human beings exhibit similar behaviors of desire, aversion, and competition in order to seek the satisfaction of desires for what is perceived to be good in accordance with our nature or individual preferences. Distinct from other animals, however, human beings can also exercise a degree of *rational control* over our sensory appetites (q. 81, a. 3). First, rational principles inform the estimation of particular goods or evils as perceived by the senses. Thomas thus renames the estimative capacity of other animals as the "cogitative" capacity in the case of human beings, since it is not merely an *instinctive* assessment, but a rational judgment, that determines whether a particular object should be pursued, avoided, or fought against. Second, the will has final control over a human being's bodily activity—at least for those actions that one consciously intends and for which one can be held morally responsible. Sensory appetites do not dictate human behavior. A non-rational animal, for example, cannot go on a "hunger strike" based on a rational decision that a political victory for the sake of justice is more important than the satisfaction of its desire for food; if the animal feels hungry, it will be instinctively motivated to find food and eat—although an animal's emotional state may cause it not to feel hungry when it otherwise would. A human being, on the other hand, can make such a rational determination and, despite feeling hungry and concupiscibly desirous of food, can will not to eat; human beings can also rationally decide to "fast" for the sake of attaining certain moral and spiritual benefits (II–IIae, q. 147).

In describing the *extent* to which reason exercises control over the sensory appetites, Thomas utilizes a political analogy (q. 81, a. 3 *ad* 2). He affirms that, with respect to various parts and capacities of the body, reason rules them *despotically*; hence, for example, when one wills to walk, her legs—assuming they are functioning normally—cannot help but move. When it comes to the sensory appetites, however, reasons rule them *politically*—that is, in a more democratic fashion. The hunger-striker, for instance, is able to will herself not to eat, but cannot will herself not to feel hungry; her concupiscent desire for food will continue to clamor for satisfaction, like the citizens of a state, until the political leader (the will) responds appropriately. Similarly, a married man who rationally understands that he ought not to cheat on his spouse and does not will to do so, may still find attractive women concupiscently desirable. He may even will his imagination to conjure up sexually stimulating phantasms (q. 81, a. 3 *ad* 3). His imagination, though, could generate such images even without his having willed it to do so; in which case, however, he can exercise rational control over whether to indulge or ignore such fantasies.

We now arrive at Thomas' discussion of the human *will*, which he defines as an intellectual appetite oriented toward whatever is rationally apprehended as *good* insofar as it is *perfective* of a human being according to her nature. He thus contends that the will is *necessarily inclined* toward *happiness* (q. 82, a. 1). On first glance, this claim may seem to fly in the face of Thomas' insistence that the human will is *free*; but we must carefully parse out what Thomas means by the terms "necessary" and "free." Thomas distinguishes three forms of necessity: natural necessity, necessity of end, and necessity of coercion. The last is "altogether repugnant to the will" insofar as it involves being forced to do something by an external agent. Thomas is not thinking here of a case of someone handing over his wallet because a robber is pointing a gun to his head; for it remains an option, even if an eminently irrational and undesirable one, for the person to will not to hand over his wallet and be killed as a result. Rather, Thomas is referring to a case like that in which a neurosurgeon has implanted a chip in one's brain so that she may control his motor cortex and force his body to do things he does not will to do: his actions follow from the neurosurgeon's will, not his own.

Necessity of the end is not repugnant to the will insofar as it simply refers to a case in which there is only one means that one must will in order to achieve a desirable goal. For example, if one wishes to travel someplace that is only accessible by plane, then they necessarily will to buy a plane ticket; although it remains open for them not to will to travel there. Natural necessity is not contrary to one's will either insofar as it refers to the will's fundamental inclination toward *happiness* and whatever means may contribute to the attainment of happiness. Freedom of will, according to Thomas, does not lie in the capacity to will not to be happy. Rather, it follows from the fact that there are many ways in which human beings may conceive of happiness, as well as myriad means one may employ to attain happiness. Thomas, as we will see in the next chapter, defends on objective, universal definition of human happiness and definitely considers certain means toward happiness to be better than others; nevertheless, even if one properly understands what will make her happy and wills to attain it, there may still be multiple legitimate routes she may take toward achieving that end. Thus, the only circumstance under which the will would will something necessarily would be if one were to intellectually apprehend God in His essence, "in Whom alone true happiness consists" (q. 82, a. 2). A defense of this last claim will have to await our discussion of the beginning of the *secunda pars*. What is important to note here is Thomas' contention that, given the premise that God alone fulfills all of a human being's natural desires, then no human being can resist willing to be in loving union with God if she were to apprehend intellectually God in His essence. In one's embodied life, however, a human being typically does not apprehend God in His essence and so has only an imperfect conception of God arrived at through reason or faith, which leaves room for one not to believe that God exists, or to utterly reject God, or—as is the case for many—to believe in and desire union with God, but yet still turn away from God on occasion and commit sin.

Human freedom may thus cash out in various ways. In one way, a person desires happiness, intellectually comprehends that God is the source of happiness, and thereby wills to be in loving union with God; she then comprehends that there are various means toward achieving this union and *freely chooses* one of the available means on a given occasion that she understands will lead her to happiness. In another way, a person desires happiness, does not comprehend that God is the source of happiness, but cognitively estimates that one or more other goods—e.g. wealth, power, fame, sexual promiscuity—will make her happy and freely chooses to pursue one or more of those means in an attempt to attain happiness. In still another way, a person desires happiness, comprehends that God is the source of happiness and wills to be in union with God; but she also comprehends other ends as good and thereby desirable, even if pursuing them may detract from her attainment of divine union. Hence, she may freely choose on a given occasion to pursue a desirable good—such as sleeping-in on a Sunday morning instead of attending church—to the detriment of attaining her ultimate goal of divine union. We will explore the complexities of human volition and the moral evaluation thereof as we progress through the *secunda pars*. The key point to note here is the common denominator in all three cases that a human being is, first and foremost, fundamentally oriented toward willing *happiness*—howsoever she may define it or understand the means toward achieving it.

The next two articles of Question 82 (aa. 3 and 4) discuss the relationship of the intellect and will as distinct capacities of the human soul. There is a complicated "feedback" relationship between these two capacities that Thomas will more fully describe in the first treatise of the *secunda pars*. Here, he affirms that the causal relationship between the two is bi-directional, but involves distinct forms of causality. Recall Aristotle's four types of causes dealt with in Chapter 2: formal, material, efficient, and final. In asking whether the will is a "higher" capacity than the intellect, Thomas denies that it is insofar as the will is dependent upon the intellect supplying its *final cause* (q. 82, a. 3). We noted above that the will necessarily wills happiness; however, in order to do so, one must intellectually comprehend what happiness *is* and what *means* will contribute to its attainment. The intellect thus performs an essential function in human moral psychology by comprehending both our ultimate end—happiness—and the particular desirable goods that will lead us to happiness. On the flipside, the will has the power to move the intellect, as well as the soul's other capacities—excepting the autonomic vegetative capacities—as an *efficient cause* (q. 82, a. 4). In short, the will can direct the intellect to think about something, as when one wills to meditate about God, or not to think about something, as when one wills to stop dwelling on the sports car one wants to buy but cannot afford, or to reconsider something, as when a general adopts a strategic plan to win a battle but stays up late at night going over the plans one more time before committing his troops.

Having explained how the will is necessitated by virtue of its natural inclination toward happiness, Thomas now accounts for how the will is *free* (q. 83). "Freedom of will" is actually a bit of a misnomer since the standard medieval term Thomas utilizes here is *liberum arbitrium* ("freedom of judgment"), implying that human freedom lies not in the will but in the intellect. This conclusion is, depending on the sense, both true and not true according to Thomas. On the one hand, it is the case that freedom resides in the intellect's ability to evaluate various objects as to their intrinsic or instrumental goodness—that is, to what extent a given object is desirable either for its own sake or as a means toward something else one desires (q. 83, a. 1). Sex, for example, is both intrinsically desirable due to its inherent pleasure and instrumentally desirable as a means toward procreation. Since, as noted above, only the intellectual comprehension of the divine essence would necessitate the will, and such comprehension is typically not available in the present life, all sorts of objects may present themselves to the intellect as desirable. Furthermore, even if one locks onto God as the source of happiness, one may cognitively evaluate various means toward union with God to be variably desirable: living as a contemplative monk, actively serving the poor, teaching and writing as a theologian, raising a family, serving one's society in politics, healing the sick as a physician, etc.

On the other hand, since the intellect is able to apprehend and evaluate as good various means toward attaining happiness, it is ultimately up to the will to *elect* one of those means on any given occasion to pursue: freedom of judgment leads to freedom of *choice* (q. 83, a. 3). The bi-directional dependence relationship of intellect and will involves the will requiring the intellect to present it with "willable" goods—and part of human freedom consists in the intellect providing the will with many such goods—while the will has the power to choose which of the goods will be pursued, if any at all: the will could always will *not* to will, or will the intellect to reconsider the goods it has presented or search for additional potential goods to will—but even these options would have to be presented to the will by the intellect as goods that may be willed.

It is already evident how complex human moral psychology is when considering just these two fundamental capacities. As we move through the *secunda pars*, we will not only unpack this co-dependent relationship in greater detail, but also see how the sensory appetites and human emotions affect human volition and activity. Later, when we reach the *tertia pars*, we will see how divine grace, mediated through the redemptive sacrifice of Christ and the sacraments of the Church, aids the intellect and will to attain humanity's ultimate end, which lies beyond our natural capabilities.

QUESTIONS 90–102—NATURE OF THE FIRST HUMAN BEINGS

From a purely philosophical perspective, the treatise on human nature could have ended with Question 89 and moved on to the moral treatises that constitute the *secunda pars*. Thomas did not compose a *Summa philosophiae*, however, and his primary concern is to provide a full account of humanity's *exitus* from God and *reditus* toward loving union with Him. Thomas thus gives an account of humanity's *first* condition, prior to the fall into sin as recorded in the Book of Genesis. Consideration of humanity's original state also provides insight into what existence will be like after the *parousia*—namely, Resurrection and Final Judgment—although the two modes of being will not be exactly the same.

As we have seen, Thomas' metaphysical account of human nature represents a *via media* between Platonic substance dualism and contemporary material reductionism. Thomas affirms his hylomorphic view of human nature when he contends that intellective souls do not pre-exist their bodies, but rather are created each with their respective bodies as the latter's substantial form (q. 90, a. 4). Nevertheless, the human soul's intellective capacities, insofar as they are immaterial and do not depend upon any bodily organ for their operation, entail it could not be produced through any natural, physical process. Hence, each human soul is produced directly by God in cooperation with the natural reproductive process (q. 90, aa. 3 and 4). The only human bodies not produced through natural reproduction, of course, were those of the biblical "Adam" and "Eve"—both having been directly created by divine agency (q. 91, a. 2 and q. 92, a. 4).

One of the most significant lines in all of Scripture is God's declaration, "Let Us make man to Our own image and likeness" (Genesis 1:26). Thomas thus devotes Question 93 to unpacking what this divine "image and likeness" means in terms of the human essence. He first affirms that the *imago Dei* is found in human nature, but this does not at all imply that human beings share in the divine nature—as if human beings were akin to Greek mythological demi-gods. Rather, they "exemplify" God's nature in an imperfect fashion; the divine exemplar *infinitely* exceeding the created image (q. 93, a. 1). Thomas next affirms that non-rational creatures, indeed all of creation, reflect the divine image in various degrees insofar as creation manifests *harmony* in accord with the order established by God's perfect reason. Creatures reflect the *imago Dei* increasingly from that which merely exists, to living creatures, to beings capable of knowledge and understanding (q. 93, a. 2). Thomas then considers the question of whether the *imago Dei* is found in every human being, regardless—in the question at hand—of gender, but one could easily add considerations of race, ethnicity, sexual orientation, etc. Thomas answers affirmatively, noting three ways in which human beings possess the divine image: 1) by possessing an inclination toward knowing and loving God; 2) by actually or habitually knowing and loving God; and 3) by knowing and loving God perfectly. While the latter two require the cooperative activity of each human being's will and divine grace, the first, foundational inclination, is common to all human beings (q. 93, a. 4).

Thomas now turns to specific consideration of the condition of human beings in our original, pre-Fall, condition. Key points to note here include that Adam and Eve did not fully comprehend the divine essence; otherwise, they would not have been able to sin since they would have recognized God as the source of their happiness and thereby would not have been able to turn their wills toward other, lesser goods (q. 94, a.1). Nevertheless, Adam and Eve would have had all available knowledge that is possible for the human intellect; but such knowledge does not include the divine essence itself, or an omniscient grasp of future contingent events or particular facts that are not requisite for human flourishing—e.g. how many pebbles there are in a certain stream (q. 94, a. 3). They would also have been endowed with divine grace appropriate to the perfection of human nature and potential attainment of voluntary union with God (q. 94, a. 1), one of the effects of which is that Adam and Eve would have been *immortal* (q. 97, a. 1). As noted earlier, however, Thomas does not conceive of the final immortal condition of human beings post-Resurrection to be simply a return to our pre-Fall immortal state. For instance, Thomas claims that our resurrected bodies will not require food to sustain them or engage in sexual intercourse to propagate the species, both of which would have been proper activities for the first humans and their descendants (q. 97, a. 3 and q. 98). Having raised the topic of human propagation, Thomas concludes the treatise on human nature—and the *prima pars'* explication of creation's *exitus* from God—with a metaphysical account of the process of human procreation.

QUESTIONS 118–119—PRODUCTION OF HUMAN BEINGS

We have seen throughout this chapter Thomas' hylomorphic account of human nature and the implications of an intellective soul's relationship to its body as the latter's substantial form. In defining the necessary and sufficient conditions for a body to be informed by a soul—whether vegetative, sensitive, or intellective—Thomas first notes Aristotle's definition of "soul" as "the act of a physical organic body which has life potentially," and then clarifies what "potentially" means in this context:

> The soul is said to be the "act of a body," etc., because by the soul it is a body, and is organic, and has life potentially. Yet the first act is said to be in potentiality to the second act, which is the operation; for such a potentiality "does not reject"—that is, does not exclude—the soul.
>
> (q. 76, a. 4 *ad* 1)

In short, Thomas holds that a soul's capacity—or *active potentiality* ("first act")—to perform its definitive operations—whether life, sensation, or intellectual thought—is necessary for it to exist. The actual use of this capacity ("second act"), however, is *accidental* to the soul's existence as its body's form—this distinction will be explicated further below.

Of course, a developing human embryo or fetus, and even a newborn infant, does not actually exercise all the operations proper to a human being, including intellectual activity. Nonetheless, Thomas denies that this lack implies that the body of a developing human embryo, fetus, or newborn infant is not informed by an intellective soul. All that is required for the presence of an intellective soul, and thus the existence of a human being, is a body that has the active potentiality to eventually perform the operations proper to an intellective soul.

Concerning the question of when the active potentiality for the operations proper to an intellective soul is first present in a developing human body, Thomas asserts that a body must have the proper *organic structure* if it is to have an intellective soul as its substantial form. As we have seen, the appropriate organs for an intellective soul are those associated with sensation, because it is through sensation of particular things that the mind comes to possess intelligible forms, which are the natures of things understood as abstracted from any particular material conditions (q. 84, a. 6). The abstraction of intelligible forms from the products of sensation—*phantasms*—is the essence of intellective thought as Thomas defines it: "Therefore it behooved the intellectual soul to be united to a body fitted to be a convenient organ of sense" (q. 76, a. 5).

This understanding leads Thomas to develop an account of *successive ensoulment* in a human embryo's formation. After conception occurs, which, according to Thomas' 13th-century understanding is the action of semen upon menstrual blood, a material body exists that has a vegetative soul as its substantial form—i.e. an entity that is alive at the most basic level. As the early embryo develops and its organic structure increases in complexity to the point where it can support sensitive operations, the embryo's vegetative soul is annihilated and its matter becomes informed by a sensitive soul. Since, according to Thomas, a thing's identity is determined by its having the same substantial form, the early vegetative embryo has ceased to exist and a new embryo has come into existence that is an animal life form, due to its having the capacity for sensation. The final stage of embryonic development occurs when the embryo has developed to a point where it has a sufficiently complex organic structure to support intellectual operations. At this point, the sensitive soul is annihilated and the animal embryo goes out of existence as its matter becomes informed by an intellective soul and thereby a human being begins to exist.

In sum, the basic metaphysical principle Thomas employs in his account of human embryogenesis is that an intellective soul does not inform a material body—resulting in a human being's existence—unless the body is properly disposed for the sake of that type of soul (q. 90, a. 4). The requisite disposition is the body's having sense organs and a brain capable of imagination such that phantasms of sensible objects may be generated for the mind to abstract intelligible forms, which is the nature of intellective thought. A body disposed in such a way does not seem to exist until after first a vegetative, and then an animal, embryo has existed. Thomas thus concludes that a living, sentient, and rational human being does not begin to exist until some point well after conception: "We conclude therefore that the intellectual soul is created by God at the end of human generation, and this soul is at the same time sensitive and nutritive, the pre-existing forms being corrupted" (q. 118, a. 2 *ad* 2).

Two key points merit explanation here. First, unlike vegetative and sensitive souls, which naturally inform properly organized matter, Thomas holds that the intellective soul of each human being is created directly by God (q. 90, a. 2). Nevertheless, he also holds that God does not create an intellective soul unless an appropriate body exists for it to inform; for an intellective soul has its natural perfection only insofar as it informs such a body to constitute a human being (q. 90, a. 4). Second, Thomas' claim that an intellective soul includes sensitive and vegetative capacities, and that the sensitive and vegetative souls that had previously informed a developing embryo are *annihilated* once an intellective soul is infused, is intended to counter the claim—discussed above—that there are three souls existing at the same time in a fully developed human being.

In the passage quoted above from Question 76, Article 4 *ad* 1, Thomas distinguishes between *first* and *second* act: "The first act is the form and integrity of a thing; the second act is its operation" (q. 48, a. 5). The term "first act" refers to the *active potentiality* to perform some operation. The locus of a substance's set of active potentialities is its substantial form, which, for a human being, is an intellective soul. The term "second act" refers to the actualization of an active potentiality. In contrast to an active potentiality, something has a *passive* potentiality if it can be the subject of externally directed change such that it can become what it is not already.

In addition to the difference between first and second act, it must be noted that the former comes in two varieties. The first is an object's *immediately exercisable capacity* to perform some action, which means that no further development or significant change is required for the capacity to be actualized. For example, I have the capacity to speak Spanish (having majored in it in college along with philosophy). It just happens to be the case at this moment that I am not using this capacity since I am not actually speaking Spanish right now. The second is an object's *natural potentiality* to develop a capacity to perform some action. For example, before I learned to speak Spanish and thereby developed a capacity to do so, I had a natural potentiality to develop this capacity. I have numerous other natural potentialities, some of which I have developed into capacities, such as my capacity to play chess, and others which I have left undeveloped, such as my potentiality to learn to read Sanskrit.

In applying the concepts of first and second act to the presence of an intellective soul, as noted above, Thomas contends that all that is required for an intellective soul to inform the matter of a particular body is that the body has an active potentiality to perform the operations proper to an intellective soul. The actual performance of these operations is accidental to the soul's existence. Thus, since an intellective soul is the substantial form of a human body, the existence of a body with active potentialities for life, sensation, and intellective thought entails the existence of an intellective soul informing that body. It is inconsequential whether such operations are actually exercised in a body for an intellective soul to inform it (q. 118, a. 1 *ad* 4). In Chapter 11, we will see how contemporary Thomistic scholars have sought to combine Thomas' metaphysical account of human nature with current embryological science in order to reconstruct a proper Thomistic conclusion to the vexed question of when a human being first comes into existence.

This completes both Thomas' exposition of the ontological nature of human beings, as well as his account of the *exitus* of all created beings—the physical universe, angels, and humans—from the First Being—God—thus concluding the *prima pars* of the *Summa*. The next major section of this volume will explicate the moral journey of human beings—who alone among physical creatures possess free will—in their *reditus* to God. It will be followed by an elucidation of Thomas' theological account of how divine grace is administered through the redemptive sacrifice of Christ and the sacraments of the Church to allow human beings to complete the journey toward loving union with God.

SUGGESTIONS FOR FURTHER READING

For more detailed explications of Thomas' account of human nature in the *Summa* and ancillary works, see Robert Pasnau, *The Treatise on Human Nature* (Indianapolis, IN: Hackett, 2002); Pasnau, *Thomas*

Aquinas on Human Nature (New York: Cambridge University Press, 2002); Eleonore Stump, "Non-Cartesian Substance Dualism and Materialism Without Reductionism" *Faith and Philosophy* 12:4 (1995): 505–531; Stump, "Aquinas's Account of Freedom: Intellect and Will" *The Monist* 80:4 (1997): 576–597; Anthony Kenny, *Aquinas on Mind* (New York: Routledge, 1993); Jason T. Eberl, "Aquinas on the Nature of Human Beings" *The Review of Metaphysics* 58:2 (2004): 333–365; Anton Pegis, *St. Thomas and the Problem of the Soul in the Thirteenth Century* (1934; reprint, Toronto: Pontifical Institute of Mediaeval Studies, 1978).

For Thomas' more complete polemical response to the Latin Averroists, see Ralph McInerny, *Aquinas against the Averroists: On There Being Only One Intellect* (West Lafayette, IN: Purdue University Press, 1993).

For further elucidation of Thomas' cognitive theory, see John Haldane, "The Metaphysics of Intellect(ion)" *Proceedings of the American Catholic Philosophical Association* 80 (2006): 39–55; Robert Pasnau, *Theories of Cognition in the Later Middle Ages* (New York: Cambridge University Press, 1997); a more classical treatment is Bernard Lonergan, *Verbum: Word and Idea in Aquinas*, eds. Frederick E. Crowe and Robert M. Doran (Toronto: University of Toronto Press, 1997).

Section 2

THE MORAL JOURNEY
(*SECUNDA PARS*)

5

THE STRUCTURE OF
HUMAN ACTIONS

PREFACE

The *prima pars* of the *Summa theologiae* elucidates the *exitus* of all created beings from God, whose essence is Being, Truth, Beauty, and Goodness itself. The discussion culminates in Thomas' account of human nature. Human beings straddle the ontological divide between material and immaterial substances by virtue of possessing an intellect capable of understanding universal, conceptual truths about the essential nature of various types of beings; at the same time, we exist physically as animals of the biological species *Homo sapiens*. Human beings are thus akin to other members of the animal kingdom insofar as we are living, sentient organisms with desires and emotions particular to our animalistic appetites. But human beings are also akin to God and the angels—who exist as purely immaterial intellects—insofar as we possess the capacities for both intellective thought and free will.

The *secunda pars* comprises Thomas' exhaustive treatment of human moral activity, in which we utilize our intellect and will to determine what actions we ought to perform and, even more importantly, what character traits we ought to cultivate in order to move ourselves closer to union with the source of our being—that is, our *reditus* to God. As we will see though, our complete return to God cannot be accomplished by our own natural capacities; thus, in both the *secunda pars* and the *tertia pars*, Thomas will discuss the ways in which God bestows upon humanity the "grace" necessary to attain perfect union with Him. The *secunda pars* is subdivided into two main parts: *prima secundae* (Ia–IIae) and *secunda secundae* (IIa–IIae). *Prima secundae* mixes both philosophical and theological elements, wherein Thomas lays out his account of human moral psychology and the modes of divine assistance necessary for human beings to live morally upright lives even in our present existence. *Secunda secundae* delves into the specific key virtues that are fundamental to human moral living and discusses particular meritorious and sinful acts, and character traits, in detail. As the longest part of the *Summa*—comprising 189 questions—this was the most copied and disseminated among pastors and missionaries who required a concrete guide to Christian morality so as to evangelize, preach to the faithful, give counsel, and hear confessions.

We will divide our discussion of *prima secundae* into three chapters. In this chapter, we will first examine Thomas' *psychological* theory of human moral action, in which he establishes the ultimate foundation of human *motivation* and develops in richer detail the *interaction* between intellect and will discussed briefly in the *prima pars*. Chapters 6 and 7 will illuminate Thomas' criteria by which human action may be *morally evaluated*. We will discuss Thomas' account of the *sources* of moral evaluation for human beings with respect to both their character and actions; of which there are both *internal* principles—namely, passions, virtues, vices, and sin—and *external* ones— namely, law and grace.

QUESTIONS 1–5—HAPPINESS

In analyzing the moral psychology of human beings, Thomas first determines whether there is a *purpose* to human activity and, if so, whether it is one or many, followed by the nature of said purpose(s). He first establishes that human beings always act for the sake of some *end* (purpose); in other words, human activity is essentially *goal-oriented* (q. 1, a. 1). Here, Thomas makes two important distinctions. First, he distinguishes between a "human act" (*actus humanus*) and an "act of a human" (*actus hominis*). The first refers to acts that follow from a human being's intellect and will, which are thereby *deliberate*, *purposeful*, and *free*; as such, they are also *morally evaluable* and the person who performs a human act may be held *morally responsible* for its goodness or evil. The latter refers to acts that are physically performed by a human being, but do not follow from her intellect and will, which are thereby *mindless* and *unintentional*—e.g. absent-mindedly scratching one's chin or unconsciously gesticulating while speaking—such acts are not subject to moral evaluation. So, for instance, if I unintentionally wave my right arm as I speak and accidentally strike the person standing next to me, I cannot be faulted for having performed an act of physical violence as I did not intend to hit him; although, I might be held accountable for negligence in not being aware of his standing next to me while knowing that I have an unconscious tendency to wave my arms about when speaking passionately.

The other key distinction Thomas makes in this very first article is between the *order of intention* and the *order of execution*. In affirming that every human act is for the sake of some purpose, Thomas places the purpose as "last in the order of execution, yet it is first in the order of the agent's intention" (q. 1, a. 1 *ad* 1). "Agent" refers to a being—in this case, a human person—who performs an intentional action. The "order of intention" refers to the formation of the agent's *reason* for performing an action. The "order of execution" refers to the actualization of the agent's intention by the performance of said action. As we will see in the latter half of this chapter, both orders involve complex interactivity between the agent's intellect and will. Thomas' initial point here is that the fundamental requirement for an agent to formulate an intention is that she has an *ultimate purpose*—or "last end"—toward which she is aiming by her action; the fulfillment of this purpose is the final goal of the action she executes.

The structure of Thomas' reasoning here is similar to his first two arguments for God's existence (Ia, q. 2, a. 3), in that all three arguments rely on the foundational premise that there cannot be an *actually infinite ordered series*. In the case of his arguments for God's existence, Thomas concludes that there cannot be an infinite chain of moved movers or caused causes; hence, there must be a first "unmoved mover" and "uncaused cause." In the case of human psychological motivation, there cannot be an infinite series of *instrumental ends*—that is, ends that are pursued insofar as they are also means toward the achievement of another end (Ia–IIae, q. 1, a. 4). For example, I pour myself a cup of coffee. Why? Because I want to fight fatigue and stay alert. Why? Because I want to continue writing my book this afternoon. Why? Because I want my book to be completed and published. Why? Because I want to help others learn and receive professional accolades for my work. Why? Because acting beneficently and professional recognition satiates my ego. Why? . . . This chain of motivations for my seemingly simple action of pouring a cup of coffee could go on *ad infinitum* unless there is some ultimate goal toward which I am striving. So, why do I want to satiate my ego or, for that matter, do anything else? Because I want to be happy. *Happiness* constitutes the ultimate end of human activity, as evidenced by the apparent absurdity in asking someone the question, "So, why do you want to be happy?"

Thomas derives the term "happiness" from Aristotle's term *eudaimonia*, which refers to the *flourishing* of human beings in our essential nature. To flourish means to fully actualize the inherent capacities that define our nature as living, sentient, social, and rational animals, rationality being the highest and most definitive capacity of the human species; thus, *contemplation* of truth is the most fulfilling activity in which a human being can engage. Thomas agrees with Aristotle's account as far as it goes; nevertheless, it does not go far enough insofar as human beings, according to Thomas, are oriented toward flourishing in both natural and *supernatural* ways. Human beings can attain perfect fulfillment only through intellectual and affective union with the ultimate source of being, truth, beauty, and goodness: God. Thomas thus utilizes the term *beatitudo* to refer to the ultimate end of human activity insofar as it implies both natural and supernatural modes of flourishing.

Thus far, Thomas has established that there is an ultimate end of human activity to which the term "happiness" refers, that there is only one such end (q. 1, a. 5), and that this end is the same for all human beings (q. 1, a. 7). Two challenges immediately come to mind. First, it does not appear that human beings *always* act for the sake of ultimate happiness, particularly when it comes to either mundane or self-destructive activities. Second, it is evident that what makes one happy differs among various human beings, so Thomas' last claim appears manifestly false.

In response to the first challenge, Thomas contends that even small, everyday actions are oriented toward an ultimate end, although an agent may not be consciously thinking about that ultimate end (q. 1, a. 6 *ad* 3). Referring to the previous example, if you ask me why I poured myself a cup of coffee, I will likely not respond, "Because it is the source of my happiness," or, even less likely, "Because it fulfills me as a rational animal," or "Because it brings me closer to God." Yet, these responses are implicit in the answer I am likely to give, "Because it will help me stay alert so I can write." Writing this book, as outlined above, ultimately makes me happy, and the reason it does so, in part, is because it essentially involves a higher-order exercise of my intellect; furthermore, exercising my intellect—particularly in writing a book about Thomas' *Summa theologiae*—helps facilitate—I hope!—my growing closer to God. Thomas affirms, as another example in response to a specific objection, that speculative scientific study aims at the perfective good of the scientist (q. 1, a. 6 *ad* 2). So, even writing routine lab reports, while perhaps a boring chore at the time, ultimately contributes to the scientist's happiness; otherwise, why would she do it?

More problematic are cases in which an agent willfully engages in *self-destructive* behavior. As I write this chapter, people are mourning, and attempting to understand, the suicide of the acclaimed comedian and actor Robin Williams. We can view Williams'—and any other person's—suicide in two ways. First, it could be the result of some form of psychological depression, perhaps coupled with the influence of psychotropic drugs, that results in an act that does not meet Thomas' criteria for being an *actus humanus*; in short, suicide, in many cases, may not be an act that follows from a rational judgment and free volition such that the agent can be held morally responsible for his self-destructive act. Second, an act of suicide could be the result of a rational deliberation leading an agent to the conclusion that he would be better off dead than continuing to live a life of unbearable physical or psychological suffering. For example, a terminally ill patient living in the state of Oregon, who has reached the limits of what medical treatment can do to cure or comfort him, may decide to opt for physician-assisted suicide. This would constitute an *actus humanus* and would thereby be subject to moral evaluation—we will see later Thomas' three-pronged argument against the moral permissibility of rationally chosen suicide (IIa–IIae, q. 64, a. 5). For now, the key point is that the suicidal agent is pursuing his own demise *as a good*. Regardless of how one may *objectively* assess the rationality or morality of his suicidal act, from his *subjective* perspective, the suicidal agent is pursuing a goal that he perceives to be good for him given his suffering. In short, according to the Thomistic analytical framework, a person who deliberately commits suicide, upon rational reflection, is doing something that he believes will make him happy—or at least end his misery.

My fulfillment in writing an expository text on Thomas' *Summa*, a research scientist's joy in discovering a new type of bacteria, a Wall Street banker's thrill in making a high-yield trade, or Hugh Hefner's delight in being surrounded by beautiful Playboy "bunnies" exhibits the second challenge noted above: namely, that there is not a single ultimate end of human activity for all human beings. It seems as clear as anything could be that all sorts of different types of things make different human beings happy. As just discussed, one may rationally deliberate to the conclusion—whether right or wrong—that non-existence may be a source of happiness, or at least the cessation of insurmountable unhappiness. In responding to this challenge, we must first note that there is an important distinction between the *conceptual definition* of happiness and in what happiness, so defined, *consists*. Conceptually, Thomas has defined happiness as the ultimate end toward which all human activity is oriented, which is perfective of human beings both naturally and supernaturally. In Question 2, Thomas now explores various proposals for what happiness, so defined, consists in and, in so doing, further refines his conceptual definition.

Thomas runs through the gamut of various potential sources of human happiness that have been, with equal vigor, promoted and vilified. More specifically, he discusses those alleged sources of happiness that have been—and continue to be—popular among the majority of human beings, while being—both historically and contemporarily—shunned by philosophers, theologians, and psychologists attempting to provide a sober analysis of what human happiness *ought* to consist in and why.

Thomas first discusses *wealth* and cites two reasons why the accumulation of such cannot suffice for human happiness. First, wealth is never rationally sought for *its own sake*, but always as a *means* toward something even more desirable: one does not merely want a ton of cash, but rather wants a ton of cash in order to buy stuff she wants even more (q. 2, a. 1). Second, the accumulation of wealth does not *perfectly fulfill* one's desires; even if a person had more wealth than she could spend in her, or her children's, lifetime, there would still be other goods she would desire: companionship, a fulfilling career, peace of mind, etc. (*ad* 3). Next, Thomas dispatches with *honor* as a source of happiness insofar as honor *follows from* an "excellence" one possesses which is the genuine source of happiness (a. 2). In other words, honor is *concomitant* with true happiness when it is recognized as such by others; it is not that which one should seek for its own sake in order to be happy. Otherwise, one could be mistakenly honored for excellence that he does not in fact possess, as when a brilliant scientist is honored for a new discovery that he in fact had plagiarized. A *true* scientist finds his happiness in the honest discoveries he makes, and then enjoys the attendant honors that follow, rather than fabricating or plagiarizing discoveries merely to receive ersatz honors; while he might enjoy them in the moment, deep down he knows that such honors are falsely given and that his perceived "excellence" as a scientist is a mere sham. Thomas makes similar points in reference to the false reception of *fame* or *glory* (a. 3 *ad* 2 and 3). Finally, Thomas considers whether *power* could be a source of happiness and dismisses it for two reasons (a. 4). First, power is not an end in itself, but serves as a principle of human activity that makes the achievement of ends possible; it thus serves an *instrumental* purpose like wealth. Second, power may be utilized for either good or evil purposes, and only the former contributes to human happiness while the latter detracts from it.

Turning to anthropological considerations, Thomas next analyses whether any goods of the *body* or of the *soul* may function as the source of human happiness insofar as we are essentially soul/body—or more precisely form/matter—composite entities, as discussed in Chapter 4. Thomas rules out any bodily goods as the source of happiness for the same reason that many philosophers following him have—namely, that there is much more to human nature than our animalistic tendencies and, furthermore, that bodily goods are "good" insofar as they contribute toward actualizing the goods of the soul (a. 5). *Health*, for example, is a bodily good that ought to be promoted and preserved so that one may engage in intellective activities and allow his will to fulfill itself in physical activities; nevertheless, one would not rationally sacrifice his intellect for his health. Would Stephen Hawking accept a cure for his physically debilitating ALS if an unavoidable side-effect was the total loss of his immense intellectual ability? Relatedly, Thomas counters the hedonistic thesis that *pleasure* is the ultimate constituent of human happiness by noting that, while pleasure may be concomitant with happiness, it does not itself perfectly fulfill a human person's fundamental natural desires as a rational animal (a. 6). It is worth emphasizing that Thomas does not consider bodily pleasure to be *bad*, but merely *imperfect*. There is nothing wrong with enjoying the pleasure that follows from the achievement of some sort of fulfilling human good—such as the orgasmic pleasure attendant upon sexual union between a loving, committed couple—but, according to Thomas, one misses what is truly good in the human sexual experience if mere physical gratification is pursued at the expense of a mutually loving relationship.

Having ruled out any bodily good as essentially constitutive of human happiness, it may appear that happiness must consist in some good of the *intellective soul*. Thomas denies this as well, however, insofar as the intellectual and moral virtues that ought to constitute the fundamental dispositions of one's soul—we will discuss these virtues in detail in later chapters—are psychological tools *orienting* one toward happiness (a. 7). Happiness is not simply *courage* in the face of danger or the *temperate* moderation of one's sensual appetites; rather, these and other virtues help lead one toward happiness. A courageous person who lacks temperance, or who misuses her courage—e.g. a Nazi soldier who courageously fights Allied forces—would not thereby be happy according to Thomas.

Thomas thus concludes that no *created good* can constitute human happiness insofar as all such goods—even if one possessed the totality of them—would fall short of the basic criterion of happiness: namely, the *complete satisfaction* of one's desires (a. 8). No matter what a human being may achieve, experience, or possess in this life, there will always be something she lacks—specifically, knowledge of the *ultimate cause* of being and union with the *ultimate good*. The human intellect and will are respectively inclined toward these ends and only God can fulfill these fundamentally constitutive desires of the human soul. Moreover, the attainment of these ends results in *permanent* satisfaction, which no created good can offer. It is worth emphasizing that happiness, once attained, manifests itself in both the *intellect* and the *will* insofar as a person's will is naturally oriented toward the attainment of happiness and thus "delights" in the ultimate experience of God; however, the experience itself is an intellectual activity wherein one finally knows the *truth* her intellect has always sought (q. 3, a. 4). Thomas' ultimate answer, then, to the question of what human happiness consists in is "the vision of the Divine Essence" (q. 3, a. 8). All other "goods" one may pursue are either *means* toward happiness, or merely *appear* to be means toward happiness but in fact detract from its attainment. Of course, not everyone *recognizes* God as the source of human happiness; nevertheless, everyone desires happiness and pursues it as each understands it (q. 5, a. 8). It is simply the case that many people *misunderstand* what would be truly fulfilling, satisfying, and delightful to them according to their essential nature as rational animals, and thus attempt to content themselves with lesser goods while still remaining at some level *discontent*.

Two key points merit discussion before leaving the topic of human happiness. The first concerns the relation of the *body* to one's happiness. The second regards the distinction between Thomas' understanding of happiness and that of his intellectual predecessor Aristotle, whose account he otherwise liberally adopts.

As noted earlier, Thomas denies the hedonist thesis that human happiness can consist in bodily pleasure; nonetheless, he affirms that bodily pleasure may be *concomitant* with happiness. This logically follows from his *hylomorphic* conception of human nature—as elucidated in Chapter 4—in which a human being is not identical with an immaterial soul that is merely conjoined with an animal body between birth and death—as Thomas' Platonic interlocutors held—but rather human beings are *composites* of soul and body, essentially defined as "rational animals." As to the question, then, of whether one's body is *necessary* for his happiness, Thomas answers negatively insofar as the vision of the divine essence involves one's intellect and will, and these are capacities possessed by the intellective soul alone. Hence, during the interim state of disembodiment between death and bodily resurrection—which we will discuss in detail in Chapter 10—one's soul can experience knowledge and union with God and thereby be perfectly happy (q. 4, a. 5). Thomas' hylomorphic anthropology, though, allows for an "overflow" of the happiness experienced by one's soul into her body. To understand this relationship, think of watching your favorite movie. There is nothing lacking in your enjoyment of the film while watching it alone in your living room; however, if a friend were to watch it with you, your enjoyment of the film would be *intensified* by his enjoyment of it as well.

One consequence of the body's participating in one's happiness upon its resurrection is that it would have to be *perfect* itself, suffering no defect. Hence, Thomas affirms that one's resurrected body, while still physical, will nevertheless be fundamentally transformed from its previously corruptible and imperfect state (q. 4, a. 6). Furthermore, if one's body is not necessary for happiness insofar as God alone perfectly fulfills all of a human being's natural desires, then neither are *external goods* required (q. 4, a. 7) or even *friends* (q. 4, a. 8). Love of one's friends, though, is, like bodily pleasure, *concomitant* with happiness. Thomas contends that if there were but one human soul in loving union with God, that person would be perfectly happy; but if there were another human soul enjoying the same union, the two persons would love each other through their mutual love of God (q. 4, a. 8 *ad* 3).

In terms of his basic conceptual definition of human happiness, Thomas is directly inspired by the first book of Aristotle's *Nicomachean Ethics*. He also concurs with Aristotle's conclusion that the most noble of human activities is to engage in *intellectual contemplation*. Thomas departs from Aristotle, however, in three primary ways. First, Thomas identifies the *object* of intellectual contemplation as the divine essence insofar as God is the ultimate cause of all beings, and in fact is Being, Goodness, Beauty, and Truth itself, as discussed in Chapter 2. Second, Thomas affirms that happiness has not only an intellective dimension, but an *affective* one as well insofar as one does not merely come to know God, but enters fully into a loving relationship with Him. Third, following from the preceding considerations, Aristotle's understanding of what happiness consists in can only be *imperfect*. It thus follows that no one can be perfectly happy in this present life since knowledge of and union with the divine essence cannot be attained until after death (q. 5, a. 3); nor can one attain happiness through his own natural capacities since the infinite nature of the divine essence transcends the inherent limits of such capacities (q. 5, a. 5). Hence, God's *grace* is required to bring one into a state of knowledge and union with Him; nevertheless, a human being *participates* in the attainment of happiness by virtue of his good deeds, leading to the cultivation of a virtuous character, that opens himself to the *reception* of grace (q. 5, a. 7). We will explore the relationship of human moral activity to divine grace in the next chapter.

QUESTIONS 6–7—THE NATURE OF VOLUNTARY ACTION

Building upon his account in *prima pars* of the respective natures of the human intellect and will—see Chapter 4—Thomas now provides a detailed elucidation of how these two faculties of the intellective soul cooperate in the formulation and execution of intentional human action. At this point, he is still only providing an analytical account of human psychological motivation and activity without an explicitly moral component. This account, however, will set the stage for his later importation of moral concepts such as virtue, vice, sin, law, and grace that are the subject of the remaining questions of the *prima secundae* and the subsequent chapters of the present volume.

The first crucial concept that must be defined is what constitutes a *voluntary* act, for only such acts are subject to moral evaluation. As the term implies, a voluntary act is one that follows directly from an agent's *will* (*voluntas*); nevertheless, the *intellect* plays a necessary role insofar as it provides the will with knowledge of what to will. Thomas thus defines a voluntary act as one that follows from an agent's awareness of a goal to pursue and her self-movement in pursuit of that goal (q. 6, a. 1). Based on this broad conceptual definition, Thomas concludes that not only human beings—that is, *rational* animals—can act voluntarily, but so too can *non-rational* animals insofar as the latter have an "imperfect" knowledge of goals worth pursuing (a. 2); recall from Chapter 4 that all animals are capable of sensation and also of "estimating" whether what they are sensing is something to be pursued, avoided, or fought against in relation to the animal's natural appetites. Non-rational animals are also self-movers, instinctually driven to seek the satisfaction of their natural appetites; although they do not possess a *free* will. As we will see in the next chapter, when discussing the *passions* that serve as a powerful motivator for human activity, there is a great degree of psychological similarity among humans and other higher-order animal species, as well as significant categorical differences.

A human being can voluntarily act or not-act, as well as will or not-will (a. 3). This leads to the question of whether anything can affect the will such that one ends up acting/not-acting or willing/not-willing *in*voluntarily. Thomas analyzes several potential factors that could cause involuntary action. First, he considers *violence*. Could someone *force* me to will something against my will? The very way this question is phrased reveals the inherent absurdity of such an occurrence if we are referring to the same sense of "will" both times those terms are used. Thomas notes, however, that one may speak of an "act of will" with two distinct referents: first, there are acts *immediately elicited* by the will—namely, the very act of *willing* itself, expressible in other terms as what one *wishes* to do; second, there are acts *commanded* by the will—such as *to walk, to speak, to hand money over to an armed robber*, etc. (a. 4). The first type of act of will cannot suffer violence insofar as follows *immediately* from one's will.

One may think here of the fictional "Manchurian Candidate," psychologically programmed to assassinate an important politician, and wonder whether such programming does violence to the agent's will. About such cases of "brainwashing," Thomas would say that it is not that the agent's will is violently forced by another, but rather that his will is *displaced* by the brainwashing agent's will. When the brainwashed victim pulls the trigger to assassinate the politician, it is an *actus hominis*, not an *actus humanus* issuing from the agent's own intellect and will such that he can be held morally accountable for the act. Part of the inherent evil in the brainwashing is not only that the victim is being used for a nefarious purpose, but also that the victim has been "dehumanized"—converted from being a *person*, an *agent* responsible for his actions, to being a mere *instrument*, a *tool*, of the brainwashing agent's will. Insofar as the brainwashed victim's will has not been violently turned, but rather *sublimated* altogether once the programmed behavior is activated, the act of assassinating the politician is not *involuntary*—it does not go *against* the victim's will; rather, it is *non-voluntary*—the victim's will is *absent* altogether.

When it comes to the second type of acts of will, Thomas affirms that violence can be done to an agent such that he may be forced to do something involuntarily (aa. 4 and 5). For example, in an altered version of the Manchurian Candidate, instead of being psychologically manipulated, the victim has had a microchip implanted in his brain's motor cortex such that another agent can take control of his bodily functions and cause his hand to pick up a gun and pull the trigger to assassinate the politician. All the while, however, the victim is aware of what he is doing and *does not wish* to do it. The victim has an immediately elicited act of will not to shoot the politician, but his commanded act has been violently taken over by the other agent via the microchip. Unlike the original version in which the victim's will has been completely supplanted by the brainwashing agent (non-voluntary), in this version the victim is forced to do an action that he consciously wills not to do (involuntary).

Less extraordinary are cases in which an agent is motivated by *fear* to do something that he would otherwise not will to do (a. 6). Consider one of the above examples of a commanded act of will: handing your money over to a robber who is holding a gun to your head. On the one hand, you willingly give the robber your money insofar as your bodily movements issue directly from your intellectual awareness of the situation at hand and your volition to do what is necessary to avoid being fatally shot. On the other hand, your action appears involuntary insofar as, absent the fear caused by the robber's threatening gun, you would not will to give him your money. The most accurate way of describing this type of case is that your fear *motivates* you to will what you would otherwise not will; nevertheless, strictly speaking, your action of handing over your cash is voluntary as you have the option, irrational as it may be, to refuse and risk the robber shooting you.

Thomas next briefly discusses how *concupiscence*—a sensory appetite he had previously defined in the *prima pars* (Ia, q. 81, a. 2), see Chapter 4—far from being a potential cause of involuntariness, is actually one of the potential *foundations* of voluntary action insofar as an agent wills what she *desires*, and one of the primary sources of desire for humans and other animals is our concupiscent desire to acquire what we perceive to be good in accord with our respective natures (Ia–IIae, q. 6, a. 7). Finally, he considers the effect *ignorance* may have on voluntariness due to the fact that an agent can only will what she is consciously aware of: "If ignorance cause involuntariness, it is in so far as it deprives one of knowledge, which is a necessary condition for voluntariness" (a. 8). He immediately notes, though, that not every form of ignorance has the same effect on voluntariness and describes three ways in which ignorance may be related to an agent's will.

The first relation is *concomitance*, which occurs "when there is ignorance of what is done; but, so that even if it were known, it would be done" (a. 8). Thomas cites the example of someone killing his foe when he mistakenly thought he was killing a stag; but, having realized that he killed his foe, does not regret his action and would have done it anyway even if he did know that he was killing his foe. The next type of ignorance is *consequent* to an agent's act of willing due to the fact that the ignorance itself is *willed* by the agent. Such voluntary ignorance can occur in two ways: in the first way, an agent wills *not to know* certain pertinent information; in the second way, an agent is *negligent* in acquiring and giving due consideration to all the pertinent information at her disposal. This type of ignorance has the effect of rendering the action eventually willed and performed due to the lack of knowledge to be involuntary; yet the ignorance itself is the product of a volition for which an agent could be held accountable.

An example of the first type of consequent ignorance is a politician who wants to vote in support of certain industrial interests, and so does not want to be influenced by scientific data evidencing the harmful environmental impacts of the pollutants generated by such industries. He elects not to read certain scientific articles written by well-credentialed environmentalists promoting conclusions on the basis of well-confirmed data, nor published studies by physicians documenting manifest negative health impacts from these pollutants. He thereby casts his vote with a subjectively clear conscience and can plausibly deny to constituents who oppose his vote that he was unaware of the existence of validated studies contradicting his position.

As an example of the second form of consequent ignorance, consider again the hunter who takes aim at something moving in the woods, not being sure if it is a stag or a person, and ends up shooting a person. Because he shot his gun without having confirmed what he was shooting at, the hunter is responsible for his ignorance and subsequent act due to negligence. Only the final type of ignorance, which is *antecedent* to one's will, excuses an agent from potential moral culpability insofar as it causes him to will "what he would not will otherwise." In this case, the hunter exercises due diligence in confirming as best he can that he is aiming at a stag and not a person; unbeknownst to him, however, a college freshman is running through the forest in a convincing deer costume as part of a fraternity initiation stunt, resulting in a tragic and undesirable consequence for all concerned.

Thomas concludes his discussion of the nature of voluntary action by considering whether and to what extent the *circumstances* under which an action is performed factor into the determination of the *type* of action one does (q. 7). His discussion here is brief as he will more fully consider later how circumstances factor into the moral evaluation of voluntary actions (q. 18, aa. 3, 10–11; q. 73, a. 7). The key point Thomas makes is that circumstances—such as when, where, or in what manner—an action is done is an *accidental* feature of the action (q. 7, a. 1). This undergirds his later conclusion that circumstances do not change the *specific nature* of an action—with certain exceptions—but can render a good action better or an evil action worse. He thereby concludes that theologians should take account of the circumstances in their moral evaluation of human actions (a. 2).

QUESTIONS 8–17—INTERACTIVITY OF INTELLECT AND WILL IN VOLUNTARY ACTION

Having just stressed the importance of knowledge for voluntary action, we are now in a position to examine the interdependent, interactive relationship between the intellect and will in the formulation of an intentional human act. It is important to keep in mind that the intellect and will are two faculties of the *one* intellective soul. Although it may sound sometimes as if the intellect and will were two homuncular entities within a person, referring to the intellect and will as distinct faculties is just a shorthand way of referring to "a person knowing" versus "a person willing."

The starting point of any human act is the will's fundamental, natural orientation toward *goodness* (q. 8, a. 1). The will is basically like a "good-seeking missile." However, just as the analogous heat-seeking missile requires sensory equipment and a rudimentary computer program so that it can locate and identify heat sources toward which it steers itself, the will requires the intellect to locate and identify good things for it to will. Thus, the will is constantly willing the intellect to "seek good." In this way, then, the will moves the intellect as an *efficient cause*. The intellect, once it locates and identifies one or more goods potentially worth willing, provides the will with its *potential formal cause*—"potential" because, until the will actually *chooses* which good it is to pursue on a given occasion and the intellect in turn *commands* the will to pursue the chosen good, it does not yet have an *actual* formal cause of its volition. In short, while the will moves itself, the intellect, and all of a human being's other capacities—excluding autonomic vegetative capacities—efficiently, the intellect moves the will formally (q. 9, a. 1).

The will can *only* will what the intellect perceives to be good. Even when one wills something that is, or appears to be, objectively bad or evil, he does so only because he perceives it as something good. As noted earlier, even someone who rationally decides to commit suicide does so because he perceives death to be good as a means to end his unbearable physical or psychological suffering. This example shows the extent to which other factors may impact the intellect's assessment of what is good, such as desires and passions of the sensitive part of the human soul. Thomas notes that something—e.g. quitting one's job and telling off the boss—may appear good to someone who is in a state of anger, but which he would not judge to be good if he calmly assessed his prospects at landing another, better job promptly with a supportive letter of recommendation (q. 9, a. 2).

Insofar as the will's essential function is to will what the intellect perceives as good, the primary object of the will is the *end*—that is, the *goal* toward which one's act is oriented. Of course, the will also wills whatever *means* allow one to attain the end, but the willing of means is subordinate to the overall willing of the end (q. 8, a. 2). Furthermore, one could will an end and then later, in a distinct volition, will some particular means toward achieving that end—for example, I may have an overall volition to be healthy without willing any particular means toward being healthy until later when I am presented with a choice of eating fried food or steamed vegetables (q. 8, a. 3).

The will's fundamental orientation toward goodness also means that there is a *remote extrinsic cause* of the will's volitions: God. For God not only directly causes the creation of each intellective soul (Ia, q. 90, aa. 2–3; q. 118, a. 2), of which the will is a faculty, but also gives the will its fundamental orientation (Ia–IIae, q. 9, a. 6). It is important to stress the word "remote" here, as it is not the case typically that God *directly* moves the will as an efficient causal agent; such would do violence to the will and render any resulting act involuntary—like the Manchurian Candidate. Rather, having created each individual person's will with its fundamental orientation toward goodness, it is now up to each person to search out intellectually what is good and then will or not will to pursue any perceived good on particular occasions (q. 10, a. 4). Insofar as God is omnipotent, it is possible for Him to efficiently move one's will directly; but God's goodness internally restricts His use of this power to situations in which a person has voluntarily opened herself up to this sort of direct movement, constituting an act of divine grace (q. 9, a. 6 *ad* 3), as we will discuss toward the end of the next chapter.

Thomas thus defends the will's *freedom* by virtue of its capacity to will, on any particular occasion, one of various potential means that the intellect has identified would lead to the attainment of some intermediate end toward which the will is oriented—e.g. health, safety, power, humility—which in turn contributes toward the ultimate end pursued by the will: happiness. While the will is naturally oriented toward happiness and whatever the intellect perceives will contribute to one's happiness (q. 10, a. 1), it does not *necessarily* will any particular perceived good, since any such good would be limited and thus perceptible as not-good in some way that would allow the will not to will it (q. 10, a. 2). The only object the will would be compelled to will by the necessity of its nature, if one were to intellectually comprehend it, would be the divine essence itself. In this life, however, even fervent religious believers who devote their lives to contemplation and communion with God lack a sufficiently perfect understanding of the divine essence that would compel their will. Thus, even for the most devout ascetic, it remains possible to turn away from God and say, like Lucifer as depicted in Milton's *Paradise Lost*, "evil be thou my good."

Fundamentally oriented toward happiness, however it is intellectually conceived, the will formulates an *intention* to achieve what the intellect has determined happiness consists in and whatever intermediate steps are required to attain it (q. 12). A university student, who has discerned that a career in medicine will contribute to her happiness, formulates an *absolute* volition to become a physician (q. 12, a. 1 *ad* 4) that will inform her further deliberations and volitions concerning *particular means* by which she may fulfill this intention (q. 12, a. 4). Thus, she wills, on a particular Friday evening, to study biochemistry instead of going to a party so that she may fulfill her intended goal and ultimately rest in the *delight* of her achievement once she dons the white coat of a physician. Even becoming a physician, however, would not completely fulfill her natural desire for happiness; Thomas thus distinguishes between the delight that she would feel in achieving her educational and professional goals from the *enjoyment* she would experience only upon attainment of her ultimate goal of knowledge of and loving union with God (q. 11, a. 3). In sum, the basic elements involved in a human being's motivational structure are 1) a fundamental, natural orientation toward happiness; 2) intellectual discernment of what happiness consists in, which, if one reasons properly, should lead to the conclusion that only God can be the source of happiness; 3) willful intention to pursue specific goods that one discerns will contribute to the attainment of happiness and delight in their achievement; and finally 4) enjoyment of the ultimate happiness one attains.

A crucial element missing from this structure is the deliberation and choice of particular means by which one may fulfill her specified intentions and ultimately attain happiness (q. 13). This is precisely where human freedom lies, according to Thomas, for the intellect is able to discover all sorts of potential means by which one may pursue an intended good, and the will has the power to *choose* to pursue any of these means or to *refrain* from choosing if none of the options presented by the intellect are deemed sufficiently choiceworthy (q. 13, a. 6). Having discerned and formulated a willful intention to become a physician, a university student must still select what her undergraduate major will be—whether a pre-medical track if her school offers one, or one of the basic physical sciences such as biology or chemistry, or perhaps even a humanities discipline—as well as whether she will pursue an allopathic (M.D.) or osteopathic (D.O.) medical education, and finally which medical school she will attend if she is accepted into more than one.

Having made each of these decisions, she must then deliberate and choose ever more particular means by which she may attain each intermediate goal, all the way down to whether she should stay up late to study the night before her biochemistry final or get a good night's rest so she is not exhausted while taking the exam. Her intellect and will are intimately cooperative in this process, for the intellect must *inquire and analyze* (q. 14, a. 5) which means are appropriate for leading her to her goal—ruling out, for instance, means that would be impossible for her (q. 13, a. 5)—a process Thomas terms "counsel" (q. 14, a. 1), while her will ultimately *chooses*, from among the various options presented by the intellect, the means she actually pursues on a particular occasion (q. 13, a. 1 *ad* 2).

Prior to making its ultimate choice, though, the will first *consents* to a subset of the options presented by the intellect's counsel (q. 15). This winnowing process consists of the will affirming certain options the intellect has presented as good in some respect to be sufficiently *choiceworthy*. While deliberating about various options for getting into medical school, a university student may entertain the fantasy of "buying" her way in if her father happened to be a wealthy alumnus of a prestigious school that sometimes favors "legacy" students whose parents make large donations to support the school. Her disposition toward *integrity*, though, may result in her will not consenting to this option as choiceworthy; she thus no longer even considers picking up the phone to call her influential father.

As we will discuss in detail in subsequent chapters, one's moral *dispositions*—that is, the *virtues* or *vices* one cultivates—regulating the relation of one's *passions* to the dictates of *practical reason*, factor crucially into the consent process insofar as some possible options for acting presented initially by one's intellect will be dismissed as impossible for a particular moral agent due to the cultivated dispositions of her moral *character*; whereas, for another moral agent, such options may be consented to insofar as they accord with the dispositions of his character. For example, while two persons, who are married to others, may assess each other as sexually desirable and their respective intellects initially consider the possibility of engaging in an adulterous affair, one of them, having cultivated the virtue of marital *fidelity*, will not consent to an affair as a "live option" and thereby cease considering it; whereas the other, lacking this virtue and perhaps possessing the vice of *licentiousness*, may not only consent to seriously consider the option but actually choose to act upon it.

Finally, having made one's choice from among the previously consented to options, the agent's intellect *commands* her will (q. 17) to *use* her intellectual and physical capacities to employ the chosen means (q. 16). The intellect's command constitutes the *actual formal cause* of the agent's act, all the previously considered options before the agent makes her choice being *potential* formal causes of her act (q. 17, a. 4). The extent of the will's commanded use of the agent's capacities applies to every aspect of her nature other than her autonomic vegetative capacities (q. 17, a. 8). Having chosen to stay up late and continue studying for her biochemistry final, our university student cannot help feeling tired; so she tells herself that she needs to brew a cup of coffee and do whatever else is necessary to stay awake and focused. Her body then moves appropriately to make the coffee, assume an attentive posture at her desk, and visually focus on the textbook in front of her. The story is not so simple, however, as she has a choice whether to drink coffee or tea—or (inadvisably) to take an amphetamine—whether to study at her desk or on her bed, whether to listen to music while she studies or do so in silence, whether to study alone or see if her classmate across the hall is also up studying, etc. Each of these choices involves the same interactivity of intellect and will identifying, evaluating, and ultimately choosing and doing what she discerns to be the most desirable means at the moment to attain her immediate and long-term goals, fulfill her intention to become a physician, and eventually rest in the enjoyment of happiness—assuming that her vocational career as a physician is in accord with God's will for her and that she cultivates all the requisite virtues to be not only an excellent physician, but also a morally well-rounded human being in all aspects of her life.

Understanding all of the factors that go into living an ethically informed and fulfilling human life requires an analysis of the *passions* that drive human behavior, rooted in the sentient aspects of our nature; the *virtues* and *vices* we ought to cultivate in order to properly order our passions in accord with reason; the *laws* that reason is able to discern and utilize in guiding the deliberative process of practical reason; and finally, the *grace* that human beings require in order not only to live an authentically fulfilling human life in this world, but also to attain our ultimate happiness in the next world—enjoying knowledge of and loving union with the source of Being, Truth, Goodness, and Beauty: God. Careful consideration of each of these topics will occupy Thomas' attention throughout the remainder of the *prima secundae*, leading into more detailed discussion of specific virtues and salvific divine graces in the *secunda secundae* and *tertia pars*.

SUGGESTIONS FOR FURTHER READING

Some excellent introductions to Thomas' account of moral action are Ralph McInerny, *Ethica Thomistica: The Moral Philosophy of Thomas Aquinas*, rev. ed. (Washington, D.C.: Catholic University of America Press, 1997); Rebecca Konyndyk DeYoung, Colleen McCluskey, and Christina Van Dyke, *Aquinas's Ethics: Metaphysical Foundations, Moral Theory, and Theological Context* (Notre Dame, IN: University of Notre Dame Press, 2009); Steven J. Jensen, *Living the Good Life: A Beginner's Thomistic Ethics* (Washington, D.C.: Catholic University of America Press, 2013). A more in-depth introduction and analysis is provided by Denis J. M. Bradley, *Aquinas on the Twofold Human Good: Reason and Human Happiness in Aquinas's Moral Science* (Washington, D.C.: Catholic University of America Press, 1999).

Readers who wish to delve into issues of scholarly interpretation and debate regarding Thomas' moral theory should consult the following edited collections: Scott MacDonald and Eleonore Stump, eds., *Aquinas's Moral Theory: Essays in Honor of Norman Kretzmann* (Ithaca, NY: Cornell University Press, 1999); Stephen J. Pope, ed., *The Ethics of Aquinas* (Washington, D.C.: Georgetown University Press, 2002).

For more detailed analyses of Thomas' theory of human action and moral evaluation, see Stephen L. Brock, *Action and Conduct: Thomas Aquinas and the Theory of Action* (Edinburgh: T&T Clark, 1998); Kevin L. Flannery, *Acts Amid Precepts: The Aristotelian Logical Structure of Thomas Aquinas's Moral Theory* (Washington, D.C.: Catholic University of America Press, 2001).

6

THE MORALITY OF HUMAN ACTIONS

PREFACE

In the remainder of the *prima secundae*, having laid out the structure
of human beings' moral psychology—how the intellect and will
function interactively to motivate voluntary human activity—Thomas
analyzes the various factors that inform the *moral evaluation* of human
actions. First, he describes the features of human actions themselves
that are subject to classification as either "good" or "evil." Second,
he discusses how the *passions*—the emotive aspects of human psychology that we share with non-rational animals—influence both
the intellect and will in the process of moral deliberation and choice.
Third, Thomas invokes Aristotelian *virtue theory* to account for the
proper formation of human beings' moral *character* in order to enjoy
a proper ordering of the passions to reason; as we will see, Thomas
augments Aristotle's account with Christian teaching concerning the
necessity of *beatitude* in order to combat *sin*. Thomas then outlines a
foundation for a set of rational principles that ought to guide human
moral behavior both individually and politically, which he terms

natural law. Finally, he discusses how divine *grace* functions as a necessary element in order for human beings to attain our ultimate end of *happiness* in loving union with the source of our existence: God. In this chapter, we will review all of these discussions with the exception of Thomas' account of virtue (Ia–IIae, qq. 49–89), reserving that discussion for the next chapter, followed in Chapter 8 by Thomas' treatment of specific virtues and vices in the *secunda secundae*.

QUESTIONS 18–21—GOOD AND EVIL IN HUMAN ACTIONS

As we saw in the previous chapter, in the very first article of the *prima secundae*, Thomas distinguishes between two types of actions that a human being may perform: a "human act" (*actus humanus*) and an "act of a human" (*actus hominis*) (Ia–IIae, q. 1, a. 1). A human act follows from one's intellect and will and is thereby *morally evaluable* as either good or evil, while a mere act of a human that "does not proceed from deliberate reason" is not subject to moral evaluation (q. 18, a. 9). Every *human act* can be considered as good or evil with respect to four different categories:

> Accordingly a fourfold goodness may be considered in a human action. First, that which, as an action, it derives from its genus; because as much as it has of action and being so much has it of goodness, as stated above (a. 1). Secondly, it has goodness according to its species; which is derived from its suitable object. Thirdly, it has goodness from its circumstances, in respect, as it were, of its accidents. Fourthly, it has goodness from its end, to which it is compared as to the cause of its goodness.
>
> (q. 18, a. 4)

An action's *genus* is merely the action as such insofar as, due to convertibility of the transcendentals *being* and *goodness*, everything that exists is good at some level (Ia, q. 5, a. 1). An action's *species* is the particular kind of action it is—the "form" or "object" of the action: "what is done." *Circumstances* are the accidents attendant upon an action—e.g. the place and time the action occurs, and any other quality that is not part of the action's definition as the kind of action it is. An action's *end* is its intended goal.

Thomas asserts, "The primary goodness of a moral action is considered from its suitable object" (q. 18, a. 2; q. 19, a. 2). An action's "object" refers to the *nature* of the action itself—its "species"—as determined by that at which it is *directly aimed*. The object of an action differs from its "end" insofar as its direct aim cannot be separated from the action's specific nature, while the same specific type of action could be oriented toward different ends. For example, a physician injects a terminally ill patient with a sufficiently high dose of morphine to immediately kill her. The specific nature of the action is that it is a "killing" due to its directly intended aim that the injected patient dies. However, the physician may perform such an action for any of a number of ends: to alleviate the patient's suffering, to assist the patient's family to collect her life insurance, to free up a needed ICU bed in the hospital, to test the effective dosage to kill someone, etc.

Thomas contends that an action must be good not only in its object, but in all four of the above-named respects (q. 18, a. 4 *ad* 3). Thomas argues that whether an action is good or evil is part of its species (a. 5). For one considers an action's object as either good or evil—e.g. if the object is to steal something, it is evil; whereas if the object is to help someone, it is good. Thomas then refers to the circumstances: "For the plenitude of [an action's] goodness does not consist wholly in its species, but also in certain additions which accrue to it by reason of certain accidents: and such are its due circumstances" (a. 3). He later addresses whether an action's circumstances can change its species from good to evil (aa. 10–11). He answers that circumstances do not change an action's species, but they can make a good action better or an evil action worse (a. 11).

There is a caveat, though. Whenever a circumstance can be understood "as the principle condition of the object that determines the action's species . . . has a special relation to reason, either for or against, it must needs specify the moral action whether good or bad" (a. 10). By "principal condition of the object," Thomas means that the circumstance is part of the object's definition. His example is stealing from a holy place as opposed to stealing merely someone else's possession. The circumstance of "place," in this case, defines the act as one of "sacrilege" and not merely "theft." It is thus a different kind of action. This example is one in which an already evil action—theft—is changed into another worse kind of evil action—sacrilege. Thomas also states that the appropriation of property, which is *per se* morally permissible, becomes evil if the action includes the defining circumstance of the appropriated property being "another's." Here, a good action is changed to an evil action due to one of its circumstances.

Concerning an action's *consequences*, Thomas states that they "do not make an action that was evil, to be good; nor one that was good, to be evil" (q. 20, a. 5 *s.c.*). Although, if the consequences are *foreseen*, he states, "it is evident that they increase the goodness or malice" (q. 20, a. 5). Thomas does not assert that foreseen consequences can change an action's specific nature from good to evil; but they can make a good action better or an evil action worse.

Thus, one cannot ignore the fact that such a defect in an action's attendant circumstances prevents the action from being good "simply" (*simpliciter*) or having the "plenitude of goodness." Does this entail that the action is morally impermissible? Thomas states:

> Evil is more comprehensive than sin, as also good than right. For every privation of good, in whatever subject, is an evil: whereas sin consists properly in an action done for a certain end, and lacking due order to that end.

> (q. 21, a. 1)

We will see in Chapter 8 how Thomas utilizes this analysis of the moral ontology of human action to justify acts aimed at a good end, but in which an agent foresees an unavoidable concomitant negative consequence; such acts may be permissible if they satisfy the criteria established by the so-called "principle of double-effect."

Finally, Thomas considers the question of whether there may be any *morally neutral* actions, which are neither good nor bad. He affirms that the specific nature of certain actions may not be inherently good or bad, but rather are "indifferent"—e.g. picking up straw from the ground or walking through a field (q. 18, a. 8). Nevertheless, since there is fourfold measure of the goodness or evil of any *individual* deliberate action, then an action that is morally neutral in its species may become good or evil due to the attendant circumstances or the agent's intended end. For example, while picking up a rock from the ground is itself morally neutral, to do so with the intention of throwing it at a puppy would be morally bad. And while walking through a field is not inherently good or bad, walking through a farmer's newly planted crops would be wrong due to the circumstances. If, however, one's intended end in running through the new planted field was not maliciously to ruin the farmer's crops, but rather to save someone's life in an emergency, then the overall action would be good since its species is neutral and its end is good. On the other hand, Thomas later cites an example of running through a planted field and unintentionally damaging the crops because one is racing to commit a sinful deed; in this case, the overall action is bad due to its intended end, and the negative consequence that ensues—harming the crops—aggravates the wrongfulness of the action (q. 73, a. 8). In sum, *every* deliberately willed individual human action is subject to moral evaluation due to its specific nature, the intended end for which it is done, or the circumstances in which it is performed.

QUESTIONS 22–48—THE INFLUENCE OF PASSIONS

Only human beings—as *persons*—are capable of morally evaluable action, according to Thomas, insofar as we are able to intentionally determine our own wills toward certain ends and particular means of achieving those ends. Furthermore—as delineated in Chapter 5—a human being's will is informed by her intellect. Nevertheless, the will is not a human being's only appetitive faculty and the *passions* human beings share with other non-rational animals have a significant influence on the intellect's practical reasoning process in discerning what goods one ought to pursue. This can occur in two ways. First, passion may focus one's attention in such a way that the intellect is distracted from its moral evaluation; thus, for example, one's over-whelming desire for sex, food, or alcohol may interfere with, or altogether impede, one's moral assessment of carrying on an adulter-ous affair, eating a triple cheeseburger, or indulging in an entire bottle of whiskey (Ia–IIae, q. 77, a. 1). Second, passion may affect how the intellect morally evaluates some object such that it appears good to her, whereas it would not appear good otherwise; in this case, one may engage in a rational assessment of the relative merits of the affair, cheeseburger, or whiskey and, instead of objectively perceiving them as not contributing to one's flourishing, her desire colors her perception so that they appear more good than they actually are (a. 2). The key point here is that passion cannot directly move an agent's will; rather, passion influences the will indirectly by means of affecting an agent's intellect, which in turn informs her will.

In the *Summa*'s longest treatise, Thomas explores how the *concupiscible* and *irascible* appetites—previously introduced in the *prima pars* (see Chapter 4)—are characterized by certain specific passions—what we would today call, albeit imprecisely, "emotions"—that affect how the intellect perceives and evaluates certain objects as either good or bad. This analysis will lead into his treatment of the *virtues* insofar as part of the essential function of virtue is to align one's emotional response with rational judgment so that the will may be properly informed and thereby oriented toward what is objectively good with respect to human flourishing. After providing a general characterization of the passions (qq. 22–25), Thomas describes each of the passions he enumerates in detail: first, those related to the *concupiscible appetite* aimed at obtaining what one desires (qq. 26–39)—namely, love, hatred, concupiscence, pleasure/delight, and pain/sorrow—second, those related to the *irascible appetite* aimed at removing obstacles to the attainment of what one desires (qq. 40–48)—namely, hope, despair, fear, daring, and anger.

The organizing rubric around which Thomas enumerates and interrelates the concupiscible passions is a triad of evaluation, movement, and possession: "Accordingly every concupiscible passion in respect of good, tends to it, as love, desire and joy; while every concupiscible passion in respect of evil, tends from it, as hatred, avoidance or dislike, and sorrow" (q. 23, a. 2).

If one perceives some object and evaluates it as good, she will *love* it, leading to her *desire* to possess the object and thereby motivate her to act; upon attainment of the desired object, she will experience *joy*. Conversely, if one perceives and evaluates some object as evil, then she will feel *hatred* toward it, leading her actively to *avoid* the object; ultimately, if she is unable to avoid encountering the hated object, she will feel *sorrow*.

The principle by which Thomas sorts the irascible passions is the difficulty or arduousness of either obtaining a desired good or avoiding a hated evil:

> Now the good which is difficult or arduous, considered as good, is of such a nature as to produce in us a tendency to it, which tendency pertains to the passion of *hope*; whereas, considered as arduous or difficult, it makes us turn from it; and this pertains to the passion of *despair*. In like manner the arduous evil, considered as an evil, has the aspect of something to be shunned; and this belongs to the passion of *fear*: but it also contains a reason for tending to it, as attempting something arduous, whereby to escape being subject to evil; and this tendency is called *daring*.
>
> (q. 23, a. 2)

If one desires something that is difficult to obtain, but nevertheless obtain*able*, then she experiences hope; whereas, if she perceives the difficulty in obtaining the desired good to be insurmountable, then she will despair of obtaining it. If one encounters difficulty in avoiding something evil, she may fear it due to its perceived unavoidability; on the other hand, she may perceive the evil as a challenge that may be overcome and so will daringly meet it head-on. Ultimately, if one cannot avoid the feared evil or fails to overcome it, then she may either simply feel sorrow at having to suffer the evil or actively fight against it, which is the passion of *anger* (q. 23, a. 3).

Many philosophers before and after Thomas have argued either that the passions are hindrances to the cultivation of moral virtue—e.g. the Stoics—or that morality can only be defined with respect to our passions—e.g. David Hume. Seneca (4 BCE–65 CE), a Stoic, argues in his essay *De ira* ("On Anger") that anger cannot possibly serve any constructive purpose insofar as it cannot ever be subject to rational control. Hume, in his *Enquiry Concerning the Principles of Morals* (1751), contends that all judgments of good or evil can be reduced to *sentiments* of approval or disgust, with reason functioning only to ensure that our sentimental reactions are based on a proper understanding of the facts of the matter at hand. Thomas, following Aristotle, understands the passions generally as neither good nor evil in themselves; nor does he take them to be the ultimate arbiters of what is good or evil. He does cite certain exceptions, however: *shame*, which is one's fear of disapproval for a moral wrong one has committed, is inherently good; while *envy*, which is sorrow for lacking some good another possesses, is inherently evil (q. 24, a. 4). In all other cases, passions can become good or evil based on whether they are subject to rational control (q. 24, a. 1). Thomas explicitly differentiates himself and the rest of the Aristotelian school of thought from the view of the Stoics, who considered not just anger, *per* Seneca, but all passions as "diseases of the soul" (q. 24, a. 2). Furthermore, he disagrees with the position, which we have seen Hume adopt, that reason can *inform* but cannot ultimately *direct* the passions. Reason, as we will see in Thomas' elucidation of the *natural law*, is the faculty that discovers what is objectively good or evil; and when one has cultivated certain virtues, the relevant passions align with one's rational discernment: "The passions of the soul, in so far as they are contrary to the order of reason, incline us to sin: but in so far as they are controlled by reason, they pertain to virtue" (q. 24, a. 2 *ad* 3).

In Chapter 8, we will see how the virtue of *moderation*, present in an agent's will and passions, inclines one to align both with the determinations of reason. Thomas' analysis does not rule out the possibility that a passion may overwhelm one's reason to the point where one cannot at all think rationally; but then whatever action one does under the influence of that passion would not be voluntary. Thomas would thus agree that an authentic "crime of passion," while still inherently evil, may mitigate the culpability of the agent involved since he acted out of uncontrollable passion and not his rationally informed will. In all other cases where an agent *gives into* their passions, there is a movement of the will in accord with the passion and so whatever action follows is voluntary and thus one may be held morally accountable for it (Ia–IIae, q. 10, a. 3).

With just a few exceptions— namely, hatred and desire—Thomas follows a threefold structure in analyzing each particular passion. He first defines the general *nature* of the passion, followed by its *causes*, and then its *effects*. Thomas begins with the first of the concupiscent passions: *love* (q. 25, a. 2). He defines love as an *inclination* of the concupiscible appetite toward something a person perceives to be fulfilling for him according to his nature (q. 26, a. 1). Love is thus a movement of the appetite caused by the object one perceives to be *good*, in the sense of being fulfilling to one's nature in some way, and thus *desirable* (q. 26, a. 2; q. 27, a. 1). This initial movement is a *tending* toward the beloved object, not a fully-formed *volition* to actively pursue that object (q. 26, a. 3). Love, as a passion, is part of the sensitive appetite, and thus a further *choice* involving one's intellect and will is necessary for one to act upon his tendency toward pursuit of the beloved object.

Love involves two basic tendencies: toward the *object* that one perceives as good (love of *concupiscence*) and toward the *subject* for whose sake one desires that good (love of *friendship*) (q. 26, a. 4). The latter form of love can be directed not only toward *another* with whom one shares an authentic friendship, as defined by Aristotle (*ad* 3), but also toward *oneself*; in fact, Thomas goes so far as to assert that love for oneself precedes all other forms of love (q. 27, a. 3). Another way of characterizing this distinction is that what one loves out of concupiscence is loved *relatively*—that is, merely for the sake of something else— namely, the beloved friend for whose sake one desires said object. The beloved friend, on the other hand, is loved *simply*—that is, for her own sake.

Analyzing what causes love, Thomas' starting-point is one's love for oneself. Self-love leads to a natural attraction toward whatever one perceives to bear some sort of *likeness* (*similitudo*) between them. There is something in the beloved object that draws one toward union with it insofar as he perceives it as reflective of his own self: "Hence the affections of one tend to the other, as being one with him; and he wishes good for him as to himself" (q. 27, a. 3). Alternatively, one may love another insofar as the beloved possesses in *actuality* some quality that the lover possesses in *potentiality*. Thus, for example, a student may love his mentor insofar as he perceives his mentor as the type of scholar and teacher he would like to become.

Insofar as what causes one's love is the perception of the beloved object as *good* for the person, one cannot love something that is evil *for its own sake*. One may certainly love something that is objectively evil, insofar as it has been misperceived as contributing to one's happiness, or is simply not the optimal good one could love on a given occasion. However, one's love for what is evil or a lesser good than what one ought to love is not due to one's loving the object *because* it is evil or a lesser good, but because one has misperceived its moral nature or one loves it as a means to something else he perceives to be good (q. 27, a. 1 *ad* 1).

Turning to love's effects, Thomas affirms that love is the *root cause* of all the other passions, for they all presuppose love in some sense

(q. 27, a. 4); and thus love is also the root cause of all voluntary human action (q. 28, a. 6). Other effects of love include, first and foremost, *union* of the lover with the beloved (q. 28, a. 1). Such union immediately causes two other effects: "mutual indwelling" of the lover and the beloved (a. 2) and "ecstasy," in which the lover is taken out of himself to dwell in the beloved (a. 3). It is important to note that this union is something between a merely figurative "bond"—as may be shared by, for example, a group of acquaintances or one's community of "Facebook friends"—and a literal "absorption" of the lover into the beloved. As any good marriage counselor would advise, being in love does not mean that one ought to "lose oneself" completely and surrender the totality of his being to his beloved spouse. Nevertheless, Thomas notes that the ecstatic union one shares with his beloved leads to a certain *zeal* for the good of his beloved (a. 4) and, given human beings' psychosomatic nature (see Chapter 4), *physical* effects as well (a. 5). Furthermore, one's zeal for the sake of his beloved may also lead to *hatred* of whatever opposes the beloved or their union (a. 4 *ad* 3), reaffirming Thomas' claim that all of the passions, even hatred (for one), is grounded in love (for another against whom the hated one is opposed) (q. 29, a. 2).

Expanding further his discussion of hatred, Thomas characterizes it in terms of *dissonance* between one's natural appetite, oriented toward one's own flourishing, and the hated object (q. 29, a. 1). Once again, Thomas emphasizes the importance of *perception* insofar as, just as one may inadvertently love something that is not objectively good for her—i.e. contributing toward her flourishing as a human being—so one may inadvertently hate something that is objectively good for her (*ad* 2). Another nuance is that the object one hates is not the object *per se*, since everything that exists has some measure of goodness and thus nothing can be *wholly* hated as evil, but rather some *quality* of the object that is apprehended and evaluated as "repugnant" (*ad* 1). Finally, Thomas addresses the question of whether a person can hate *himself*, to which Thomas responds that such is "impossible" since "everything naturally desires good, nor can anyone desire anything for himself, save under the aspect of good" (a. 4). Applying this reasoning to the ultimate example of apparent self-hatred, *suicide*, Thomas theorizes, "For even they who kill themselves, apprehend death itself as a good, considering as putting an end to some unhappiness or pain" (*ad* 2). Thomas' analysis here does not preclude death as something objectively bad, nor excuses suicide as an objectively evil act—we will see his triple indictment of suicide in Chapter 8 (IIa–IIae, q. 64, a. 5). Nevertheless, to the extent that forces outside of one's control may have shaped one's conscience such that one misperceives the value of death or the morality of suicide as a means of escaping one's unhappiness or pain, one's *culpability* for such an act may be mitigated.

It may seem odd at first that Thomas, after having discussed love and hatred as passions of the concupiscible appetite, next discusses *concupiscence* as a specific passion of said appetite. Nevertheless, he affirms that this passion exists as such (q. 30, a. 2) and defines it as "the craving for pleasurable good" (a. 1), as distinct from one's rational desire for *intelligible* good, such as wisdom—the latter desire, however, may involve ancillary concupiscent effects (*ad* 1). Thomas further distinguishes concupiscence in terms of a) the *natural* desire human beings and other animals have toward those things that are pleasurable to them in accord with their specific nature, and b) the desire for something that is *rationally* perceived to be good for someone beyond what is "suitable" according to one's animal nature (a. 3). Thus, while concupiscence is a passion of a human being's *sensitive* appetite (a. 1), it can be informed and thereby oriented by one's reason.

Thomas next applies his threefold analysis to the passion of *delight*—or *pleasure*—and adds a further question discussing its moral value, which makes sense given the long history of debate over whether pleasure is the ultimate good—as the Greek *hedonists* argued—or is an inherently evil distraction from intellectual and spiritual pursuits—as held by the classical Stoics and extremes dualists such as the Manichees. Thomas follows Aristotle in, once again, negotiating a *via media* between these extreme positions to argue that, while not all pleasures are good by virtue of being in accord with reason (q. 34, a. 2), neither are all pleasures inherently evil (a. 1). Furthermore, while pleasure itself is not the highest or most proper good a human being ought to strive to attain, it nevertheless is a concomitant good that properly attends to a virtuous person's attainment of happiness (a. 3). Thus pleasure, in relation to the objects in which one takes pleasure or whether the taking of pleasure in such objects accords with reason, serves as an indication of one's moral character: "that man is good and virtuous, who takes pleasure in the works of virtue; and that man is evil, who takes pleasure in evil works" (a. 4).

Thomas' valuing of pleasure applies to both *bodily/sensual* and *intellectual/spiritual* forms of pleasure—*delectatio* and *gaudium*, respectively—though not equally. Thomas gives several reasons affirming the greater inherent value of intellectual pleasure in terms of both the quality of the object in which one delights and quantity of delight one experiences (q. 31, a. 5). He explains, however, why most people seem to prefer bodily pleasures due to their familiarity, ease of attainment compared to intellectual pleasures, and the fact that they serve as "remedies for many kinds of sorrow and sadness" (*ad* 1). He further elaborates that while the general experience of pleasure is natural for human beings in accord with our sentient nature, some particular forms of pleasure certain individuals experience may be "unnatural" insofar as they diverge from our natural conditions— e.g. the pleasure one may take from eating dirt, or cannibalism, or sado-masochism (a. 7).

As noted above, Thomas considers pleasure to be good in itself and appropriately attends the culmination of rational activity (q. 33, a. 4). A person of sound mind will thus prefer higher intellectual goods to lower sensual goods insofar as the pleasure attendant upon attainment of the former is inherently more delightful than the latter. However, pleasure can also distract reason from its proper functioning by focusing its attention on a pleasurable object instead of a more appropriate good, or even inhibit it altogether—akin to how reason is inhibited when one is intoxicated (q. 33, a. 3). Thomas observes, though, that sometimes reason is appropriately inhibited by certain natural pleasures— such as the pleasures of sleep or sexual orgasm (q. 34, a. 1 *ad* 1). In sum, while pleasure is not evil *per se*, it is nevertheless not an *unqualified* good insofar as the value of specific forms of pleasure or instances of pleasure must be rationally assessed in relation to what is ultimately good for human beings according to our nature.

The passions contrary to bodily pleasure or intellectual delight are, respectively, pain (*dolor*) or sorrow (*tristitia*)—sorrow, as experienced by the intellect, being a species of pain (q. 35, a. 2). Pain or sorrow is caused by one's apprehension of something as evil, just as pleasure or delight is caused by one's apprehension of something as good (q. 35, a. 3). Thomas elaborates that the desire to avoid pain and sorrow is parasitic upon one's desire for what is good, analogous to his conception of evil as a privation of goodness; pain and sorrow thus presuppose desire (q. 36, a. 2). He thus concludes that the desire for pleasure is stronger than the desire to avoid pain (q. 35, a. 6), and that sorrow is caused by the loss of something good when such loss is perceived as evil if, for instance, the lost good did not allow one to attain an even greater good (q. 36, a. 1). While pain—considered apart from sorrow—refers to a sensory experience of bodily ailment, Thomas clarifies that bodily ailment *per se* is distinct from pain, as one's body could be damaged or disabled in a way that is not perceived by one's soul as painful (q. 35, a. 1 *ad* 1).

Pain and sorrow are natural elements of the human constitution, but may lead to significant impairments when experienced immoderately (q. 37): impeding intellectual activity, burdening one's soul, and harming one's body. Nevertheless, Thomas sees instrumental value in the *moderate* experience of sorrow insofar as it may, for example, inspire one toward discovering what may free her from sorrow (a. 1 *ad* 1), or hoping for forgiveness of sins for which she sorrows (a. 2 *ad* 1). In proposing various remedies for pain or sorrow, it is worth noting that Thomas identifies potential remedies involving every aspect of human existence: internal physical—i.e. tears and groans (q. 38, a. 2), external intellectual—i.e. sympathy and consolation of friends (a. 3), internal intellectual—i.e. contemplation of truth (a. 4), and external physical—i.e. sleep or a bath (a. 5).

According to Thomas, pain and sorrow *per se*—that is, in their *formal* nature—are evil insofar as they inherently involve one's experience of something perceived as evil. Nevertheless, pain and sorrow are not to be avoided at all costs. As noted above, a moderate experience of sorrow may have some *instrumental* benefit (q. 39, a. 3). Thomas thus concludes that at least some experiences of pain or sorrow may be "for that which is apparently evil, but really good"; hence, such experiences "cannot be the greatest evil, for it would be worse to be altogether separated from that which is truly good" (a. 4). The key point here is that the value of one's experience of pain or sorrow is only relative to its usefulness for producing some good.

As noted above, the passions related to the irascible appetite have as their object either something good, but which is difficult to attain, or something evil, but which is difficult to avoid. As such, they involve movement either toward (hope) or away from (despair) some good depending on how arduous one perceives its attainment to be, as well as movement either toward (daring) or away from (fear) some evil depending on one's assessment of the possibility of one's avoiding or overcoming it (q. 23, a. 2).

Hope (*spes*), then, is a passion experienced when one perceives some future good that is nevertheless difficult to attain; however, one assesses the value of the good to be worth the arduousness of working toward it and believes its attainment is possible (q. 40, a. 1)—note that Thomas is not here discussing the *theological virtue* of hope, which we will examine in Chapter 8. Conversely, one despairs (*despera*) of attaining the perceived good if it seems impossible (a. 4)—Thomas will later discuss despair as a type of sin (IIa–IIae, q. 20), but for now it is a morally neutral passion. *False* hope occurs when one mistakenly perceives a difficult future good to be attainable when it is in fact beyond one's power—Thomas cites drunkards and the young as especially prone to false hope (a. 6). He concludes that hope is a source of *activity* insofar as it excites one's attention and causes pleasures, which then spurs one into action to attempt to attain the hoped for object (a. 8).

One experiences fear (*timor*) when faced with some future evil perceived to be extremely difficult or nearly impossible to overcome or escape from (q. 41, a. 2); although there is at least a slim hope of avoiding it (q. 42, a. 2). Fear is intensified in cases where the evil comes upon one suddenly (q. 42, a. 5) or no remedy for it is readily apparent (q. 42, a. 6). Conversely, in cases where the perceived possibility of overcoming the evil is greater, one may daringly (*audaciter*) meet it head-on in the hope of conquering it (q. 45, aa. 1–2). Similar to false hope, Thomas identifies drunkenness (q. 45, a. 3 *ad* 1) and inexperience (*ad* 2) as causes of daring premised upon a misperception of one's ability to conquer the evil one faces.

Thomas analyzes fear into six distinct types (q. 41, a. 4): *laziness* is the fear of too much work; *shamefacedness* is the fear of ruining one's reputation before one does something immoral or otherwise disgraceful; *shame* is the same fear but with respect to actions already performed; *amazement* (or *wonder*) is fear related to something that exceeds one's power to rationally comprehend, at least fully—note that Thomas distinguishes amazement, as a form of fear related to an incomprehensible *evil*, from amazement in the face of something *good* that causes pleasure (q. 32, a. 8; q. 41, a. 4 *ad* 4); *stupor* is fear related to something one encounters that is unusual or extraordinary; finally, *anxiety* is fear related to something unexpected that catches one off-guard. As with other passions such as anger—as discussed below—fear has an effect on both one's soul and body (q. 44); this accords with Thomas' *hylomorphic* construal of human nature—see Chapter 4.

Anger (*ira*), according to Thomas, is provoked by one's rational perception that another person purposely harmed her unjustly; the slighted individual thus desires *vengeance* (*vindicta*) against the other as a matter of just dessert (q. 46, aa. 1–2; q. 47, aa. 1–2). Anger thus differs from *hatred* insofar as the latter involves a desire for evil inflicted upon one's enemy *as such* (a. 6); whereas anger only seeks punishment for one's enemy as a matter of *justice* (a. 7). One of the primary effects of anger in motivating one's vengeful pursuit is the *pleasure* resulting from the hoped for harm she intends to inflict upon the other, intensified once the harm is actually inflicted (q. 48, a. 1). It may seem odd for a "turn the other cheek" Christian such as Thomas to advocate defining anger in terms of vengeance, but note that he is merely being *descriptive* here of what he observes to be a fact of human psychology; he is not *normatively* advocating that a person seek vengeance out of anger. He in fact warns of the extent to which anger can have disturbing effects on one's body and reason (q. 48, aa. 2–4), corrupting one's reasoning such that, for example, one metes out a disproportionate degree of harm to the other person (q. 46, a. 4 *ad* 3). Nevertheless, Thomas does not agree with Seneca and other Stoics that anger is inherently disruptive and cannot serve any useful, rational, good purpose. Thomas even affirms that Christ experienced anger (IIIa, q. 15, a. 9)—for example, when He overturned the merchants' tables in the Temple, being "eaten up by zeal for the house of God" (John 2:14–17). As another example, anger at a *bona fide* injustice—say, on the part of a disenfranchised minority against those who are oppressing them—may lead to justifiable acts of civil disobedience. As a caveat, one's actions, though motivated by anger, must nevertheless be tempered by reason so that one metes out *just*—i.e. proportionate—retribution; otherwise, anger can lead to sin. Thomas would thus differentiate non-violent acts of civil disobedience from violent acts—except in cases of immediate self-defense (IIa–IIae, q. 64, a. 7).

QUESTIONS 90–114—LAW AND GRACE

Thomas' treatise on law is today one of the best known and most often anthologized treatises from the *Summa*. This is somewhat ironic insofar as it represents a small fraction of his overall moral theory—merely 19 questions compared to the 41 questions composing his treatment of virtue and sin in the *prima secundae*, let alone the detailed analysis of the theological and cardinal virtues that compose the massive *secunda secundae* which, in earlier centuries, was the most widely disseminated section of the *Summa*. This treatise evolves the discussion from the animalistic *passions* that motivate human behavior—whether good or evil—to the *rational* foundation for determining whether such behavior counts as morally good or evil.

Thomas defines "law" as "nothing other than a certain ordinance of reason for the common good, made by whoever has care of the community, and that is promulgated" (q. 90, a. 4). In order for some principle to count as a law, it must fulfill all four of these criteria. For example, a law against driving while intoxicated is a valid law because it is made by a legitimate legislative government, the members of which used their collective reasoning capacity to determine that it would promote the common good if people were not allowed to drive while their judgment is impaired by alcohol consumption, and is announced to the citizenry so that they are aware that this law is binding upon them.

This example represents one type of law Thomas recognizes: *human law*, also known as civil or positive law (q. 91, a. 3; qq. 95–96). Thomas defines three other types of law: *eternal law* (q. 91, a. 1; q. 93), *natural law* (q. 91, a. 2; q. 94), and *divine law* (q. 91, aa. 4–5; qq. 98–108). Eternal law is the ultimate foundation for all other types of law. It is formulated in the mind of God, who has care of everything that exists, for the good of the entire created universe. It is the inherent order of the universe created by God and governed by God's providence. According to Thomas, God creates the universe with a specific order that is manifested in the laws of nature—e.g. the laws of physics, such as gravity—and the natural inclinations of the various species that populate the universe—e.g. a plant's natural inclination to take in nourishment and grow in the direction of sunlight. Thomas thus asserts, "It is evident that all things participate to some extent in eternal law; namely, insofar as from its impression on them they are inclined toward their proper acts and ends" (q. 91, a. 2).

Thomas contends that God creates and sustains all that exists other than His own self (Ia, q. 2, a. 3; q. 44, a. 1). Furthermore, God does not create things in a haphazard or random way, but in an *ordered* way that will allow for the maximal realization of the universe's overall perfection and that of the individual beings that constitute it. In order for God to create the ordered nature of the universe—an act of *providence*—God must first have such an ordered nature in mind: "Now it is evident, supposing that the world is ruled by divine providence (Ia, q. 22, aa. 1–2) . . . that the whole universal community is governed by divine reason" (Ia–IIae, q. 91, a. 1). Thomas thus argues that God's *knowledge* is the cause of things (Ia, q. 14, a. 8)—in the Aristotelian sense of *formal* cause—just as the form, or idea, in an artisan's mind causes her to create something which reflects that idea (q. 15, a. 1). Furthermore, God does not have in mind just one idea of the ordered universe as a whole, but many ideas corresponding to the manifold types of beings that populate the universe and materially instantiate its ordered nature (q. 15, a. 2).

In his account of eternal law, Thomas succinctly states, "eternal law is nothing other than the order (*ratio*) of divine wisdom, according to which is directed all acts and motions" (Ia–IIae, q. 93, a. 1). This statement does not imply that God literally directs all actions and movements. Rather, eternal law, in establishing the ordered nature of the universe, "imprints on the whole of nature the principles of its proper acts" (q. 93, a. 5). For non-rational beings, such principles constitute the physical laws of nature by which each thing acts in a determinate fashion—at least at the macro-level. For rational beings, these principles constitute the natural law (q. 91, a. 2).

Thomas describes human beings as able to participate in eternal law more fully than other material beings by virtue of having the capacity for rational thought. Human beings are able to understand, albeit imperfectly, the eternal law; non-rational beings are unable to do so. It is the human understanding of eternal law which Thomas terms "natural law." Natural law is one of two ways in which eternal law is promulgated to rational creatures. The second way is through direct revelation, which Thomas terms "divine law" and which he considers, due to his Christian heritage, to consist of the so-called "Old" and "New" Laws found in the Hebrew and Christian Scriptures.

The faculty by which a human being's natural inclinations, and the correlative precepts of natural law that tend toward their fulfillment, become apparent to her is termed *synderesis*: "*Synderesis* is called the law of our intellect, insofar as it is a habit containing the precepts of natural law, which are the first principles of human actions" (Ia–IIae, q. 94, a. 1 *ad* 2; cf. Ia, q. 79, a. 12).

The ultimate foundation for synderesis is eternal law; nevertheless, eternal law is not the *proximate* cause of human volition in accord with what is good versus what is evil: "Now there are two rules of the human will: one is proximate and homogeneous—viz., human reason; the other is the first rule—viz., eternal law—which is God's reason, so to speak" (Ia–IIae, q. 71, a. 6; cf. Ia–IIae, q. 19, a. 4; q. 21, a. 1; IIa–IIae, q. 17, a. 1). *Reason* gives a human agent the precepts which are the ultimate measure for all human actions. Eternal law cannot be denied, however, as the *ultimate* cause of the precepts of natural law understood synderetically by human reason. It is because of this second-order meta-ethical relationship that natural law is said to *participate* in eternal law.

While synderesis is the *habit* of knowing the precepts of natural law, *conscience* is the active application of such principles in order to determine what one ought to do in particular circumstances (Ia, q. 79, a. 13). The actualization of the synderetical habit in the form of the moral determinations of one's conscience is not an automatic process, but one requiring *formation*; as such, the lack of certain intellectual virtues—most importantly *prudence*—could lead to the formation of an *erroneous* conscience. Thomas thus considers the question whether an agent is morally bound to follow the determination of her conscience even when it is in error. His, perhaps surprising, answer is that "the will is evil when it is at variance with erring reason" (Ia–IIae, q. 19, a. 5 *s.c.*). This seemingly paradoxical response implies that it is morally permissible to will something that is objectively evil so long as one's reason informs it to do so. To understand how Thomas could hold this thesis that "an erring conscience binds" an agent morally, it is necessary to recall the analysis presented in Chapter 5 of how the intellect informs the will to produce a volitional act. The key element is that an agent only wills what her intellect perceives to be *good* in some respect; one does not will evil for its own sake. Thus, if one's conscience informs her will that performing, say, an act of fornication under a certain set of circumstances is good, then, if she were to act against her conscience, she would be acting contrary to what her reason understands to be good—in short, she would be willingly rejecting the good as she understands it, and the willful rejection of what one understands to be good constitutes sin. Even more so, Thomas states, by willfully rejecting what one's reason has presented as *true* in accord with God's eternal law or a revealed divine command, although erroneously understood, one willfully rejects God's law, which constitutes the very essence of sin (q. 19, a. 5 *ad* 1–2). Of course, this does not mean that the agent is completely morally innocent insofar as she may be responsible for the errant formation of her conscience such that she wrongly perceives fornication to be good under certain circumstances; but there may have also been external factors that had negatively influenced the formation of her conscience such that her culpability is mitigated. Thomas refers back to his discussion of how *ignorance* may or may not excuse one's moral culpability depending on whether one is responsible, either voluntarily or through negligence, for the malformation of one's rational judgment (q. 19, a. 6).

Natural law principles, as will be shown below, are quite general so as to be universally applicable to all human beings, no matter what their cultural background or station in life. Thomas thus recognizes the need for what he terms "human law," which is the particular determination of general natural law principles made by human legislators using prudent practical judgment. Human laws are crafted with respect to particular communities to help train each community's members in becoming virtuous; in this sense such laws can be considered culturally relative because the same human laws would not be appropriate for every community: "The general principles of natural law cannot be applied in the same way to all, because of the great variety of human affairs. And accordingly there appears a diversity of positive [human] laws among diverse people" (q. 95, a. 2 *ad* 3). Thomas further notes the important role that "custom," relative to different communities, plays in specifying and applying natural law principles (q. 97, a. 3).

Nevertheless, human laws must be crafted in accordance with the general principles of natural law that are universal and thus binding upon all human beings regardless of culture or circumstance. Any valid human law, Thomas contends, must be somehow derived from the natural law; otherwise, it would be a "perversion of law" (q. 95, a. 2). For example, a law permitting racial segregation is not a valid human law because it violates the natural law mandate to treat all human beings justly and maintain social harmony. Racial segregation does not treat all human beings justly and leads to a fundamentally disharmonious social state. Even if such a practice has the force of "custom" supporting it, Thomas maintains that the customs of human communities, useful as they may be in specifying and applying natural law, cannot change the universally binding principles of natural law and must yield when they conflict (q. 97, a. 3 *ad* 1).

Another example applying the natural law precept that human beings ought to live in social harmony involves providing for each other's material needs. Natural law thus arguably requires that there be social mechanisms to provide funds to help alleviate the effects of poverty and "level the playing field" as much as possible. But it is up to human law to determine the nature of such a mechanism—whether it be, for example, taxation of the wealthy, incentives to prompt the wealthy to philanthropic acts, or redistribution of public funds used for other things such as national defense or infrastructure.

Thomas defines natural law as "nothing other than the participation in eternal law by rational creatures" (q. 91, a. 2). By virtue of our capacity for rational thought, human beings are able to understand the general principles which underlie the existence of particular beings, actions, and events. For example, everything that exists is governed by the principle of non-contradiction, which states that the same thing—whether it is a substance, action, or event—cannot both *be* and *not be* at the same time, in the same place, in the same respect. Hence, it cannot be both raining in this very spot at this very moment and not raining in this very spot at this very moment. As another example, I can be both tall with respect to my seven-year-old daughter and not tall with respect to an NBA basketball center; but I cannot be both tall and not tall with respect to my daughter at this very moment.

Just as there are general principles that underlie what Thomas terms "speculative" matters, such as the nature of reality, mathematics, geometry, etc., there are also general principles that underlie what Thomas terms "practical" matters, such as what a moral agent ought to do in a particular situation (q. 94, a. 2). Some of these general principles are "self-evident" (*per se nota*) because they are immediately knowable by the human mind without any empirical investigation required. Everyone acts, for example, on the principle of non-contradiction, even if they had never seen it formulated before reading the above paragraph. No one in their right mind would think that, if Vladimir Putin is the current president of Russia, that it is true that Vladimir Putin is not the current president of Russia. By the same token, Thomas thinks that certain general practical principles are self-evident to any rational mind.

This leads Thomas to formulate the first, fundamental principle of natural law that is understood by the human mind: "Good is to be done and pursued, and evil avoided" (q. 94, a. 2). He then contends, "And upon this are founded all other principles of natural law; such that everything which practical reason naturally apprehends to be good [or evil] for human beings belongs to the natural law principles to be done or avoided" (a. 2). Hence, natural law mandates us to use our reasoning capacity to determine what is "good" in accordance with our nature as rational animals and go after it, and avoid whatever we determine to be "evil" because it is opposed to our flourishing as human beings.

Knowledge of natural law thus entails knowledge of both self-evident "first principles" and additional principles discovered through reflection on human natural inclinations toward certain goods that are fulfilling to human nature. Such goods, insofar as they are good and are perceived as such by the human mind, provide a sufficient rationale for human beings to pursue them. This does not imply that knowledge of the good is a sufficient motivation to do the good; Thomas agrees with Aristotle that the cultivation of *virtue* is necessary to ground human beings' proper moral motivation. Rather, the normative foundation for the precepts of natural law is their accordance with what is objectively good for human nature in terms of fulfilling our natural inclinations toward what is perfective of our nature—such perfection constituting our *happiness*. God remains, however, the ultimate meta-ethical foundation for the inherent goodness of beings in the universe.

Thomas cites the following "goods" with respect to human nature toward which human beings are naturally inclined: life, sexual inter-course, education of offspring, knowing the truth about God, and living in society (q. 94, a. 2). Thomas acknowledges that this list is not complete and exhorts the prudent use of practical reason to deter-mine the set of goods and evils relative to human nature, and then to define the principles of natural law which promote the goods while avoiding the evils. For example, since human beings are "social" by nature, it is good for us to live in community; fulfilling this good requires that we be honest with one another and keep our promises (IIa–IIae, q. 88, a. 3 *ad* 1), avoid deception (IIa–IIae, q. 110, a. 3), as well as respect others' property and not injure one another. As a gen-eral natural law principle to guide human beings in our relationships with each other for the sake of forming a stable society, Thomas cites the Golden Rule: "Do not have done to another what you do not wish to be done to you" (Supp., q. 65, a. 1 *ad* 7). As mentioned above, it also follows from our social nature to treat each other justly and not segregate different racial groups from one another.

Thomas cites further specific natural law principles that follow from the natural inclination to educate one's offspring. Such educa-tion is not simply the imparting of knowledge, but the more general sense of "upbringing" that includes moral education and everything else a child needs to learn in order to pass successfully into adulthood (IIa–IIae, q. 57, a. 4). Thus, for example, one ought not to engage in "simple fornication"—i.e. casual sex—that may result in a pregnancy for which one does not intend to take responsibility. Lack of parental responsibility, on the part of both fathers and mothers, hinders the fulfillment of a child's upbringing (IIa–IIae, q. 154, a. 2).

Thomas contends that various natural law principles can be known by the human mind either immediately, with little reflection, or only with a great deal of reasoning (Ia–IIae, q. 100, a. 1). Nevertheless, it is expedient, on Thomas' view, for God sometimes to reveal directly certain general natural law principles. One reason for the existence of *divine law* is that human beings are naturally inclined to know, as well as love (Ia, q. 60, a. 5 *ad* 4), God as the ultimate source of being and goodness, but this is not achievable by human beings' own capacities

(Ia–IIae, q. 5, a. 5; q. 62, a. 1). The fact that the purpose of divine law is to direct human beings toward our supernatural end supports the thesis that acknowledgment of God's existence as our ultimate end is irrelevant to—and thus not required for—a sufficiently coherent and sound theory of natural law, the purpose of which is to direct human beings toward the fulfillment of our natural capacities.

Divine law is not only a "supplement" to natural law, but also another means by which natural law is revealed to human reason; while such revelation helps human beings to understand natural law in cases where sin or some other defect has clouded our reason, it remains that case that what divine law reveals, for the most part, is also discoverable by human reason alone. As a prime example, the Decalogue, or "Ten Commandments," contain a number of natural law principles which, though divinely revealed, are discoverable by human reason alone (q. 100, a. 3). The natural law thus includes prohibitions against murder, theft, adultery, covetousness, lying, and dishonoring one's parents. Thomas notes, however, that some precepts of the Decalogue, while part of natural law, nonetheless require "Divine instruction" in order for human reason to comprehend them—e.g. not making a graven image or taking God's name in vain (q. 100, a. 1).

Thomas affirms the ordered relationship of divine law to natural law and so contends, for instance, that all the moral precepts of the Old Law belong to natural law (q. 99, a. 2 *ad* 1; q. 100, a. 1) and are thereby universally applicable to all rational beings; although some non-moral precepts are binding only on the Jewish people to whom the Old Law was revealed (q. 98, a. 5). Finally, Thomas holds that the two "greatest commandments" that sum up the precepts of the Old Law— namely, love of God and love of neighbor—"are the first and common precepts of natural law, which are self-evident to human reason, either through nature or through faith" (q. 100, a. 3 *ad* 1). Hence, divine law, though superior to natural law insofar as it is promulgated to humanity directly by God, is nonetheless subordinate to natural law insofar as the rule of reason, grounded in humanity's natural inclinations, remains the primary, proximate foundation for the existence and normative value of natural law. Thomas even holds that, in certain cases, the requirements of natural law—specifically, in this case, natural *justice*—may supersede what would otherwise appear on first glance to be a divine commandment. The case in question involves baptizing Jewish children against their parents' wishes. While Thomas would understand it to be God's will that children be baptized so that they may receive Christ's salvific grace, he nonetheless holds that the rational conclusion that baptizing a child against her parents' wishes would violate the naturally just relationship between parent and child is the more accurate indicator of what is truly God's will and our ethical duty in this matter (IIa–IIae, q. 10, a. 12; IIIa, q. 68, a. 10).

An important issue concerns the relationship of Thomas' concept of natural law and the existence of God. Is God's existence necessary for a coherent and sound Thomistic account of natural law? Does the nature of God's relationship to human morality, if there is a relationship, entail a "divine command ethic"? This is an important consideration because Thomas' moral theory is often taken to be theologically defined due to his description of natural law as rational beings' participation in God's eternal law. It thus seems that we must add eternal law as a necessary meta-ethical foundation for Thomas' natural law theory. But the fact that Thomas cites God as a meta-ethical foundation of human morality, just as he cites God as the metaphysical foundation of human existence, does not entail that the nature of human existence or morality requires divine determination. It is the consideration of human natural inclinations that grounds our understanding of natural law principles, and not an arbitrary set of revealed divine commands (q. 94, a. 2). Even the commandments of the Decalogue *reflect* what is in accordance with the natural law as opposed to *defining* morality. Despite Thomas' appeal to God as a meta-ethical foundation for human morality, actual belief in God and divinely revealed law is not required for moral knowledge or the validity of natural law principles.

Another way of describing the *theonomous* character of natural law is that it requires eternal law as its *ultimate* foundation; in other words, a *complete* accounting of natural law cannot be given without reference to eternal law. This is undeniably Thomas' view insofar as the precepts of natural law are defined relative to human natural inclinations, which follow from the nature of human beings, which is ultimately defined in reference to an idea of humanity in the mind of God that constitutes part of eternal law (Ia–IIae, q. 71, a. 2 *ad* 4; a. 6 *ad* 3).

How strong is the participatory connection between natural law and eternal law? In particular, is it the case that natural law has its moral force *only* if eternal law exists to ground it? Thomas contends that what is dictated by natural law is based not only on natural inclinations, but also out of reverence for divine commands. He further asserts:

> Now it is from eternal law, which is the divine reason, that human reason is the rule of the human will, from which its goodness is derived (Ia–IIae, q. 19, a. 3) . . . Hence, it is evident that the goodness of the human will depends much more on eternal law than on human reason; and when human reason fails, it must have recourse to the eternal reason.

(q. 19, a. 4)

For Thomas, God is the creative source by which beings in the universe have a specific essence or belong to a natural kind, have certain dispositional properties relative to their essence, and have obligatory ends that promote their well-being relative to their essence. God also provides rational beings with the epistemological apparatus and practical reasoning capacity required to be aware of their essence and the ends to be pursued that promote their well-being. Thomas, however, argues that the human mind cannot apprehend the eternal law itself, because we are not God (q. 19, a. 4 *ad* 3; q. 93, a. 2). Therefore, apprehension of natural law principles must be based upon something knowable by the human mind—namely, human natural inclinations. One could respond that the revealed divine law provides a better epistemological foundation for moral awareness, and that morality is thus best understood as theologically defined. Thomas, though, contends that divine law is something distinct from natural law that is added to it, and in fact presupposes natural law (q. 99, a. 2 *ad* 1). Therefore, the existence of natural law principles knowable by the human mind is logically prior to the principles of divine law, which serves to define more clearly and enforce the natural law.

Not only does God provide the ultimate meta-ethical foundation for the natural law, God also directly gives human beings specific help required to overcome the morally debilitating effects of *original sin*, re-orient our wills toward the source of our existence, and transcend the limits of our natural condition to merit our *supernatural* end of happiness in experiencing the Beatific Vision—that is, knowledge of and loving union with God in His essence. The common theological term for the "divine help" offered to human beings that Thomas utilizes is "grace." In the final questions of the *prima secundae*, Thomas describes the *essence* (qq. 109–111), *cause* (q. 112), and *effects* (qq. 113–114) of grace.

Thomas first examines whether grace is *necessary* for various human beings to achieve various purposes (q. 109). In so doing, he generally differentiates between those actions a human being can perform due to her own natural capabilities, for which grace is not necessary beyond God's providential endowment of a human being with her nature, and actions undertaken to fulfill a purpose that transcends a human being's natural condition—such as attaining knowledge of God in His essence—for which grace is required (a. 1). When it comes to the crucial question of whether a human being can will to perform any good deed without grace, Thomas differentiates between human nature in its pre-Fall and post-Fall state (a. 2). In either state, human beings depend upon God as the ultimate foundation for our very existence, as well as for any activity we do, voluntarily or otherwise—as Thomas has just established in the previous article. Before humanity's Fall, additional grace was required only for human beings to attain our supernatural end of knowledge and loving union with God; however, we could perform any other good deed by virtue of our own natural capacities. After the Fall, though, humanity requires grace in order to *heal* each of our souls so that we can be re-oriented toward first desiring, and then voluntarily willing to move toward loving union with God. Thus, one of the primary effects of grace is the *justification* of sinners (q. 113).

Clearly, human beings require grace in order to merit *perfect happiness*—consisting in the supernatural gift of the Beatific Vision (a. 5). But do we require grace even in order to be able to receive grace? Thomas answers this question positively (a. 6). He defines two types of grace. The first is *habitual*—in the same sense as virtues or vices are *habits*—that is, a *disposition* toward receiving further grace that allows the human will to perform objectively good, and thereby *meritorious*, actions that will lead us to the completion of our *reditus* to God (q. 114, a. 2). The second is a *gratuitous* movement of the will by God toward the reception of the habitual grace necessary to perform meritorious actions (q. 112, a. 2). The source of grace in both cases is God (a. 1). This creates an inherent tension in Thomas' account since he holds both that a human being has free will and thereby can—and must if she is to be morally assessed—*move herself* toward what she perceives to be good, but also that a human being's will must *be moved by God* if it is to turn itself toward God as the ultimate good (a. 6 *ad* 1 & 4). In order to preserve both the necessity of grace and human freedom, Thomas must make the case that the two can *cooperate* in effecting a human being's re-orientation toward what is objectively good and the source of her happiness (q. 111, a. 2). Furthermore, this cooperative functioning of divine grace and the human will continues beyond the initial re-orientation of one's will toward God (q. 109, a. 7), but is also needed in order to avoid further occasions of sin (a. 8), do good (a. 9), and persevere in a "graced" state throughout life (a. 10). In sum, Thomas concludes that the effects of grace are: 1) to heal the soul; 2) to desire good; 3) to carry into effect the good proposed; 4) to persevere in good; and 5) to reach glory (q. 111, a. 3).

SUGGESTIONS FOR FURTHER READING

In addition to the suggested readings at the end of Chapter 5, detailed expositions of Thomas' account of the passions and their relationship to virtue and vice can be found in Robert Miner, *Thomas Aquinas on the Passions* (New York: Cambridge University Press, 2009); Nicholas E. Lombardo, *The Logic of Desire: Aquinas on Emotion* (Washington, D.C.: Catholic University of America Press, 2011); Diana Fritz Cates, *Aquinas on the Emotions: A Religious-Ethical Inquiry* (Washington, D.C.: Georgetown University Press, 2009).

An English translation of Seneca's *De ira* is available at www.sophia-project.org/uploads/1/3/9/5/13955288/seneca_anger.pdf (accessed May 26, 2015).

Hume's *Enquiry Concerning the Principles of Morals* is available in an edition by P. H. Nidditch (Oxford: Clarendon Press, 1975).

More in-depth analyses of Thomas' theory of natural law are offered by R. J. Henle, ed., *The Treatise on Law* (Notre Dame, IN: University of Notre Dame Press, 1993); Anthony J. Lisska, *Aquinas's Theory of Natural Law: An Analytic Reconstruction* (New York: Oxford

University Press, 1996); John Goyette, Mark S. Latkovic, and Richard S. Myers, eds., *St. Thomas Aquinas and the Natural Law Tradition: Contemporary Perspectives* (Washington, D.C.: Catholic University of America Press, 2004); Jean Porter, *Nature as Reason: A Thomistic Theory of the Natural Law* (Grand Rapids, MI: Eerdmans, 2005).

There are several good syntheses, analyses, and defenses of the natural law moral tradition beyond Thomas' own account; see Heinrich A. Rommen, *The Natural Law: A Study in Legal and Social History and Philosophy*, trans. Thomas R. Hanley (St. Louis, MO: Herder, 1948); Jacques Maritain, *Natural Law: Reflections on Theory and Practice*, ed. William Sweet (South Bend, IN: St. Augustine's Press, 2001); John Finnis, *Natural Law and Natural Rights* (New York: Oxford University Press, 1980); David S. Oderberg and Timothy Chappell, eds., *Human Values: New Essays on Ethics and Natural Law* (New York: Palgrave Macmillan, 2004).

Readers who wish to explore the larger political ramifications of Thomas' moral theory should consult John Finnis, *Aquinas: Moral, Political, and Legal Theory* (New York: Oxford University Press, 1998).

A helpful elucidation of Thomas' treatment of divine grace is provided by Bernard Lonergan, *Grace and Freedom: Operative Grace in the Thought of Thomas Aquinas*, eds. Frederick E. Crowe and Robert M. Doran (Toronto: University of Toronto Press, 2000).

7

VIRTUE AND BEATITUDE, VICE AND SIN

PREFACE

The previous chapter laid out the theoretical foundations for Thomas' detailed analysis of human moral action. We saw how the capacity to understand rationally how one ought to act—which Thomas terms "natural law"—as well as divine grace cooperate in allowing one to will what is objectively good. Grace, however, does not take control of a human being's will, turning her into a puppet or automaton; nor is mere knowledge of what is objectively good sufficient for a human being to be inclined to actually pursue the good. The latter point invokes the problem of "incontinence" (Greek: *akrasia*), which is the psychic dissonance that follows when one knows what she ought to do, but does not will to do it. In the Christian Scriptures, this problem is noted by St. Paul when he admits, "For I do not do the good I want, but the evil I do not want is what I do" (Romans 7:19). It is thereby vitally important that moral agents cultivate certain *dispositions* that incline them toward pursuing what they know to be good—i.e. *virtues*. However, dispositions in the opposite direction may also be cultivated—i.e. *vices*.

In this chapter, we will elucidate Thomas' general, theoretical account from the *prima secundae* of virtues—which are aimed toward happiness or beatitude—and vices—which are aimed toward sin. In the next chapter, we will canvass his detailed treatment in the *secunda secundae* of the three "theological" virtues—faith, hope, and charity—and the four "cardinal" virtues—prudence, justice, fortitude, and temperance—along with their counterpoint vices.

QUESTIONS 49–56—THE CONCEPT OF VIRTUE

Virtues, according to Aristotle, whom Thomas closely follows, are *habits* cultivated in order to define a moral agent's *character* (q. 55, a. 1). If, for example, a human being develops the virtue of courage, then she will be considered a courageous person. On a virtue theoretic construal of human morality, the goal is not merely to do virtuous actions, but rather to become a *virtuous person*. In other words, the central moral question one should ask oneself is not, "What ought I to do?" but rather, "How ought I to live?" or "What type of person should I be?" Nevertheless, one becomes a virtuous person only by *cultivating* specific virtues, which is accomplished by doing virtuous *actions* (q. 51, a. 2; q. 63, a. 2). A human being thus becomes courageous by performing acts of courage, generous by performing acts of generosity, etc. Nevertheless, Thomas departs from Aristotle in holding that God may directly *infuse* some virtues into a human being so that we may be equipped to attain our supernatural end of loving union with God (q. 51, a. 4; q. 63, a. 3).

Since a human being's moral development depends upon doing virtuous actions, it is necessary to understand which actions count as "virtuous." According to Aristotle and Thomas, a virtuous action is one that, if done, will promote a human being's "flourishing"—i.e. the fulfillment of her "nature" as a human being (q. 49, a. 2). A human being's nature, as described in Chapter 4, is determined by her substantial form, which provides the set of capacities—vegetative, sensitive, and rational—that define her as a "rational animal." Human flourishing involves actualizing these definitive capacities such that a virtuous human being is the most "perfect"—i.e. most complete or fully actualized—human being she can be: "virtue implies a perfection of power" (q. 55, a. 3). A human being may also develop habits that detract from her flourishing: vices (q. 54, a. 3).

As habits, virtues and vices are dispositions that a moral agent *possesses* such that they become "second nature" to her—disposing her to act in certain ways just as the customs of a particular culture disposes its members to act in certain ways (q. 58, a. 1). But human beings are not born with any such habits; nor are these habits formed simply by nature (q. 51, a. 1)—though Thomas notes that certain natural conditions of one's body may predispose one toward developing certain habits. Rather, virtues and vices must be "cultivated," much as a plant or any other living thing needs to be, through the action of both principles *internal* to the agent—her own intellect, will, and passions—as well as *external* influences—upbringing, education, laws, and other forms of social conditioning. While a certain degree of external "conditioning" is involved, human moral development differs from the way one might *train* a non-rational animal to behave itself since one's intellect and will are essential players in this process (q. 50, a. 3 *ad* 2). Although we are not born with any virtues or vices, Thomas recognizes the need for certain *inchoate* principles in human nature that allows for virtues to be cultivated in the first place (q. 63, a. 1)—e.g. our *synderetical* apprehension of the first principles of natural law (Ia, q. 79, a. 12; Ia–IIae, q. 94, a. 1 *ad* 2).

These internal and external factors cited above contribute not only to the *formation* and *strengthening* of one's habitual dispositions (q. 52), but also to their *diminution* or *corruption* (q. 53). As a result, individual human beings will have distinct sets of such habits, as well as different levels of strength for each habit they possess; although Thomas argues that all of the *virtues* are possessed by an individual person at the same level (q. 66, a. 2). For example, a child raised by parents who practice kindness and generosity will likely develop such virtuous dispositions herself; if, however, she encounters a high school environment that is hostile to such traits, the teasing, embarrassment, and social exclusion she experiences may lead her to cease acting on these dispositions (q. 53, a. 3) or even start acting in accord with the contrary vices of meanness and selfishness—either way, she would eventually convert away from being a kind and generous person.

After discussing the nature of virtues and vices as *habits* that define each human being's moral character, Thomas is ready to define "virtue" itself and he affirms the definition provided by

Augustine: "Virtue is a good quality of the mind, by which we live righteously, of which no one can make bad use, which God works in us, without us" (q. 55, a. 4). Thomas claims that this definition "comprises perfectly the whole essential notion of virtue" insofar as it references all four *causes* of virtue—recall the four Aristotelian causes elucidated in Chapter 2. The *formal* cause of virtue—that is, its specific nature—is its being "a good quality." The *material* cause of virtue—that is, of what it is a good quality—is the mind. This may sound odd insofar as the mind—more precisely, the *intellect* and its affective disposition, the *will*—is immaterial according to Thomas; but the material cause of something does not necessarily have to be composed of matter in the sense of being extended in physical space. Rather, the term "matter" refers to any sort of *substratum* capable of bearing various forms—consider the nature and function of the "receptacle" in Plato's *Timaeus* (49a–51b). In this case, the intellect and will function as the *substratum* for the various virtues that inform an agent's character. The *final* cause of virtue— that is, its end, goal, or *telos* toward which it is aimed—is for one to "live righteously." The definition specifies further that "no one can make bad use" of a virtue, unlike other habits of which one may make good or bad use; for example, an intellectual habit of strategic thinking—which good chess players often develop—may be used to play chess, or to plan an operation to rescue innocent hostages, or to plan a terrorist attack.

The *efficient* cause of virtue is God, but only in the case of *infused* virtues. Such virtues include the three theological virtues of faith, hope, and charity, as well as infused complements of the other moral virtues that perfect them in their orientation toward a human being's supernatural end of loving union with God (q. 63, a. 3). It is crucial to note, however, that God does not infuse such virtues without one's *consent* (q. 55, a. 4 *ad* 6); and, while God alone is the efficient cause of an infused virtue, one cooperates with such infusion by performing acts in accord with it, which in turn strengthens the infused habit (q. 51, a. 4 *ad* 3). The efficient cause of *naturally acquired* virtues is a moral agent herself performing virtuous actions, with the external assistance of positive social influences and other extrinsic goods that facilitate her performance of virtuous actions.

QUESTIONS 57–67—TYPES OF VIRTUE

Having defined "virtue," Thomas next distinguishes two general categories of virtues: *intellectual* and *moral*. Under the former category, he defines three virtues of the *speculative* intellect—the part of the intellect concerned with what is true on a theoretical level (q. 57, aa. 1–2). *Understanding* is the intellectual virtue by which one possesses knowledge of foundational necessary *principles* that are intuitively knowable in and of themselves (*per se nota*). Such "first principles" include the fundamentals of logic—e.g. the principle of non-contradiction—as well as one's *synderetical* knowledge of the natural law—e.g. good is to be done and pursued and evil avoided (q. 94, a. 2). *Science* involves the application of the foundational principles of reasoning to derive further truths and to understand the nature of things in the world—this term thus includes, but has broader application than, the strictly *empirical* method of scientific investigation to which it typically refers today. Finally, *wisdom* is one's knowledge of the *ultimate cause* of things, which traces back to God in accord with Thomas' second argument for God's existence (Ia, q. 2, a. 3). Due to the greatness of the object of its knowledge, Thomas considers wisdom to be the noblest of the intellectual virtues (q. 66, a. 5).

Two other intellectual virtues are related to the *practical* intellect, concerned with determining what actions one ought to do in a given situation. The first is *art*, which is "right reason about certain works to be made" (q. 57, a. 3); although we typically think of art today in reference primarily to aesthetic creations, its wider scope, encompassing any form of technological invention, may be seen from the Greek root (*technē*) of the Latin term (*ars*). The other, and most important of the intellectual virtues, is *prudence*, which Thomas defines as "right reason of things to be done" (q. 57, a. 4). Prudence, in fact, is the *hinge* between the intellectual and moral virtues, and so could be considered under either category. Thus, it is properly labeled one of the "cardinal" virtues—the word "cardinal" is derived from the Latin *cardo*, which means "hinge." Without prudence, a person could not perform morally good actions, since—as discussed in Chapter 5—the intellect is necessary in order to provide the formal content of what one may will: in short, prudence informs a person's *choice* of which good to pursue in a particular situation, such that one could not act virtuously at all without prudence. Hence, a person requires not only speculative knowledge of the first principles of natural law—attained through the virtue of understanding—but also practical knowledge of how to apply such principles in the context of particular situations calling for rationally informed moral choice. Thomas thus concludes that "prudence is a virtue necessary to lead a good life" (q. 57, a. 5).

In discussing prudence's central role in moral action, Thomas anticipates a distinction later formalized by Immanuel Kant (1724–1804) between a moral agent who wills in accord with direction or influence from an external source (*heteronomy*) and one who wills in accord with his own internal rational understanding of the moral law (*autonomy*). Consider, for example, a person who refrains from stealing because he fears being caught and punished, compared to a person who refrains from stealing simply because he knows it is morally wrong. Or consider a child who behaves herself due to parental instruction when she lacks the maturity to reason on her own what she ought to do, compared to an intellectually and morally mature person. Thomas expresses the distinction thus,

> When a man does a good deed, not of his own counsel, but moved by that of another, his deed is not yet quite perfect, as regards his reason in directing him and his appetite in moving him. Wherefore, if he do a good deed, he does not do well simply; and yet this is required in order that he may lead a good life.
>
> (q. 57, a. 5 *ad* 2)

Again, while prudence is most properly classified as an intellectual virtue—since it concerns practical reasoning about what one ought to do—it may also be counted as a moral virtue—since it is required in order for one to will a morally good action for which she may be praised (q. 58, a. 3 *ad* 1). Prudence, however, while *necessary*, is not *sufficient* for one to will a morally good action. Other moral virtues are also required that bring one's concupiscible and irascible appetites—described in Chapter 6—into line with the dictates of prudence: "the virtue which is in the irascible and concupiscible powers is nothing else but a certain habitual conformity of these powers to reason" (q. 56, a. 4). Thomas, following Aristotle, characterizes reason's rule over one's appetites as "political," as opposed to "tyrannical," meaning that the irascible and concupiscible appetites have "a certain right of opposition" to what reason commands ought to be done (q. 58, a. 2). Thus, on the one hand, moral virtue requires both understanding and prudence so that a person may know both generally what she ought to do in accord with the natural law, as well as what she ought to do in particular circumstances (q. 58, a. 4); but, on the other hand, prudential reasoning about particular circumstances requires that a person be disposed toward doing actions that are just, temperate, or courageous in accord with what reason determines ought to be done (q. 58, a. 5).

Thomas defines four *cardinal* moral virtues on which all moral behavior "hinges" (q. 61). Prudence, as we have already seen, is an essential virtue of the practical intellect. Also related to intellect's practical reasoning function is the virtue of *justice*, by which various goods are properly ordered in relation to each other, and which Thomas considers to be the most important of the moral virtues (q. 66, a. 4). *Temperance*—or *moderation*—is a virtue of the concupiscible appetite through which sensible goods are pursued in line with prudential reasoning. Finally, *fortitude*—or *courage*—is a virtue of the irascible appetite through which a person is able to withstand obstacles or dangers to following what prudential reasoning has concluded she ought to do (q. 61, a. 2).

These virtues are essential to living a good moral life in a way that the intellectual virtues—prudence aside—are not, since one could cultivate excellence in scientific reasoning or in artistic creativity while lacking in moral rectitude. Thomas thus terms the moral, as well as the theological, virtues as virtues in the truest sense of the term (*simpliciter*); whereas the intellectual virtues—again, excepting prudence—are virtues only in a relative sense (*secundum quid*) insofar as they do not have a direct relationship to one's *will* (q. 56, a. 3). Here, Thomas once again anticipates a Kantian distinction between two senses of the term "good." Kant defines a moral agent's will as the only thing that could be called good in an "unqualified" sense, since all other good qualities an agent may possess—such as intelligence, strength, various skills—may become perverted if employed for evil ends by a will that is not good. Adolf Hitler and Dr. Martin Luther King, Jr. both possessed intelligence, perseverance, and oratorical skills that allowed them to influence the minds of millions of followers; there is, however, a clear moral difference in the *ends* to which they respectively employed these generally positive traits.

The cardinal virtues are by no means the only moral virtues; for instance, in addition to mapping temperance to the concupiscible passions and fortitude to the passions of fear and daring, Thomas links *magnanimity* to hope and despair and *meekness* to anger (q. 60, a. 4); and we will see other moral virtues emerge as we progress through the *secunda secundae* in Chapter 8. In governing one's passions, it is worth emphasizing that Thomas—unlike the Stoics, or the Vulcans on *Star Trek*—does not depict such virtues as *antithetical* to the passions (q. 59, a. 2), such that the passions ought to be sublimated or eliminated from one's psyche. Rather, moral virtues *perfect* the passions by ordering them to reason. Thomas goes so far as to assert that the moral virtues cannot even exist without the passions and that they even cause passionate responses, such as joy and pleasure: "the more perfect a virtue is, the more does it cause passion" (q. 59, a. 5). In short, there are no dour saints.

The *theological* virtues Thomas identifies, following Scripture (1 Corinthians 13:13), are faith, hope, and charity (q. 62, a. 3), of which the last is the greatest insofar as it is the "mother," "root," and "form" of *all* other virtues (Ia–IIae, q. 62, a. 4; q. 66, a. 6; IIa–IIae, q. 23, a. 8). These virtues are necessary for human beings to attain our supernatural end of loving union with God, which surpasses our natural abilities. Thomas notes that these virtues are properly called "theological" for three reasons: 1) they orient a human being's activities toward God; 2) they are infused by God as opposed to being cultivated through habitual activity; and 3) our knowledge of them is through divine revelation (q. 62, a. 1). *Faith* provides us with intellectual awareness of God as the source of human happiness. *Hope* allows us to believe that we may attain our ultimate goal of loving union with God. *Charity* inclines our will toward such union, which also extends to our desire for loving union with our fellow human beings. Upon attainment of this union after death, neither faith nor hope remain in the soul insofar as one now has direct intellectual apprehension of, and is in actual union with, God (q. 67, aa. 3–5); only charity remains since union with God is the perfection of love (q. 67, a. 6).

In addition to the theological virtues, Thomas argues that God also infuses *perfect* forms of the other virtues so that a person's intellectual and moral activity may be oriented not only toward the attainment of the *imperfect* happiness this life can offer, but also the *perfect* happiness possible only in loving union with God (q. 65, a. 2). Unlike naturally acquired moral virtues, which can be diminished or lost through one's activity, infused virtues—dependent as they are fundamentally on the theological virtue of charity (q. 65, a. 2)—can be lost only by turning away from God in the case of grave sin, resulting in God's withdrawal of the grace of infused charity and the other infused moral virtues along with it as a form of punishment (IIa–IIae, q. 24, a. 10).

Let us pause to summarize how Thomas' moral theory has developed to this point. Thomas argues that everything has goodness to the degree that it has being (Ia, q. 5, a. 1); the convertibility of being and goodness is the primary meta-ethical foundation for his moral theory. Thomas' concept of goodness includes the notion of "desirability": the more goodness something has, the more it is objectively desirable. Based on this premise, Thomas argues that all substances have a set of "natural inclinations" to pursue whatever they perceive to be good—that is, what is desirable to them. In particular, all substances are naturally inclined toward whatever they perceive that can increase their own goodness—that is, whatever will help actualize their definitive capacities. Natural law, as explained in Chapter 6, includes a set of principles which, if followed, will satisfy a human being's natural inclinations and thus lead to her perfection as a human being. By acting in accordance with the principles of natural law, a human being will perform virtuous actions and thereby become a virtuous person. Thomas thus refers to natural law principles as "nurseries" of virtue (q. 63, a. 1 and a. 2 *ad* 3).

The relationship between natural law and virtue can be understood, in a simple and direct fashion, in terms of the natural law principles providing the formal guidance—that is, the rule or measure (q. 63, a. 2) —for a human being to choose what actions to perform which will lead to her perfection as a human being. For example, if I desire to be a virtuous person, I must understand that, as a rational being, I need to actualize my capacity for rational thought. I thus choose to do actions that involve actualizing that capacity, such as getting an education, reading intellectually stimulating books, conversing with intelligent and wise people, etc. By developing a habitual disposition toward doing these and other actions that involve applying what I learn in beneficial ways, I thereby become an intellectually virtuous person.

QUESTIONS 68–70—PERFECTION OF THE VIRTUES

Complementing the infused theological and moral virtues are various "gifts of the Holy Spirit," first enumerated by St. Gregory the Great (540–604) based on a Scriptural description of the spiritual characteristics of the Messiah (Isaiah 11:2–3). These gifts dispose one's intellectual and appetitive powers for the reception of further promptings of the Holy Spirit toward performing acts conducive to attaining our supernatural end of loving union with God. In short, the Holy Spirit helps us to *operationalize* the habits endowed by the theological and infused moral virtues (q. 68). These gifts are related to various aspects and activities of the human psyche: *understanding* and *wisdom* in relation to the speculative intellect's apprehension and judgments concerning truth; *counsel* and *knowledge* in relation to the same activity on the part of the practical intellect; *piety* with respect to our appetitive relations with other persons; *fortitude* in relation to our appetitive fear of danger; and *fear* in relation to our appetitive desire for pleasure.

While the gifts of the Holy Spirit help one to operationalize the habits endowed by the theological and infused moral virtues, the gifts are nonetheless habits themselves (q. 68, a. 3). The *actualization* of the habitual dispositions endowed by the gifts constitutes the *beatitudes* enumerated in Matthew 5:1–12 (q. 69, a. 1). The beatitudes function both as a reward, providing one with a measure of happiness in the present life, as well as a means of preparation for the experience of perfect happiness in the life to come (q. 69, a. 2). As with the gifts, Thomas relates each of the beatitudes to various aspects of the human psyche (q. 69, a. 3). Three relate to our sensual nature: specifically, contempt for external goods ("Blessed are the poor in spirit"), lack of disturbance by the irascible passions ("Blessed are the meek"), and willingness to choose sorrow over indulgence in the concupiscible passions ("Blessed are they that mourn"). Two relate to our *active* life in relation to others: specifically, working for justice with "ardent desire" ("Blessed are they that hunger and thirst after justice"), as well as going beyond the limits of justice in offering "gratuitous bounty"

("Blessed are the merciful"). Two refer to perfection in our *contemplative* life: in relation to oneself, being cleansed of any defilement by the passions ("Blessed are the clean of heart"), and, in relation to others, being at peace with them ("Blessed are the peacemakers"). Finally, Thomas notes that the blessedness of those who suffer persecution for the sake of righteousness and for Christ is "a confirmation and declaration of all those that precede" (q. 69, a. 3 *ad* 5).

The beatitudes constitute *perfection* or *excellence* in the actualization of the gifts of the Holy Spirit; more generically, the gifts are also actualized by 12 "fruits" of the Holy Spirit enumerated by St. Paul (Galatians 5:22–23) in contrast to the "works of the flesh" (q. 70). The most preeminent of the fruits is *charity* insofar as the Holy Spirit is essentially love, which necessarily results in the *joy* of abiding in God's presence, as well as the *peace* of not being disturbed by external things and having our desire focused on God. Commensurate with this peacefulness, one is not disturbed when threatened by evil (*patience*) or delayed in attaining some good (*long suffering*). Other fruits of the Holy Spirit include *goodness* and *benignity* in relation to others, as well as *meekness* when one suffers harm from another and curbs his anger, and *faith* in entering into relationships of trust. Finally, *modesty* in our words and deeds, as well as *continence* and *chastity* in not being "led away" by either lawful or unlawful desires, respectively, are fruits of the Holy Spirit (q. 70, a. 3).

QUESTIONS 71–89—VICE AND SIN

Thomas' elucidation of the fundamental concepts of human morality has thus far focused on the upward trajectory of moral character formation at both natural and supernatural levels. In the final section of the *prima secundae* we will examine in this chapter, Thomas turns his attention to the opposing trajectory involving *vice* and *sin*. He first defines and differentiates these concepts (qq. 71–74), then identifies their causes (qq. 75–84), and concludes with their effects (qq. 85–89). Particularly important in this section is Thomas' discussion of the theological concept of "original sin" (qq. 81–83) and the central role it plays in his overall vision of humanity's moral nature, which will lay the groundwork for the presentation in the *tertia pars* of the salvific nature of Christ's incarnation, life, suffering, and death, as well as the graces that are administered through the sacraments of the Church instituted by Christ.

The first step in Thomas' analysis of sin and virtue is, of course, to define these concepts and show how they are related to, and differentiated from, each other. Vice is the directly contrary term to virtue insofar as the latter refers to a disposition toward acting in ways that contribute to the flourishing of one's nature; while the former refers to a disposition toward acting in ways that detract from one's natural flourishing (q. 71, a. 2). Sin is the *actualization* of vice in a specific type of disordered desire, word, deed, or failure to act (q. 71, aa. 3–5; q. 72, aa. 6–7). Sinful acts detract from a human being's natural flourishing and also violate God's eternal law, which directs humanity toward happiness in both natural (flourishing) and supernatural (beatitude) forms (q. 71, a. 6).

Specific sins are differentiated from each other in various ways. Primarily, they differ with respect to their *object*—namely, the nature of the sinful act itself and that at which it is directly aimed (q. 72, a. 1). Thus, Thomas distinguishes "spiritual" sins from "carnal" sins insofar as the former are intellectual in nature and are aimed at attaining pleasures such as praise from others; while the latter are bodily in nature and are aimed at attaining pleasures involving things like food, drink, and sex (q. 72, a. 2). Thomas considers spiritual sins to be more serious than carnal sins since the former are more directly related to God (q. 73, a. 5). It is important to emphasize that, following Augustine, Thomas does not consider such spiritual and carnal desires to be sinful in and of themselves; rather, sin involves "inordinate desire" for such goods, which are *mutable* in nature—meaning that they are temporal and thus can never be had indefinitely without any fear of losing them. Praise from others, for example, can be quite fickle. A once beloved public figure may easily fall from grace in the "court of public opinion" if implicated in a high-profile crime; the general public, fueled by the opinions of mass media personalities, may render a guilty verdict in the absence of sufficient evidence or due process and then change their view again if new evidence or a different "spin" on the case is brought to light. What maintains such desires in *well-ordered* condition is their being in accord with reason and God's eternal law.

Sins may also be categorized by the person(s) against whom they are primarily directed: whether God, oneself, or others (q. 72, a. 4).

While all sins are against God's will (*ad* 1), some are specifically directed against God alone, such as heresy, sacrilege, or blasphemy. Also, while all sins could be said to be against oneself insofar as they detract from one's own flourishing and attainment of happiness, some are more directly related to one's well-being, such as acts of gluttony or lust. Finally, sins such as theft and murder, or any other form of injustice, specifically involve one's relation to others. All three dimensions, however, may factor into the characterization of a particular type of sin—for instance, Thomas considers *suicide* to constitute a sin against God, oneself, and one's community (IIa–IIae, q. 64, a. 5).

A central categorical distinction Thomas makes in types of sin is between "venial" and "mortal" sins. This distinction is premised upon the nature of the *disorder* introduced by the sin, as well as the *punishment* incurred (q. 72, a. 5; q. 88). A *mortal* sin disrupts the fundamental principle of one's relationship to God and, by extension, the rest of the human community; it is a direct turning away from and rejection of one's loving relationship with God. The punishment incurred for mortal sin is *eternal*, according to Thomas (q. 87, a. 3), since there is no possibility of turning back toward and re-entering into a loving relationship with God except by an exercise of divine grace, to which one must open herself through repentance and the sacrament of Reconciliation (IIIa, q. 86, a. 2). *Venial* sin, on the other hand, presents an impediment, but does not involve a total disruption, of one's orientation toward loving union with God (q. 72, a. 5; qq. 88–89). Hence, such sins do not incur eternal punishment (q. 87, a. 5), nor require the same degree of formal reconciliation; although penitence on the sinner's part remains an essential requirement (IIIa, q. 87). To use bodily health as an analogy: mortal sin is akin to a fatal illness that completely disrupts ordered physiological functioning; while venial sin is akin to a broken bone that, while detrimental to physical functioning, may be more easily repaired.

In addition to the broad categorization of sins as mortal or venial, Thomas enumerates various factors that may affect the seriousness of any particular act of sin, such as the circumstances surrounding its commission (q. 73, a. 7), the amount of harm caused (a. 8), and whether the sin is against God, oneself, or another person (a. 9). The final category Thomas discusses is the "excellence" of the person who commits a sin (a. 10). In brief, the "higher" one is, in terms of moral excellence, the farther one's sinful downfall will be. One reason why this is a key factor is the potential for a morally well-regarded person to cause *scandal* by his sin, meaning that his sin influences others to sin (IIa–IIae, q. 43). For example, if a priest were to sin and this become known publicly, it may cause members of the faithful community to doubt the priest's moral authority—perhaps that of clerical leaders in general—and thereby disregard moral teachings the priest had exhorted but then hypocritically failed to follow himself.

Thomas next discusses how sin is present in various faculties of the human psyche: the will (q. 74, a. 1), the sensual appetites and integral bodily parts (aa. 2–3), and the intellect (a. 5). He then progresses to discuss the *causes* of sin, in which his previous analyses of the interaction of one's senses, sensual passions and appetites, intellect, and will serve to show how a voluntarily sinful action comes to be *internally* through the formation of *inordinate desire* (q. 75, a. 2). With respect to *external* causes of sin, Thomas affirms that the perceived objects of one's desire, as well as other potential influences on one's passions or reasoning, may play a role in "moving [one] to sin"; however, they can only do so with the *consent* of the will: "the will alone is the sufficient completive cause of sin being accomplished" (a. 3).

Two other potential external causes of sin Thomas discusses are God and the devil. Concerning the former, it is quite evident from his earlier treatise on the divine nature in the *prima pars*—see Chapter 2— that God cannot be a cause of sin; for God is *goodness* itself and sin, by definition, involves turning oneself away from the good, from God. Thus, to sin or to cause another to sin would require God turning away from Himself (q. 79, a. 1). The devil, on the other hand, is the chief of the fallen angels and thus a powerful, purely intellective mind whose will is oriented toward whatever is contrary to God (Ia, q. 63, a. 7). The devil thus has the desire and power to *instigate* a human being to sin by casually influencing her sensual appetites, with their attendant passions, and imagination (q. 80, aa. 1–2). As with any other external influence, however, the devil's instigations cannot cause a person to sin *necessarily* insofar as she is able to exercise rational control over her will (a. 3).

With respect, then, to the *origin* of sin in the physical world, both God and the devil have been ruled out as potential causes, which leaves only *humanity* as the causal origin of sin through the misuse of free will. Thomas affirms the theological traditions founded in the Book of Genesis (Ch. 3) and St. Paul's Letter to the Romans (Ch. 5) that there is an "original sin" that affects all of humanity—Christ being the only exception (q. 81, a. 3)—and that requires both Christ's salvific sacrifice and the continuing action of divine grace mediated through the sacraments of the Church—in particular, Baptism—to rectify. Thomas explains the nature of original sin by analogy to bodily illness: just as an illness disrupts a body's equilibrium necessary for its physical health, original sin disrupts a human being's *moral* equilibrium such that one's intellect and will are not properly oriented toward God as the objective source of happiness (q. 82, a. 1). The direct effect of original sin is the loss of "sanctifying grace" whereby humanity was originally oriented toward our supernatural end of loving union with God. Not possessing, however, the Beatific Vision, our intellect and will were free to choose to pursue some good other than God. As the story in Genesis goes, Adam and Eve sinned out of a prideful desire—prompted by the serpent's temptation—to pursue knowledge of good and evil and thereby become "like God." Human nature itself was not damaged or destroyed by original sin; rather, the grace necessary for humanity to be properly oriented to our divinely intended, supernatural end of loving union with God—what Thomas terms "original justice"—was lost (q. 82, a. 3). Nevertheless, the *potentiality* remained for humanity to be restored by grace to our original state, which made the achievement of Christ's salvific act possible (q. 85, a. 2).

Thomas considers all human beings to be affected by original sin, which naturally raises the question of how the descendants of the first human beings, who sinned voluntarily, could be justly held responsible for a sin they did not voluntarily commit themselves. Thomas' response again relies on an illustrative analogy involving the body (q. 81, a. 1). He first rejects the theory that original sin is passed on in a *hereditary* manner, as genetic traits are passed on from parent to offspring. Thomas' preferred explanation involves considering all human beings as members of the *same body* insofar as we all possess a "common nature." Consider, Thomas asks, a hand that is used to commit a sinful act. While a hand lacks an intellect and will, and thus cannot be held directly responsible for the sin it is used to commit, it is nevertheless an integral part of the body composing a person who willfully uses her hand to commit the sinful act. The hand is not culpable *per se*, but only insofar as it is inextricably part of a sinful person's body. Analogously, no individual human being after the Fall of Adam and Eve may be held directly culpable for their sin; yet, the effect of their sin has become an indelible part of human nature—removable only through divine grace wrought by Christ's sacrifice and mediated by the Church's sacraments.

Thomas conceptualizes the effect of original sin on human nature in three dimensions (q. 85, a. 1). First, humanity's baseline substantial nature of existing as living, sentient, social, and rational animals has been left unaffected; hence, every human being is conceived and born with the same basic set of natural capacities according to our specific nature. Second, humanity's *inclination* toward virtuous action aimed at happiness in the present life has been diminished, such that a human being cannot cultivate virtue or perform any morally good action without divine grace reorienting her intellect, will, and passions accordingly. Finally, the additional grace necessary for a human being to will in accord with her supernatural end of loving union with God was lost altogether and can be restored only through Christ and the Church. A further consequence of the loss of original justice was that bodily defects, culminating in death, naturally ensued (q. 85, a. 5).

The original sin described in the biblical story of Adam and Eve explains, according to Thomas, humanity's fundamentally depraved nature—not depraved *per se*, but only insofar as sanctifying grace has been lost and our fundamental inclination toward virtue has been diminished. But what is the origin of the original sin? Is there a common factor that underlies not only the sin of Adam and Eve, but all other sins human beings willfully commit on a daily basis throughout history? Thomas identifies two "root" causes of all sins: *covetousness* (q. 84, a. 1) and *pride* (q. 84, a. 2; IIa–IIae, q. 162). Covetousness refers to the earlier concept of *inordinate desire*: the desire for certain goods in a disordered relation of priority to other goods that one ought to desire primarily—such as truth or love for God. Pride refers to inordinately valuing oneself as equal to or above God. This is not only the fundamental sin of the devil and the other fallen angels (Ia, q. 63, aa. 2–3), but also of Adam and Eve when they were tempted by the serpent to eat the fruit of the Tree of Knowledge and thereby become "like God."

While covetousness and pride are the most fundamentally sinful vices disordering one's moral nature, Thomas follows St. Gregory the Great in identifying a total of seven "capital vices"—also known as the "seven deadly sins"—that are particularly fecund in giving rise to other vices and sins in pursuit of their actualization (q. 84, a. 4). As with his earlier analysis of the gifts and fruits of the Holy Spirit, Thomas relates these vices to various aspects of the natural human condition: thus, *pride* refers to an inordinate desire for excellence of one's soul—and external recognition of such—beyond its natural state; *gluttony* involves the inordinate pursuit of goods that maintain one's body; *lust* is the same with respect to sexual activity that perpetuates the species; *covetousness*, as noted already, is the inordinate desire for external goods. The other three capital vices involve the avoidance of good due to some perceived evil one wishes to avoid: thus, *sloth* is the disposition to avoid bodily labor at the cost of one's spiritual good; *envy* is based on the perception that another's good hinders one's own self-actualization, resulting in preoccupation with the other's good instead of focusing properly on oneself; this preoccupation may lead to *anger* if one pursues misplaced vengeance upon the envied other, seeking to deprive her of her coveted good or otherwise inflict recriminating harm upon her.

This completes our elucidation of Thomas' general account of moral virtue, culminating in the perfections—gifts and fruits of the Holy Spirit, including the beatitudes—leading to a human being's ultimate end: *happiness*, or *beatitude*, defined as one's loving union with God. We have also seen how vice and sin, especially original sin, may impede one's moral development. In the next chapter, we will make our way through the *secunda secundae*, wherein Thomas discusses each of the three theological virtues and four cardinal virtues in greater detail, utilizing each as a framework for discussing more particular moral issues. This exercise in "applied ethics" is what made this part of the *Summa* not only the longest, but also the most widely disseminated by serving as a guide for confessors and spiritual advisors to assist others on their moral journey toward loving union with their Creator.

SUGGESTIONS FOR FURTHER READING

See the "Suggestions for Further Reading" at the end of Chapter 5 for a list of introductory texts and anthologies that canvass the whole of Thomas' moral theory, including his account of virtue and vice.

The primary source for the foundation of Thomas' account of virtue is Aristotle's *Nicomachean Ethics*, trans. Terence Irwin, 2nd ed. (Indianapolis, IN: Hackett, 1999).

An in-depth discussion of the moral virtues, both naturally cultivated and infused, can be found in Romanus Cessario, *The Moral Virtues and Theological Ethics*, 2nd ed. (Notre Dame, IN: University of Notre Dame Press, 2008).

For a thorough discussion of the essential role of the virtue of prudence in moral living, see Daniel Mark Nelson, *The Priority of Prudence: Virtue and Natural Law in Thomas Aquinas and the Implications for Modern Ethics* (University Park, PA: Pennsylvania State University Press, 1992).

Immanuel Kant's distinction between moral willing that is heteronomous versus autonomous, as well as his claim that only the will could be called good unqualifiedly, can be found in his *Groundwork of the Metaphysics of Morals*, ed. Mary Gregor (New York: Cambridge University Press, 1997).

Augustine's discussion of sin as grounded in inordinate desire for temporal goods may be found in Book I of his *On Free Choice of the Will*, trans. Thomas Williams (Indianapolis, IN: Hackett, 1993).

8

THEOLOGICAL AND
CARDINAL VIRTUES
(*SECUNDA SECUNDAE*)

PREFACE

While the *secunda secundae* is the longest and was the most widely disseminated part of the *Summa* after Thomas' death, our treatment in this guidebook can be brief since he is rarely introducing novel philosophical or theological concepts, but rather is systematically applying the concepts and arguments he had developed throughout the *prima pars* and *prima secundae*. Following Thomas' order, we will first examine the three *theological virtues* of faith, hope, and charity. We will then elucidate his detailed account of the four *cardinal virtues* of prudence, justice, fortitude, and temperance. For each virtue, we will also review any opposing *vices* Thomas discusses and some of the practical issues that arise in cultivating and living out these virtues. We will focus just on his discussion of the applicability of his moral theory to people in general (qq. 1–170), leaving aside his brief discussion of those who occupy particular positions within the Christian community (qq. 171–189). Thomas focuses the latter discussion upon those who receive certain gratuitous graces, such as prophecy, rapture, speaking in tongues or the word of wisdom and truth, and miracles (qq. 171–178); those who lead a contemplative life as opposed to an active life (qq. 179–182); and those occupied with various duties and states of life, including ecclesiastical offices and the consecrated religious life (qq. 183–189).

QUESTIONS 1–16—THEOLOGICAL VIRTUE: FAITH

Faith is a theological virtue that endows human beings with "certain supernatural principles" that allow us to have some degree of understanding of God as our ultimate end (Ia–IIae, q. 62, a. 3). Faith is thus primarily an intellectual virtue infused through divine revelation (IIa–IIae, q. 4, a. 2); although the assent of one's will to the propositions revealed, motivated through divine grace, is also required (q. 6, a. 1). There is also an affective dimension to faith insofar as the object of faith is *the good* itself to which one's will is naturally oriented; Thomas thus links faith with *charity* insofar as one moves lovingly toward the good understood by faith (q. 4, a. 3). Faith and charity remain distinct, however, since one could have faithful understanding by her intellect, but remain in a state of sin by lacking a charitable orientation toward the good she understands; Thomas terms this "lifeless faith" (q. 4, a. 4). A person who has lifeless faith possesses the infused *habit* of intellectual understanding of the divine; but this habit does not qualify as a *virtue* without the complementary orientation of one's will to the good understood by faith (q. 4, a. 5; q. 6, a. 2). Demons—i.e. the fallen angels—however, lack even lifeless faith, for they have no inclination toward the good whatsoever; nevertheless, they have a certain degree of understanding of the divine essence due to their natural intellectual capacity (q. 5, a. 2 *ad* 2).

Thomas affirms the fundamental Scriptural definition of faith as "the substance of things to be hoped for, the evidence of things that appear not" (Hebrews 11:1; q. 4, a. 1). He thus differentiates knowledge by faith from knowledge through *science* (q. 1, aa. 4–5)—recall from Chapter 2 that, for Thomas, the term "science" refers not only to *empirical* scientific investigation but to any form of demonstrative knowledge attained through reasoning. What is known through science is arrived at by *demonstration* based on self-evident "first principles"—e.g. the principle of non-contradiction—and can thus be equally understood by all who reason properly. Faith, on the other hand, has for its object what cannot be rationally demonstrated and thus it must be caused by divine infusion, nor is it given equally to all. This does not mean, however, that the object of faith is *irrational*, for it is in fact the "First Truth" (q. 1, a. 1). Thomas thus concludes that the epistemic nature of faith is something between the demonstrable certainty of science and the doubtfulness of mere opinion:

> But this act *to believe*, cleaves firmly to one side, in which respect belief has something in common with science and understanding; yet its knowledge does not attain the perfection of clear sight, wherein it agrees with doubt, suspicion and opinion.
>
> (q. 2, a. 1)

Thomas considers the content of what one believes through faith to be capable of formulation into *propositions* (q. 1, a. 2) that one may verbally *confess* (q. 3, a. 1). These propositions are found in the creed formulated by the First Council of Nicea (325 AD), comprising 14 articles of faith (q. 1, a. 8):

1   God is one.
2   God is Father.
3   God is Son.
4   God is Holy Spirit.
5   God created all things.
6   God works for our sanctification.
7   God will raise us from the dead to life everlasting.
8   God became incarnate in Christ.
9   Christ was born of a virgin.
10   Christ suffered, died, and was buried.
11   Christ descended into hell.
12   Christ was raised from the dead.
13   Christ ascended into heaven.
14   Christ will come again to judge the living and dead.

Although faith is not the most important of the theological virtues— charity is—it does rank first among the virtues insofar as possession of faith is a pre-condition for hope and charity, as well as all the other virtues insofar as they are oriented toward knowledge and love of God. In short, one must first *believe in* the object one is disposed toward knowing and loving. As a result, *unbelief* constitutes the "greatest of sins," according to Thomas, since one is incapable of orienting his will toward God if he does not believe that God exists (q. 10, a. 3). Yet, when Thomas addresses the question of whether every act of an unbeliever constitutes a sin, he responds that, while unbelievers cannot perform good works that require divinely infused grace, "yet they can, to a certain extent, do those good works for which the good of nature suffices" (q. 10, a. 4). Thomas attributes this possibility to reason's natural capacity to comprehend the good and the *natural law* that leads one toward the good; he states, "Unbelief does not so wholly destroy natural reason in unbelievers, but that some knowledge of the truth remains in them, whereby they are able to do deeds that are generically good" (q. 10, a. 4 *ad* 3). Because, as discussed in Chapter 6, the natural law can be coherently formulated, and its normative value grounded, without explicit reference to its second-order meta-ethical foundation in God's *eternal law*, belief in God is not required for a human being to understand and be sufficiently rationally motivated to adhere to natural law principles. While the non-believer's understanding and adherence to the natural law will be imperfect, according to Thomas, this is only a difference of *degree* from the religious believer's understanding and adherence to the natural law insofar as the latter's will be imperfect as well due to the exigencies of human nature.

A relevant concern here is whether directly revealed *divine law* provides a check, or "safety net," for religious believers to correct any potential misunderstandings or misapplications of natural law principles. If so, then non-believers, deprived of this guarantee, may be more likely to err as moral reasoners. A response to this concern is to appeal to the larger community of moral reasoners to provide some degree of guarantee—though not as certain as a divine guarantee—that one's understanding and application of natural law principles is accurate. This is one reason why Thomas considers the *customs* of a given society to have a degree of moral force (Ia–IIae, q. 97, a. 3); although, some customs may go against the natural law and thus warrant change—Thomas is *not* a cultural relativist. He also considers it a moral obligation, as a matter of charity, to offer "fraternal correction" to those whose conscience has erred or who have cultivated potentially, or actually, vicious habits (IIa–IIae, q.33).

QUESTIONS 17–22—THEOLOGICAL VIRTUE: HOPE

Hope, as a virtue, orients a human being's will toward the object intellectually grasped through the virtue of faith as her ultimate end she may attain: God (Ia–IIae, q. 62, a. 3). Thomas draws a parallel with his earlier discussion of the *passion* of hope insofar as the object of such "is a future good, difficult but possible to obtain" (IIa–IIae, q. 17, a. 1; Ia–IIae, q. 40, a. 1). Both the passion and the theological virtue have an attainable good as their object; but the movement of the passion is in the sensory appetite, while the virtue involves movement of the intellectual appetite—the will. The future good toward which the will is inclined, in the case of the theological virtue, is God, and can be attained only through divine grace. Hope thus depends upon faith insofar as one must have intellectual certainty in the attainability of the object of hope if one's will is to be oriented toward it with the same certainty (q. 17, a. 7; q. 18, a. 4).

Thomas further specifies the nature of the good that is the object of hope:

> Such a good is eternal life, which consists in the enjoyment of God Himself. For we should hope from Him nothing less than Himself, since His goodness, whereby he [*sic*] imparts good things to His creature, is no less than His Essence. Therefore the proper and principal object of hope is eternal happiness.
>
> (q. 17, a. 2)

There is a caveat, however, insofar as Thomas distinguishes the object of the theological virtue of *charity* from that of hope. For the former, the proper object is God insofar as one loves God for God's own sake and not for reason of any personal happiness. In the case of hope, however, one's will is oriented toward God for the sake of one's own personal happiness (q. 17, a. 8). Thomas further specifies that the object of one's hope includes both eternal happiness in loving union with God (q. 17, a. 2), as well as any created good that may help us attain this union (q. 17, a. 4). In light of these specifications, Thomas concludes that neither the blessed who already enjoy eternal happiness in loving union with God, nor the eternally damned, possess this virtue: the former because they already have attained the hoped for good (q. 18, a. 2); the latter because the attainment of the hoped for good is no longer possible (q. 18, a. 3).

Thomas next discusses the Holy Spirit's gift of *fear* as related to the virtue of hope (q. 19). It is important to unpack Thomas' distinctions here carefully for the concept of the "fear of God" is one of the most vexed in both scholarly and popular theological understanding. Thomas first distinguishes two ways in which one may fear God (aa. 1–2). First, one may fear the punishment justly inflicted by God upon sinners, which Thomas terms "servile fear" (*timor servilis*). Second, one may fear separation from God through one's sinful fault once union with God has become the object of one's hope, which Thomas terms "filial fear" (*timor filialis*). It is the latter type of fear that Thomas reckons to be a gift of the Holy Spirit (a. 9), since this type of fear is not based merely on one's self-interested desire to avoid punishment, but rather one's desire for union with the object of her love: God. He thus specifies that servile fear decreases as one's loving orientation toward God increases—the theological virtue of charity—since there is less reason to fear punishment as one is less likely to sinfully turn away from the object of her love; while filial fear increases insofar as the closer one draws lovingly to God, the more one fears any potential separation from God (a. 10). The blessed in heaven, who enjoy the perfection of charity, thus also possess the perfection of fear of separation from God. As a consequence, while freedom of will, which is an essential part of human nature, remains in the blessed, it becomes impossible for them to turn their wills away from God due to the perfection of their fear of separation from Him (a. 11).

Like any virtue, hope has its contrary vices: *despair* (q. 20) and *presumption* (q. 21). Thomas characterizes despair as not only a sinful vice, but as "the origin of other sins" (q. 20, a. 1 *s.c.*). For despair is based on "a false opinion that [God] refuses pardon to the repentant sinner, or that He does not turn sinners to Himself by sanctifying grace" (a. 1). Thomas considers the three vices opposed to the three theological virtues as the greatest of all sins: unbelief opposed to faith in God's own truth, hatred of God opposed to God's goodness itself, and despair opposed to one's hope of sharing in God's goodness. While unbelief and hatred of God are objectively more grievous insofar as their object is God Himself, in terms of God's essential truth and goodness, despair is the more dangerous vice from our point of view since, once hope of eternal happiness is given up, "men rush headlong into sin, and are drawn away from good works" (a. 3).

Presumption is a vice opposed to hope, not due to a lack of hope (despair), but due to "immoderate hope" (q. 21, a. 1). More specifically, one presumes upon divine *mercy* in forgiving sinners, while neglecting divine *justice* in punishing sinners (a. 1 *s.c.*). Referring back to the basic definition of hope as the desire for "an arduous possible good," presumption ignores the *arduousness* of attaining eternal happiness by means of God's gracious mercy to which sinners must open themselves up to receive through repentance:

> For just as it is false that God does not pardon the repentant, or that He does not turn sinners to repentance, so it is false that He grants forgiveness to those who persevere in their sins, and that He gives glory to those who cease from good works.
>
> (q. 21, a. 2)

QUESTIONS 23–46—THEOLOGICAL VIRTUE: CHARITY

Union with God is hoped for so long as it is understood as attaina*ble*; the *actual* attainment of this spiritual union—which begins in this life but is only perfected in the Beatific Vision—with the attendant transformation of one's will and experience of delight, involves the theological virtue of *charity* (Ia–IIae, q. 62, a. 3). More specifically, Thomas defines charity as humanity's *friendship* with God insofar as one loves God for His own sake and not for the sake of any other good God could provide (IIa–IIae, q. 23, a. 1). It is a virtue infused in a person's *will* insofar as it constitutes her *affection* for God as understood by her intellect through the virtue of faith (q. 24, aa. 1–2); Thomas further specifies that charity is infused by the Holy Spirit, whose essence is the love between the Father and the Son (q. 23, a. 2). The *actualization* of this virtuous disposition is *to love* (q. 27).

Faith is prior to charity insofar as one must sufficiently understand something as good—in this case, as goodness itself—in order to love it. Nevertheless, charity is preeminent over *all* other virtues, since the proper end of *any* human moral action is the attainment of loving union with God (q. 23, a. 6). Charity is thus not only a virtue in its own right (a. 3), but also the "form" (a. 8) and "mother" (a. 8 *ad* 3) of all other virtues, since the very essence of a virtue is to be "ordered to the good" (Ia–IIae, q. 55, a. 4) and charity is a person's affective orientation toward the ultimate good—both in seeking and attaining it. Thomas clarifies that, unlike the other theological virtues of faith and hope, charity does not pass away upon the attainment of a person's loving union with God: "charity attains God Himself that it may rest in Him, but not that something may accrue to us from Him" (IIa–IIae, q. 23, a. 6). The perfection of charity in the Beatific Vision thus constitutes the perfect attainment of *happiness*, as Thomas had defined happiness as the self-sufficient fulfillment of all of one's desires (Ia–IIae, q. 2, a. 8): once a person is resting in God, there is no other good which she would desire. As the preeminent virtue aimed at the ultimate end that all human moral actions, and the virtuous dispositions from which those actions arise, ought to be aimed, Thomas concludes that "no strictly true virtue is possible without charity" (IIa–IIae, q. 23, a. 7). He allows, however, that, in the absence of charity, a true but *imperfect* virtue may exist if one is disposed toward some *particular* good that in itself is a true—and not merely apparent—good. Utilizing Thomas' example of such a true particular good, an atheist politician, who lacks the theological virtue of faith and therefore charity as well, may nevertheless be an imperfectly virtuous politician if she acts from an intellect and will oriented toward the proper welfare of the state.

As is clear from Thomas' definition of charity, the primary *object* of one's love is God; however, one's friendship with God extends to other persons as well (q. 25, a. 1), including oneself (a. 4) and one's body (a. 5), even sinners (a. 6) and one's enemies (a. 8). With respect to the latter two cases, Thomas invokes a key distinction between a person's *nature* and her *guilt* insofar as she may be a sinner or one's enemy—a distinction captured by the moral lemma, "Hate the sin, but love the sinner." In loving various types of persons, however, Thomas finds it natural and fitting that some should be loved more than others (q. 26, a. 1). God, of course, is to be loved first and foremost (a. 2), even more than one's own self (a. 3). Perhaps more seemingly paradoxical is Thomas' claim that one ought to love *himself* more than others—God excepted. Here, Thomas distinguishes one's *spiritual* and *corporeal* natures (a. 4). While he affirms that one "ought to bear bodily injury for his friend's sake" (a. 4 *ad* 2; a. 5), one ought not to sacrifice his spiritual happiness—that is, his friendship with God— for the sake of his friend. Thus, a person who commits sin, even if it stems from a compassionate desire to save someone else from physical or spiritual ruin, is acting from *disordered* passion and not the ordered virtue of charity.

With respect to our fellow human beings, Thomas would reject the strict impartiality imposed by Jeremy Bentham's (1748–1832) *utilitarian* ethic, in which morally right action is determined by a "utility calculus" of pleasures and pains in which everyone, including oneself, who may be affected by one's action counts as one and no more than one. Bentham's pupil, John Stuart Mill (1806–1873), states that, in calculating the appropriate moral action, "The agent must be as strictly impartial as a disinterested and benevolent spectator." Rather, Thomas finds it natural for human charitable affection to be oriented toward certain persons more than others, and considers the differing levels of human natural affection to reflect the order established by divine wisdom (q. 26, a. 6). A defender of Mill's impartiality principle might accuse Thomas here of committing the *naturalistic fallacy*— that is, deriving a normative ("ought") conclusion from a descriptive ("is") premise. As we saw in Chapter 6, however, Thomas understands the principles of natural law to be founded upon our *natural inclinations*, the satisfaction of which constitutes our *flourishing*—or happiness. In short, we can hardly flourish by denying our nature.

Thomas observes that we naturally love more intensely, and thus ought to love more, those closest to us (a. 7), especially those tied to us by blood (a. 8). With respect to the latter category, Thomas analyzes the proper love a man ought to show relatively for his father, mother, children, and wife (aa. 9–11). While Thomas acknowledges the psychological reality that a man may feel closer to his children or wife more than his father, his patriarchal worldview obliges him to place love—specified as "reverence"—for one's father above all others. A contemporary reader may reject these particular, historically conditioned, conclusions Thomas draws while still affirming his overall thesis concerning there being ordered degrees of love for various types of persons.

Like the other theological virtues, Thomas correlates charity with certain gifts of the Holy Spirit—see Chapter 7. Thomas identifies the primary spiritual benefits of charity as *joy* (q. 28) and *peace* (q. 29); as we will see below, many of the vices Thomas identifies as opposed to charity involve a disruption of peace either within one's soul or between oneself and others. Other effects of charity include mercy toward sinners or one's enemies (q. 30), beneficence (q. 31), almsgiving (q. 32), and "fraternal correction" (q. 33). It may seem as if some of these should be categorized under the virtue of *justice*; however, while the demands of justice regulate harmonious relationships among persons, the demands of charity exceed the demands of justice. In short, one may minimally treat another person justly without "going the extra mile" for her that charity would compel one to do.

Since charity essentially involves the will's orientation toward God, even after its infusion, this virtue can be lost by intentionally turning one's will away from God, thereby rupturing one's friendship with God (q. 24, a. 11). Turning one's will away from God is the essence of *mortal sin*; hence, even a single mortal sin suffices for a person to lose the infused virtue of charity (a. 12). Additionally, there are specific vices opposed to the virtue of charity, regardless of whether any of these dispositions actually culminate in a mortal sin occasioning the loss of charity. These vices include *hatred* of God or neighbor (q. 34); *sloth*, which Thomas defines as "sorrow for spiritual good" that results in, not the outright *rejection* of one's friendship with God that hatred may occasion, but rather the *dejection* occasioned by one's apathetic attitude toward divine friendship (q. 35); *envy* of another's good (q. 36); *discord*, which is directly opposed to the *peace* with one's neighbor charity ought to occasion (q. 37); *contention*, which is speech arisen from or intended to sow discord, what we would today call "hate speech" (q. 38); *schism*, which involves the disruption of peaceful unity among people and about which Thomas has *ecclesiastical* schismatics—those who reject the authority of the Church and the Pope—especially in mind (q. 39); *strife*, which refers to fighting among individuals, as opposed to state-level war (q. 41); finally, *sedition* is the disruptive mindset that precedes either strife or war and is vicious in itself, insofar as it disrupts social unity on an intellectual level, even if it does not result in actual fighting—it is the *secular* version of schism (q. 42). Two vices that merit more detailed discussion are *war* and *scandal*.

Thomas lists war among the vices opposed to charity, and this makes perfect sense insofar as war essentially involves the most violent and widespread disruption of social unity. Nevertheless, with an historical understanding of the unfortunate necessity of war at times in order to bring about peace (q. 40, a. 1 *ad* 3), Thomas rejects absolute pacifism and allows that there may be "just war." Adhering to the formula given initially by Augustine, and which remains influential among moral theologians and secular ethicists today, Thomas enumerates the following conditions, all of which must be satisfied in order for a war to be evaluated as "just" (q. 40, a. 1):

1   "First, the authority of the sovereign by whose command the war is to be waged." Wars can only be declared by *states* through their duly appointed leaders, and not by private individuals.
2   "Secondly, a just cause is required, namely that those who are attacked, should be attacked because they deserve it on account of some fault." It is evident, for example, that the Allied offensive against Nazi Germany fulfills this condition.
3   "Thirdly, it is necessary that the belligerents should have a rightful intention, so that they intend the advancement of good, or the avoidance of evil." The legitimacy of some state-level offensives— such as the conflict between Great Britain and Argentina over the Falkland Islands in 1982 or the U.S. invasion of Iraq in 2003— have been criticized by just war theorists, partly based on whether this condition was met.

Quite apart from the tabloid headlines reporting actual or alleged celebrity scandals, Thomas defines "scandal" as "something less rightly done or said, that occasions another's spiritual downfall" and occurs when someone "by his injunction, inducement or example, moves another to sin" (q. 43, a. 1). He further specifies two types of scandal. *Active* scandal occurs when someone:

> intends, by his evil word or deed, to lead another man into sin, or, if he does not so intend, when his deed is of such a nature as to lead another into sin: for instance, when a man publicly commits a sin or does something that has an appearance of sin;

whereas *passive* scandal occurs when one "neither intends to lead [another] into sin, nor does what is of a nature to lead him to sin, and yet this one, through being ill-disposed, is led into sin" (q. 43, a. 1 *ad* 4). Thomas contends that active scandal is always an occasion of moral wrongdoing on the part of one who scandalizes another, while passive scandal may not entail moral wrongdoing on one's part so long as the word or action that led to another's moral downfall was good in itself (q. 43, a. 2).

Thomas' analysis of charity may be summed up by what Christian moral tradition, following directly from Scripture, holds to be the two "greatest commandments" given by Christ as encompassing the entire moral and legal tradition of Judaism, which Christ had stated He came not to abolish but to fulfill: "Thou shalt love the Lord thy God with thy whole heart, and with thy whole soul, and with thy whole mind . . . Thou shalt love thy neighbour as thyself" (q. 44, quoting Matthew 22:37–39). Executing these commandments in this life, however, requires more than just the three theological virtues. Hence, Thomas now turns his attention to the cardinal moral virtues that are cultivated through habituation and perfected through divine infusion.

QUESTIONS 47–56—CARDINAL VIRTUE: PRUDENCE

Prudence merits preeminence among the cardinal virtues insofar as it is necessary for any morally proper action to occur: "prudence is more excellent than the moral virtues, and moves them" (q. 47, a. 6 *ad* 3). Prudence is primarily a virtue of the *intellect* by which one is able to know "what to seek and what to avoid" (a. 1 *s.c.*). More specifically, prudence informs practical reason's discernment of the proper *means* for achieving the end one wills: "prudence is right reason applied to action" (a. 2; cf. a. 6). Prudence also functions, however, by rightly ordering our *appetites* in accord with reason such that a person not only knows what she ought to do, but also wills accordingly (a. 4; a. 13 *ad* 2). Thomas thus specifies three prudential functions: *counsel*, discovering various potential means toward the end one wills; *judgment* of the discovered means to determine which one ought to will in the present occasion; and *command*, "applying to action the things counselled and judged" (a. 8).

In sum, prudence "takes counsel, judges and commands aright in respect of the good end of man's whole life" (a. 13). Humanity's "good end," as Thomas has well-established, involves not only *natural* flourishing, but also attainment of our *supernatural* end of loving union with God; hence, prudence also concerns "things necessary for salvation" (a. 14 *ad* 3). Prudence, then, like all the moral virtues, can be conceptualized in both an *imperfect* natural form acquired through a combination of "teaching and experience" (a. 15; q. 49, a. 1), as well as a *perfect* form acquired through the grace of divine infusion. Specifically, the gift of the Holy Spirit known as *counsel* perfects prudential reasoning (q. 52, a. 2); thus perfected, prudence directs acts of mercy and thereby corresponds to the beatitude, "Blessed are the merciful" (a. 4).

Prudence is also the virtue by which one discerns the virtuous *mean* between the vicious extremes of *excess* and *deficiency*, as classically formulated by Aristotle (q. 47, a. 7). Hence, for example, if generosity is a virtue that lies between being miserly and giving away all of one's wealth, then a person must prudentially reason, given her own financial circumstances, how much of her wealth she should give away, as well as to which charitable organizations or individuals in need. Prudence's role is not only calculative in this regard, but also regulates one's *passions* (a. 7 *ad* 2). Thus, a person's generous action should be motivated by the proper feelings of compassion or pity—as opposed to, say, a prideful display of one's wealth or exercise of power over the poor—and to the appropriate degree. For instance, moved by pity for a homeless man begging on a street corner who shows obvious signs of alcoholism or drug addiction, one may imprudently hand him cash; whereas the more prudential compassionate act would be to buy him food or donate to an organization that provides services of which he may avail himself.

Thomas next treats various vices opposed to prudence. Of the vices that fall under the blanket category of "imprudence," Thomas includes *precipitation*—otherwise known as "foolhardiness"—by which one rushes into action impulsively (q. 53, a. 3). Rather, prudential reasoning involves certain key steps that one ought not to neglect, but follow in an "orderly fashion": "*memory* of the past" (q. 49, a. 1), "*intelligence* of the present" (a. 2), "*shrewdness* in considering the future outcome" (aa. 4, 6), "*reasoning* which compares one thing with another" (a. 5), and "*docility* in accepting the opinions of others" (a. 3). The next vice Thomas lists is *thoughtlessness*—or "inconsideration"—by which "one fails to judge rightly through contempt or neglect of those things on which a right judgment depends" (q. 53, a. 4). This relates back to Thomas' conclusion that one could be held morally culpable for *voluntary ignorance* (Ia–IIae, q. 6, a. 8). The final vice Thomas categorizes under imprudence is *inconstancy*—or "incontinence"—by which one has prudentially judged what one ought to do on a particular occasion, but fails to *command* her will to do it (IIa–IIae, q. 53, a. 5).

In Question 54, Thomas highlights *negligence* as a vice opposed to prudence insofar as a person fails to be *solicitous* (q. 47, a. 9) in having a mind alert to all facts relevant to his rational discernment of what he ought to do on a particular occasion. Negligence includes both a lack of "due diligence" in learning all pertinent information one can in order to make a prudential decision, and a lack of execution of what one has prudentially decided. Negligence is thus similar to inconstancy insofar as both involve a lack of *command* to will what one ought; they differ, however, in that inconstancy involves something in a person's psyche—a contravening passion or desire—interfering with his will; while negligence is simply a failure to will promptly in accord with one's prudential judgment (q. 54, a. 2 *ad* 3).

Finally, Thomas discusses a vice, not directly opposed to prudence *per se*, but rather involves an *inordinate focus* of prudential concern—namely, "prudence of the flesh"—by which a person is overly concerned with "carnal goods" as if they constituted "the last end of his life" (q. 55, a. 1). It is worth noting that, while some contemporary Christians are overly concerned with issues related to sex and other forms of physical pleasure—as if inordinate desire for physical pleasure counted among the worst of sins—Thomas adopts a less puritanical attitude:

> For it happens sometimes that a man has an inordinate affection for some pleasure of the flesh, without turning away from God by a mortal sin; in which case he does not place the end of his whole life in carnal pleasure.
>
> (a. 2)

The key point for Thomas is that a person must prudentially order his desire for any sort of *temporal* good in proper relation to his *eternal* end of loving union with God. Thomas thus warns that being overly concerned with temporal matters can constitute a vice opposed to prudence (a. 6), as well as being overly concerned about what the future will bring (a. 7). Such inordinate concerns betray a lack of trust in divine providence to make available whatever one needs in this life, and thereby evidence a lack of the theological virtues of faith and hope focused on what is eternally good.

QUESTIONS 57–122—CARDINAL VIRTUE: JUSTICE

Thomas defines the object of justice as what is *right* (*ius*) with respect to one's relations with others (q. 57, a. 1). He then divides what is right into *natural* and *positive* categories (a. 2). The former refers to what counts as "equal" in one's relation with another person by its very nature. For instance, the lives of two persons are naturally equivalent and thus the life of one person cannot be arbitrarily valued above that of another; although, as we will see, Thomas considers there to be justified cases in which another's life may be forfeited. The latter category refers to what counts as equal between persons due to either private or public agreement. For instance, on a small scale, a contractor provides a service for an agreed-upon price with the consumer; and, on a large scale, the value of shares in publicly traded companies are determined by exchanges made on the floor of the stock market. A non-economic example would be the determination of a minimum voting age in a particular state: while there is arguably a natural right to participate in the government of one's state, in the U.S. only citizens of at least 18 years of age have a positive right to vote in elections for public office.

Thomas emphasizes that a positive right is valid only if it accords with natural right: "If, however, a thing is, of itself, contrary to natural right, the human will cannot make it just" (a. 2 *ad* 2). Thus, a state that grants a positive right to vote only to individuals of a particular race or gender is violating what is naturally just; the same goes for a state that allows certain basic goods essential for human life and flourishing—such as clean water, food, healthcare resources, etc.— to be commodified in ways that exclude individuals from attaining these necessities. This parallels Thomas' previous discussion—see Chapter 6—of the relation between *natural law* and *human law*:

natural right and natural law are by-and-large conceptually equivalent; while what is deemed a positive right enacted through human law must be in accord with what is naturally right.

As a cardinal *virtue*, justice does not refer merely to what is right between persons, but also the *habitual disposition* to render each person her due (q. 58, a. 1). Justice manifests in various types of relations. First, transactions between individuals are governed by what Thomas terms "commutative justice," which includes *restitution* of what belongs to another after one has either licitly borrowed or illicitly stolen it (q. 62, a. 1). Second, there is what an individual owes to her *community*, which Thomas terms "legal justice" whereby one "is in harmony with the law which directs the acts of all the virtues to the common good" (q. 58, a. 5). Finally, there is the complement of what a community owes to its individual members "which distributes common goods proportionately"—termed "distributive justice" (q. 61, a. 1). The term "proportionately" refers to justice's aim being the *rational mean* between too much and too little that Aristotle defines as the practical orientation of all virtuous action (q. 58, a. 10).

Injustice is, of course, the contrary vice to the virtue of justice. As a vice, Thomas is careful to specify that simply doing an unjust action on some particular occasion does not suffice to make one an unjust person, but rather possessing the *habit* of—i.e. a disposition toward— performing unjust actions:

> Accordingly, to do what is unjust intentionally and by choice is proper to the unjust man, in which sense the unjust man is one who has the habit of injustice: but a man may do what is unjust, unintentionally or through passion, without having the habit of injustice.
>
> (q. 59, a. 2)

Thomas devotes several questions (qq. 63–78) to explicating the nuances of various forms of injustice, being careful to specify when an action that may *prima facie* seem like an unjust act may in fact be just—e.g. certain cases of killing or taking what another person claims as her property.

The first form of injustice Thomas discusses is *favoritism* or *partiality*—what he terms "respect of person." Favoritism is a violation of distributive justice insofar as one bestows some good upon someone, not due to any relevant *cause*, but arbitrarily due to the *person* himself:

> For instance if you promote a man to a professorship on account of his having sufficient knowledge, you consider the due cause, not the person; but if, in conferring something on someone, you consider in him not the fact that what you give him is proportionate or due to him, but the fact that he is this particular man (e.g. Peter or Martin), then there is respect of the person, since you give him something not for some cause that renders him worthy of it, but simply because he is this person.
>
> (q. 63, a. 1)

Thomas observes that favoritism particularly occurs in the case of *judicial sentences* (q. 63, a. 4); he thus exhibits a careful regard for *due process* in judicial proceedings with respect to judges (q. 67), prosecutors (q. 68), defendants (q. 69), witnesses (q. 70), and advocates (q. 71). Concerning the last, Thomas adopts a peculiar position from the perspective of modern democratic judicial systems. He contends that a lawyer should *not* defend an accused individual whom he knows *without doubt* to be guilty:

> It is unlawful to co-operate in an evil deed, by counselling, helping, or in any way consenting, because to counsel or assist an action is, in a way, to do it . . . Now it is evident that an advocate provides both assistance and counsel to the party for whom he pleads.
>
> (q. 71, a. 3)

In practice, though, this principle may not be as restrictive as it seems; for the judicial process is aimed precisely at *establishing* whether the accused is guilty or not. Thus, throughout the process, and perhaps even after a guilty verdict is rendered, a defense lawyer may have sufficient reason to doubt whether the accused he is defending is actually guilty.

Without doubt the most cited question from this part of the *Summa* is Question 64: "Of Murder." This is the first case Thomas analyzes of a violation of commutative justice "whereby a man inflicts the greatest injury on his neighbor." Nevertheless, not all forms of *killing* constitute the evil of "murder." First of all, Thomas holds that it is permissible to kill plants and non-human animals insofar as he understands such forms of life to have an inherent purpose in serving the needs of more perfect forms of life. Hence, just as animals eat plants to sustain themselves, it is just for human beings to eat animals or otherwise utilize them for essential purposes (a. 1). As we will discuss in Chapter 11, however, Thomas' justification for using and killing animals does not imply that human beings may *abuse* other animals, or use or kill them without a *proportionate cause*. Thus, for example, some contemporary Thomists have adopted vegetarianism or even veganism on the premise that the killing or use of non-human animals is no longer essential for human dietary purposes. Other Thomists have drawn a distinction between utilizing animals for potentially life-saving medical research and experimenting upon them for the sake of developing cosmetic products or non-essential pharmaceuticals.

Turning to the killing of human beings, Thomas first takes up the question of *capital punishment* for grievous wrongdoers. Recall that, for Thomas, there are complementary forms of justice between an individual and his community. While Thomas conceptualizes human beings, as *persons*, to each have his own inherent *dignity* due to our shared rational nature (Ia, q. 29, aa. 1, 3), each person is also inextricably a member of a particular community. He thus concludes,

> Now every individual person is compared to the whole community, as part to whole. Therefore if a man be dangerous and infectious to the community [akin to a gangrenous limb threatening the whole body's health], on account of some sin, it is praiseworthy and advantageous that he be killed in order to safeguard the common good.
>
> (IIa–IIae, q. 64, a. 2)

Thomas further justifies killing one who voluntarily threatens the common good by claiming that such an individual actually loses his dignity as a person insofar as he "departs from the order of reason" and has thereby reduced himself to the moral status of "a beast" (a. 2 *ad* 3). By-and-large, contemporary Thomists either do not share Thomas' rationale for justifying capital punishment—affirming that all human beings, even grievous wrongdoers, retain their inherent dignity as persons and thus cannot be licitly killed—or accept that capital punishment may be justified in *extreme* circumstances to safeguard the common good, but that the circumstances of most contemporary societies do not necessitate killing violent offenders since they can be successfully incarcerated for life. Even though Thomas allows for the execution of grievous wrongdoers, he requires that due process be observed and that only those invested with "public authority . . . and not private individuals, can lawfully put evildoers to death" (a. 3). Thomas does not sanction so-called "vigilante justice."

Turning from killing another to killing oneself, Thomas gives a triple indictment of *suicide* (a. 5). His first argument can be split in two. He begins by stating, "everything naturally loves itself." He then asserts first that suicide violates the *natural law*, because "everything [which loves itself] naturally conserves itself in being and resists corruptions so far as it can." Since everything naturally seeks to maintain its own being and avoid any type of corruption, suicide, which is the termination of a person's being and the instantiation of the physical corruption of her body, violates that principle of natural law. Thomas' second assertion is that, since suicide goes against one's love for oneself, suicide is a violation of *charity* to oneself and Christ's commandment to "love your neighbor *as yourself*" (Matthew 22:39).

Thomas' second injunction against suicide is derived from Aristotle: "every part as such, is of the whole. Now every man is part of the community: and so as such, is of the community. Hence in the case that he kills himself, he causes injury to the community" (a. 5). As noted above, human persons do not exist purely as individuals, but are essentially interrelated in variously defined political communities. We can also be said to belong to one overall *human* community, which transcends nation, race, and gender boundaries. As a result of this conception of human nature as essentially *communitarian*, Thomas holds that each individual is responsible not only to himself, but also to every other member of the human community. Thus, suicide is not a purely private action, which has implications only for the suicidal agent.

Thomas' third contention against suicide refers to the theological assertion that all human persons are ultimately subject to God:

> Life is a certain gift from heaven bestowed on man, and is subject to his power who *kills and brings about life*. And thus whoever takes his

own life sins against God: just as whoever kills another's servant sins against the master of whom he is the servant; and just as he sins who usurps to himself judgment of something not entrusted to himself. For to God alone belongs the judgment of death and life: according to *Deuteronomy* 32, *I will kill and I will make live.*

(a. 5)

In sum, Thomas' triple indictment against suicide is that it is a sin against oneself, against the human community, and against God.

Some forms of killing, though—even suicide—may be morally permissible insofar as they do not violate God's sovereignty over human lives. An example is *martyrdom*. Martyrdom takes many forms, one of which involves a person committing suicide to avoid some greater sin. In treating this issue, Thomas acknowledges the problematic nature of this form of martyrdom by citing an argument raised by an objector to his own position:

> To kill oneself is illicit . . . yet through this martyrdom is accomplished: for Augustine says, in Book I of the *City of God*, that *certain holy women, in time of persecution, so that they may avoid the persecutors of their chastity, threw themselves into a river, and by this means they were dead; and their martyrdom is celebrated in the Catholic Church with solemn veneration.* Therefore [concludes Thomas' objector] martyrdom is not a virtuous act.
>
> (q. 124, a. 1 *obj.* 2)

Thomas responds to this objection against the virtuousness of martyrdom by suicide through an appeal to Augustine as well: "it may be possible that *the divine authority persuaded the Church by a number of worthy testimonies by faith to honor the memory of these Saints* [i.e., holy women]" (a. 1 *ad* 2).

As unsatisfying as this answer may seem *prima facie*, it points to something more sublime than the questionable belief in some supposed "worthy testimonies." It points to the sovereignty of "divine authority." As discussed in Chapter 6, Thomas describes the necessity of *divine law*, which is the direct revelation of God's *eternal law*. He cites the "Old Law" of the Hebrew Scriptures and the "New Law" of the Gospels as examples of divine law (Ia–IIae, q. 91, a. 5). Thomas holds that the revealed divine law is necessary due to the limitations of human reason to fully comprehend the general precepts of natural law, which is also derived from God's eternal law. The revealed prescriptions of divine law demonstrate how general natural law principles are to be properly applied in particular cases. This assists human reason in formulating proper *human laws* for such particular cases, based on the general principles of natural law.

On this understanding of the necessity of divine law and its relation to natural law, Thomas can be interpreted as holding that divine law overrides any understood precepts of natural law; for the human mind's understanding of natural law is limited and subject to error, but not "the given divine law, of which it is certain that it cannot err" (q. 91, a. 4). Relating this conclusion to the issue of the women who committed suicide rather than have their chastity forcibly violated, Thomas can offer the following explanation: while the normal understanding of natural law would place a higher value on life than on chastity, for some reason, in this case, God judged the women's suicides as fulfilling his will; as a result, God revealed to the Church that these women should be honored. I will refrain from discussing the epistemic worries this account entails. The point is that, without an overriding revealed divine law related to a particular case, one should judge in accord with the precepts of natural law. While suicide, in certain cases of martyrdom, may be permissible under divine law, suicide is a violation of natural law and is impermissible in the absence of contravening divine law.

As one might expect, although he allows for the killing of grievous sinners who threaten the common good, Thomas takes a firm stance against the moral permissibility of killing an *innocent* person. Thomas' supportive rationale does not rely only upon each individual person's inherent dignity as a rational being; although he does affirm that "we ought to love the nature which God has made." He also cites each person's essential relation to her community and that the life of "righteous" persons "preserves and forwards the common good" (q. 64, a. 6).

Thomas next addresses the question of whether it is permissible to kill an aggressor in *self-defense*. In answering this question, Thomas lays the theoretical foundation for what is known today as the *principle of double-effect* (PDE). This principle basically states that an action taken to produce some consequence, which is good *per se*, may be permissible even if the action produces a foreseen but unintended negative consequence, which is *per se* morally impermissible. PDE holds provided that the relative value of the negative consequence does not outweigh that of the good consequence, and the negative consequence is not *directly intended* as an end or the means by which the good consequence is brought about. In Thomas' original formulation,

> Nothing hinders one act from having two effects, only one of which is intended, while the other is beside the intention. Now moral acts take their species according to what is intended, and not according to what is beside the intention.
>
> (q. 64, a. 7; cf. Ia–IIae, q. 73, a. 8)

In the type of case in question, by performing an act of preserving one's own life, a person brings about the aggressor's death, but under the stricture that the aggressor's death is unavoidably necessary in order to achieve the good of preserving her life and that it is "outside" of her intention (*praeter intentionem*). A moral agent in a *bona fide* double-effect case does not directly intend the negative consequence of her action; rather, it is a *foreseen concomitant consequence* of her directly intended action and, as such, is an *accidental circumstance* that cannot fundamentally alter the action's specific nature—defending one's own life—as morally good. Nevertheless, since there is a defect in the goodness of the circumstances, due to the negative consequence, the action is not good "simply" (*simpliciter*). This defect, however, need not entail that the action is morally impermissible or that the agent has "sinned."

In the case at hand, the self-defending agent does not *seek* the aggressor's death, but merely to stop the aggressor by the least harmful, but effective, means available under the circumstances; all the while, the agent foresees that she is at least *risking*, or even causing *with certainty*, the aggressor's death. Consider three different examples of shooting someone in self-defense. In each example, someone is threatening an innocent person's life and the person shoots the aggressor and he dies:

1   The shooter is unskilled with a gun and aims for the aggressor's "center mass" as this presents the optimal means of assuredly stopping him; the bullet pierces the aggressor's heart and he is killed almost instantly.

2   The shooter is skilled and aims for the aggressor's left thigh in order to incapacitate him; the bullet, though, nicks the femoral artery and the aggressor begins to bleed profusely. The shooter, having disarmed the now helpless aggressor, attempts to stop the bleeding and calls for medical assistance; however, despite her life-saving efforts, the aggressor dies.

3   The shooter incapacitates the aggressor such that he will likely survive if medical attention is sought; however, out of anger at the attack or fear that the aggressor may pose a continued threat if he survives, the shooter fires three more bullets into the aggressor's head at point-blank range.

The first two examples would satisfy Thomas' conditions for a justified killing in self-defense. In the third example, however, such killing "with extreme prejudice" would not be justified by Thomas' formulation of PDE.

Another example of a justified act of self-defense, but which does not involve an unjust "aggressor," would be a case in which a pregnant woman discovers she has a form of cancer which, if left untreated by aggressive means, will be terminal. By undergoing radiation and chemotherapy, it is almost certain that her unborn fetus will either be severely harmed or spontaneously abort (miscarry). Assuming that the value of both the mother's and the unborn fetus's lives are of equal value—given Thomas' strict prohibition of killing an innocent human being (q. 64, a. 6)—it is morally permissible for her to undergo the aggressive treatment in order to preserve her life, even though it is foreseen to produce what would, under normal circumstances, be an impermissible consequence. By respectively administering and consenting to receive the aggressive treatment, both the physician and the mother cannot avoid being accused of performing an action that resulted in the innocent fetus's death. This action, however, may be justified by explaining that the fetus's death was not directly intended. Rather, the preservation of the mother's life was directly intended and the resultant harm or miscarriage was a foreseen accidental consequence, which was unavoidably concomitant with the act of providing the treatment necessary to preserve the mother's life. Thomas differentiates this type of case from one in which a person *accidentally* kills an innocent person, but does so through *negligence* or while in the process of committing another wrongful act. Hence, while a physician is not morally culpable for a fetus's death when it is an unintended—though foreseen—side-effect of a necessary medical intervention to save the mother's life, if someone violently attacks a pregnant woman with the unintended result that either she or her fetus dies, the assailant is culpable of *homicide* (q. 64, a. 8 *ad* 2).

Thomas next treats wrongs done, not against another person directly, but against her *property*. He first affirms that there is a natural right for individuals to own private property (q. 66, aa. 1–2). Hence, *theft* constitutes not only a sin (a. 5), but a *mortal* sin insofar as it is opposed to the theological virtue of charity (a. 6). Nevertheless, Thomas does not affirm an *absolute, unqualified* right to private property. Each person is permitted to secure for her own use whatever she needs to survive and flourish; but whatever she owns "in superabundance is due, by natural law, to the purpose of succoring the poor" (a. 7). It is not merely "charitable" to give of one's superabundant wealth to the poor, but a matter of *justice*. Thomas even goes so far as to assert that, in cases of "manifest and urgent" need or "imminent danger," as a last resort, one may take from another's superabundance: "It is not theft, properly speaking, to take secretly or use another's property in a case of extreme need: because that which he takes for the support of his life becomes his own property by reason of that need" (a. 7 *ad* 2).

Finally, while Thomas affirms that *obedience* to one's superiors—whether religious or civil—is a moral duty following from justice and charity (q. 105), he once again invokes certain caveats. The primary caveat is that the commands of one's superior are in accord with natural and divine law, for "all wills, by a kind of necessity of justice, are bound to obey the divine command" (q. 104, a. 4). Thomas thereby concludes, "Now sometimes the things commanded by a superior are against God. Therefore superiors are not to be obeyed in all things" (a. 5 *s.c.*). Hence, while one is required to obey just laws enacted by legitimate civil authorities, *civil disobedience* is justified in cases of manifestly unjust laws. Dr. Martin Luther King, Jr. explicitly appeals to Thomas in this regard in his famous "Letter from a Birmingham Jail" (April 16, 1963):

> How does one determine whether a law is just or unjust? A just law is a man made code that squares with the moral law or the law of God. An unjust law is a code that is out of harmony with the moral law. To put it in the terms of St. Thomas Aquinas: An unjust law is a human law that is not rooted in eternal law and natural law. Any law that uplifts human personality is just. Any law that degrades human personality is unjust. All segregation statutes are unjust because segregation distorts the soul and damages the personality. It gives the segregator a false sense of superiority and the segregated a false sense of inferiority . . . Is not segregation an existential expression of man's tragic separation, his awful estrangement, his terrible sinfulness? Thus it is that I can urge men . . . to disobey segregation ordinances, for they are morally wrong.

As has become evident, the application of the general principles of justice may differ in various types of circumstances. Legislators craft a variety of human laws to specify and operationalize the more general principles of what is naturally right. Nevertheless, there is a particular need for virtuous *prudence* in knowing when one might need to depart from the strict "letter of the law" or discern what to do in a particular case not clearly covered by extant laws. Thomas thus identifies the virtue of "equity" (Greek: *epikeia*) as essential for an individual moral agent to prudently interpret and apply the general requirements of justice (q. 120).

Insofar as justice is essentially defined as giving to each person what is her due, it does not encompass only one's obligations toward other human beings; but, as seen in Thomas' indictment of suicide, one also has just obligations toward *God*. Thomas thus identifies *religion* as a moral virtue, defined as a person's disposition toward giving God what is His due through external actions—such as vocal praise (q. 91, a. 1)—as an explicit expression of her *affection* for God (q. 81). Forms of religious practice include devotion (q. 82), prayer (q. 83)— with the "Lord's Prayer" (or "Our Father") being the "most perfect" (a. 9)—adoration (q. 84), sacrifice (q. 85), oblations (q. 86), tithes (q. 87), vows (q. 88), and oaths (q. 89). Acts that Thomas identifies as contrary to pious religious affection for God, insofar as they defy faith in divine providence, include superstition (qq. 92–93), idolatry (q. 94), divination—i.e. fortune-telling (q. 95)—appeals to magic (q. 96), tempting God to perform some deed (q. 97), perjury—i.e. violating one's oath (q. 98)—sacrilege (q. 99), and simony—i.e. the buying or selling of spiritual indulgences (q. 100), the institutional abuse of which the Protestant Reformer Martin Luther (1483–1546) rightfully complained.

In concluding his treatise on the virtue of justice, despite all the subtle applications analyzed throughout to help theological instructors, spiritual advisors, and confessors to appropriately guide the Christian faithful, Thomas recommends the Decalogue—the Ten Commandments—as formulating the first principles of natural law in relation to various relations of justice among different types of persons (q. 122, a. 1). The first three precepts concern religious acts oriented toward God (aa. 2–4). The fourth precept—to honor one's parents—encapsulates a specific form of justice Thomas terms "piety" (a. 5; cf. q. 101). And the remaining six cover, in general terms, the ways in which human beings ought to relate to one another justly *as equals* (a. 6).

QUESTIONS 123–140—CARDINAL VIRTUE: FORTITUDE

Fortitude—also termed "courage"—is a moral virtue by which one is disposed toward restraining her fear, moderating her daring, and thereby remaining *steadfast* in her moral convictions amidst dangers or difficulties in order to do what reason dictates she ought to do (q. 123, aa. 1–3). Thomas identifies the primary act that follows from this disposition as *endurance*: "that is to stand immovable in the midst of dangers rather than attack them" (a. 6). To be clear, Thomas is not restricting the virtuous person from actively confronting dangers or difficulties through *daring*, but one's aggressive response must be *moderate*. Thus, in addressing a debate between the Aristotelian (Peripatetic) and Stoic philosophical schools on the natural and normative value of *anger*, Thomas sides with the former: "Accordingly the brave man employs moderate anger in his action, but not immoderate anger" (a. 10). Thomas labels immoderate daring—i.e. *foolhardiness*—as a sin contrary to fortitude (q. 127). Relatedly, although the goal of fortitude is the moderation of fear, it does not entail the absolute *sublimation* of fear, which has as its proper object love for one's own life. Thomas thus labels both *excessive fear* (q. 125) and *fearlessness* (q. 126) as sins contrary to fortitude.

Again, endurance in the face of fear of danger or difficulty is the exemplar act of fortitude (q. 123, a. 11 *ad* 1). Hence, while a brave soldier may daringly engage her enemy in battle, her fortitude is most properly exemplified, not in her attack, but rather in her willingness to endure *death* (aa. 4–5). Although a soldier's courage on the battlefield may be a paradigmatic example of this virtue, Thomas notes other types of cases in which one may virtuously face the risk of death:

> Moreover, a brave man behaves well in face of danger of any other kind of death; especially since man may be in danger of any kind of death on account of virtue: thus may a man not fail to attend on a sick friend through fear of deadly infection, or not refuse to undertake a journey with some godly object in view through fear of shipwreck or robbers.
>
> (a. 5)

Another key example of one who faces death with the equanimity afforded by the virtue of fortitude is a *martyr*, who endures suffering and death rather than violates the truth she believes by faith, ordering her love for God above her love for her own life (q. 124). As these examples show, Thomas conceptualizes fortitude as manifesting itself in "sudden occurrences" in which one's life is immediately threatened; nevertheless, the *habit* of fortitude must have already been cultivated as an ingrained part of one's moral character in order for it to become manifest in emergency situations (q. 123, a. 9).

Thomas identifies fortitude as a *cardinal* virtue insofar as it constitutes "steadfastness" in the face of threats that might influence one "to recede from that which is in accordance with reason" (a. 11). Thus, while it ranks less in importance as a virtue than prudence or justice—which are essential for one's intellect and will to be properly ordered toward the good in the first place—fortitude, along with temperance, plays a crucial role in moderating one's passions "lest they lead man away from reason's good" (a. 12). As with other cardinal virtues, additional virtues are associated with fortitude, such as *patience* (q. 136) and *perseverance* (q. 137). There is also a correlative gift of the Holy Spirit (q. 139, a. 1), which allows one to endure the difficulties associated with doing virtuous deeds "with an insatiable desire" and thereby attain beatitude for those "that hunger and thirst after justice" (a. 2).

One of the virtues associated with fortitude Thomas discusses extensively is *magnanimity*, the etymology of which "denotes stretching forth of the mind to great things" (q. 129, a. 1). This virtue is associated particularly with public figures or others who possess the political means to achieve great good due to the honor that has been bestowed upon them (a. 2). Such rightly honored individuals possess the *confidence* of hope (q. 6) and the *security* of mind (a. 7)— i.e. freedom from fear—to attain a difficult goal for the sake of the common good. Consider, for example, the type of political leadership displayed by two fictional U.S. presidents: Martin Sheen's Josiah Bartlet on *The West Wing* and Kevin Spacey's Francis Underwood on *House of Cards*. Both are accorded tremendous public honor by virtue of their office. Bartlet, however, pursued such high public office after conscientious reflection on his God-given gifts, and cultivated talents and virtues, which would allow him, while in the executive office, to potentially bring about great good for others. Underwood, on the other hand, exhibits various vices Thomas identifies as contrary to magnanimity: *presumption* in doing what is above his power (q. 130), *ambition* in inordinately desiring honor for himself (q. 131), and *vainglory* in ranking one's own good as higher than that of others and more worthy of praise (q. 132). Another contrary vice is *pusillanimity*, which is the opposite of presumption insofar as one does not exceed what is in his power to accomplish, but rather falls short of employing his power toward attaining the good ends toward which the honorable office bestowed upon him ought to be aimed (q. 133).

Related to magnanimity is the virtue of *magnificence*, which is a disposition toward utilizing one's wealth and other material goods for the sake of benefitting the common good: "goods of fortune are useful organs or instruments of virtuous deeds: since we can easily accomplish things by means of riches, power and friends. Hence it is evident that goods of fortune conduce to magnanimity" (q. 129, a. 8). The etymology of magnificence is *magna facere* ("to make great things") (q. 134, a. 2). Thus, magnificence involves expending one's wealth "in order that some great work may be accomplished in becoming manner" (a. 3). One may easily think of *philanthropists* such as Warren Buffet, Bill and Melinda Gates, the Eli Lilly family, etc. Thomas places magnificence under the broader category of fortitude, even though it does not involve facing the threat of death, insofar as it "tends to something arduous and difficult"—namely, "the dispossession of one's property" (a. 4). The vice opposed to magnificence is *meanness*, by which one of great wealth spends little in order to accomplish only some small good, as opposed to spending much to accomplish something great (q. 135, a. 1). At the other end of the moral spectrum is the vice of *waste*, by which one spends too much in relation to the good accomplished (a. 2). The virtue of magnificence constitutes the *rational mean* between these extremes.

QUESTIONS 141–170—CARDINAL VIRTUE: TEMPERANCE

Temperance is a virtue aimed at the harmonious ordering of concupiscible passions (Ia–IIae, q. 61, a. 2), *moderating* those passions that may orient us toward something contrary to reason (IIa–IIae, q. 141, aa. 1–2). More specifically, temperance "is chiefly concerned with those passions that tend towards sensible goods—viz. desire and pleasure—and consequently with the sorrows that arise from the absence of those pleasures" (a. 3). The particular desires and pleasures of concern are those "which chiefly regard the preservation of human life either in the species or in the individual"— namely, food, drink, and sex (aa. 4–5). To be clear, temperance does not entail the *sublimation* of these desires, as food, drink, and sex are good in themselves insofar as they are ordered toward fulfilling human necessities in the present life (a. 6). Thomas does not share the negative view of sensual pleasures espoused by Plato and the Manichees.

In fact, one of the vices Thomas specifies as contrary to temperance is the deficiency of "lack of feeling" or *insensibility* (q. 142, a. 1). Hence, temperance involves the moderate enjoyment of pleasure in accord with reason; although reason may lead some individuals to either a temporary withdrawal from such pleasures—e.g. fasting during Lent—or even permanent abstentions—e.g. avowed celibacy—for the sake of spiritual benefits, just as one may temporarily or permanently abstain from certain forms of food or drink for the sake of health benefits. The other primary opposing vice to temperance is the excess of "unchecked concupiscence" or *intemperance*, which Thomas characterizes as a "childish" state (a. 2). He also labels intemperance "the most disgraceful of sins" insofar as it is "most repugnant to human excellence" by focusing inordinately on pleasures common to both humans and other animals, as well as interfering with clear reasoning (a. 4).

As a cardinal virtue, temperance includes various other virtues under its umbrella (q. 143). One of two integral sub-virtues of temperance is *shamefacedness*, which Thomas describes as a "praiseworthy passion" (q. 144, a. 1) through which one "refrains from vicious acts through fear of reproach" or "while doing a disgraceful deed avoids the public eye through fear of reproach" (a. 2). The other integral sub-virtue is *honesty*, which does not refer to truth-telling as we typically think of it, but rather to the "spiritual beauty" of one's actions as "well proportioned in respect of the spiritual clarity of reason" (q. 145, a. 2). In short, while shame disposes one to hide his disgraceful actions, honesty disposes one to transparently display his rationally tempered actions (a. 4).

Thomas next describes various sub-virtues and vices associated with each of the three primary objects of concupiscent desire that temperance moderates. With respect to food, the virtue of *abstinence* involves a disposition toward regulating one's intake of nutritional sustenance. It does not refer to a total disregard for food, which Thomas states is not a virtuous attitude. Rather, he exhorts, "in abstaining from food a man should act with due regard for those among whom he lives, for his own person, and for the requirements of health" (q. 146, a. 1). He further notes that abstinence is in accord with right reason when done "with gladness of heart" and for the sake of "God's glory and not one's own" (a. 1 *ad* 4). The *act* of the virtue of abstinence is *fasting*, which serves three purposes: 1) to bridle one's concupiscent desires; 2) to free one's mind for spiritual contemplation; 3) to serve as penance for one's sins (q. 147, a. 1). Despite Thomas' recognition that fasts may be imposed by ecclesiastical authorities for any of these reasons, he nevertheless construes the overall aim of fasting as one's spiritual well-being and not merely as a burdensome punishment for sin (a. 3). He thus recommends Christ's "austere" life as a model for the virtuous regulation of food and drink for the sake of one's natural and supernatural flourishing (IIIa, q. 40, a. 2; q. 41, a. 3).

Gluttony is the contrary vice in which a person desires food *inordinately* (q. 148, a. 1). This vice may constitute a *mortal* sin insofar as one "adheres to the pleasure of gluttony as his end" and thereby despises God and disobeys God's commandments to obtain such pleasure (a. 2). Thomas specifies various forms gluttony may take, including eating food that is inordinately expensive or refined, eating too much food, or eating in a hasty or greedy manner (a. 4). He also cites Gregory the Great (540–604) in identifying various offspring that gluttony may produce: "dullness of sense in the understanding," "unseemly joy," "loquaciousness," "scurrility"—the latter two referring to someone talking too much or about inappropriate matters—and bodily "uncleanness" (a. 6). Especially when gluttonous eating is paired with drunkenness, one can easily picture a Jabba the Hutt-like individual embarrassing himself and those around him with loud, obnoxious, offensive words and behavior, resulting from the voluntary surrendering of rational control to more animalistic desires and passions. To be clear, gluttony or any other disposition toward an unhealthy intake of food counts as a moral vice only insofar as it is a *voluntary* component of one's character. While Thomas was unaware of eating disorders such as anorexia nervosa and bulimia, he would certainly not hold someone morally accountable for the resulting unhealthy eating habits; although he would exhort them to rationally understand their condition and seek appropriate medical or psychotherapeutic aid.

Temperance with respect to drinking alcoholic beverages consists in the virtue of *sobriety* (q. 149, a. 1), which is especially important insofar as immoderate alcohol consumption "disturbs the brain by its fumes" and thereby constitutes a "special hindrance to reason" (a. 2). Nevertheless, the moderate consumption of alcohol is not sinful except in particular circumstances where one may be especially susceptible to alcohol's harmful effects—such as someone genetically predisposed toward alcoholism—or has made a vow to abstain from drinking—such as a recovering alcoholic—or would scandalize others by her display of alcohol consumption—such as a teacher while on school property (a. 3). *Drunkenness* is obviously the excessive vice of consuming too much alcohol that constitutes a *mortal* sin in cases where one "willingly and knowingly deprives himself of the use of reason, whereby he performs virtuous deeds and avoids sin, and thus he sins mortally by running the risk of falling into sin" (q. 150, a. 2). In cases where one becomes intoxicated and subsequently commits a sin due to the lack of rational control, Thomas allows that "drunkenness may be an excuse for sin," but only in cases where one is not voluntarily responsible for having become intoxicated in the first place (a. 4). As is typical in U.S. court cases involving deaths that result from drunk-driving accidents, while the intoxicated driver is not guilty of "murder" insofar as he did not *intend* the victim's death, he is charged with "involuntary manslaughter" or "negligent homicide" in acknowledgment of his voluntary state of drunkenness while driving. Though drunkenness is the more common of the vices opposed to temperance in alcohol consumption, and abstinence from alcohol for the sake of one's health or spiritual well-being can be virtuous, Thomas nevertheless identifies the "insensibility" inherent in abstaining from alcohol for no good reason to be a vice (a. 1 *ad* 1).

Whereas abstinence from food and sobriety in drink are concerned with moderating goods related to the maintenance of individual human bodies, the virtue of *chastity* focuses on moderating the good related to the perpetuation of the human species: sex (q. 151). While Thomas devotes more questions to this virtue than the other two, the basic parameters of the discussion remain consistent. The desire for and enjoyment of sex is inherently good insofar as it is rationally ordered toward the inherently valuable end of producing and rearing offspring (q. 153, a. 2). Thus, insensibility with respect to sex constitutes a vice of deficiency. Thomas, however, lauds *virginity* as a virtue under the broader category of chastity insofar as it involves complete abstinence from "the greatest bodily pleasure" (q. 152, a. 1) so that one may "have leisure for Divine contemplation" (a. 2). While it would be disastrous for the human species if everyone practiced virginity, few individuals are given the grace necessary to attain this higher level of chastity. Thomas compares the relation between chastity and virginity with the virtues of liberality and magnificence: while liberality is a virtue of moderation that applies to all uses of money, only those of great wealth can be magnificent (q. 134, a. 3 *ad* 2); analogously, while chastity applies to all uses of one's sexuality, only some are called to virginity (q. 152, a. 3).

Thomas views chastity as a moral virtue in the fullest sense of the term insofar as it involves one's sexual desire and attendant passions having been brought into accordance with reason, such that one desires sex only insofar and to the extent that it is rational for her to do so. A lesser form of virtue is *continence*, whereby one acts in accordance with reason, but only after having to wrestle with "vehement passions contrary to reason" (q. 155, a. 1). *Incontinence* is the opposing vice whereby one gives into the pull of such passions, sometimes labelled today as "weakness of will" (q. 156).

Lust is the vice of excessive desire for sexual pleasure (q. 153), which manifests itself in six different forms (q. 154, a. 1): *simple fornication*, which Thomas deems wrong primarily on account of the harm that may accrue to any resultant offspring who may not be raised in a supportive familial environment (a. 2); *seduction*, which specifically refers to the "unlawful violation of a virgin, while still under the guardianship of her parents" (a. 6); *rape* (a. 7); *adultery* (a. 8); *incest* (a. 9); *sacrilege*, in cases where one desires or engages in sexual intercourse with a religiously consecrated person (a. 10); and finally what Thomas terms "unnatural vice," which is a category comprising *effeminacy*, *bestiality*, and *homosexuality* (a. 11). While contemporary Thomistic moral theorists debate the soundness of specific conclusions regarding, for example, extramarital intercourse, use of contraception, homosexual orientation and activity, or transvestitism and transgenderism, Thomas' conclusions are in line with his historical context and follow from his fundamental premise that human sexuality is rationally ordered toward the begetting and rearing of offspring.

Beyond the concupiscent desires prompted by basic human needs for food, drink, and sex, temperance is also applicable to the powerful irascible passion of *anger*. Thomas thus defines *clemency*, which mitigates external punishment that may be inflicted due to excessive anger, and *meekness*, which curbs the passion itself, as appropriate sub-virtues of temperance (q. 157). Nevertheless, contrary to the view of Stoic philosophers such as Seneca, Thomas does not consider anger in itself to be immoral (q. 158, a. 1); furthermore, an act of *vengeance* motivated by righteous anger in the face of injustice can be virtuous (q. 108). Vengeful anger becomes sinful, however, when it is "in any way contrary to the order of reason": for instance, one desires to punish someone who does not deserve it, or inflicts a punishment disproportionate to the offense, or punishes a wrongdoer for some end other than "the maintaining of justice and the correction of defaults" (q. 158, a. 2). Yet, just as excessive anger—culminating perhaps in *cruelty* (q. 159)—constitutes a vice, so does insufficient anger in cases where such passion ought to motivate one's will to respond to injustice (q. 158, a. 8).

Finally, Thomas examines *modesty* as a sub-virtue of temperance, which concerns—as the term often refers today—bodily movements (q. 168) and outward dress and appearance (q. 169), but also includes the virtues of *humility* and *studiousness*. Thomas defines humility as a virtue that moderates one's hope in daring to attain some difficult good; though he cautions that such moderation ceases to be virtuous if one *despairs* of attaining the difficult good altogether. Thus, an individual with the complementary virtues of both magnanimity and humility will have the strength of mind to dare to pursue the good she hopes to attain, while rationally acknowledging her limits and not allow her reach to exceed her ability to grasp (q. 161, a. 1). *Pride* is the contrary vice to humility, denoting "immoderate desire of one's own excellence" (q. 162, a. 4). Pride not only negatively impacts a human being's flourishing insofar as she irrationally strives to attain what is beyond her abilities, but also constitutes the "most grievous of sins" insofar as one disregards what is properly appointed to her by God's eternal law (aa. 5–6). Pride, of course, is what precipitated the Fall of Adam and Eve (q. 163)—see the discussion of "original sin" in Chapter 7.

Thomas identifies studiousness as virtue referring to the moderation of one's desire for knowledge (q. 166, a. 2). Opposed to this virtue is immoderate *curiosity*, which can arise in several ways: 1) one studies to learn something in order to sin; 2) the mode of one's study is inherently inordinate—e.g. one desires to know the future by consulting demons (*superstition*); 3) one studies creation without any regard for the ultimate end of knowledge— namely, the creator, God; 4) one studies to know some truth beyond his intellectual capacity, which may easily lead him into error (q. 167, a. 1).

We have arrived at the end of Thomas' detailed consideration of the theological and cardinal moral virtues, which are applicable to all human beings in whatever station of life or socio-cultural circumstance. As noted in the preface to this chapter, he concludes the *secunda pars* with a discussion of particular graces, spiritual gifts, and virtues associated with specific states of life, especially those involving clerical and religious orders (qq. 171–189). We will dispense with an examination of these more esoteric concerns and move on in the next chapters to Thomas' conclusive treatment in the *tertia pars* of the essential element for human beings to complete our *reditus* to God— namely, the salvific grace wrought by Christ's incarnation and passion mediated through the sacraments of the Church—followed by his treatment of human beings' post-mortem existence and our life in the world to come.

SUGGESTIONS FOR FURTHER READING

An accessible illumination of Thomas' account of the theological and cardinal virtues can be found in Josef Pieper, *Faith, Hope, and Love* (San Francisco, CA: Ignatius Press, 1997); and Pieper, *The Four Cardinal Virtues* (Notre Dame, IN: University of Notre Dame Press, 1966).

Jeremy Bentham's formulation of the "utility calculus" can be found in his *An Introduction to the Principles of Moral and Legislation* (Oxford: Clarendon Press, 1907). The quotation from John Stuart Mill is from his *Utilitarianism*, ed. George Sher, 2nd ed. (Indianapolis, IN: Hackett, 2001).

Aristotle's practical definition of virtue as the means between the extremes of excess and deficiency can be found in his *Nicomachean Ethics*, trans. Terence Irwin, 2nd ed. (Indianapolis, IN: Hackett, 1999), bk. II, ch. 6, 1107a1–3.

An in-depth presentation of Thomas' concept of the "common good" and its Aristotelian foundation can found in Mary M. Keys, *Aquinas, Aristotle, and the Promise of the Common Good* (New York: Cambridge University Press, 2006).

For a thorough analysis of Thomas' theory of just punishment, including capital punishment, see Peter Karl Koritansky, *Thomas Aquinas and the Philosophy of Punishment* (Washington, D.C.: Catholic University of America Press, 2012).

For detailed discussion of the "principle of double-effect" and its evolution from Thomistic ethics, see T. A. Cavanaugh, *Double-Effect Reasoning: Doing Good and Avoiding Evil* (New York: Oxford University Press, 2006); Cavanaugh, "Aquinas's Account of Double

Effect" *The Thomist* 61 (1997): 107–112; P. A. Woodward, ed., *The Doctrine of Double Effect: Philosophers Debate a Controversial Moral Principle* (Notre Dame, IN: University of Notre Dame Press, 2001); Gareth Matthews, "Saint Thomas and the Principle of Double Effect" in *Aquinas' Moral Theory: Essays in Honor of Norman Kretzmann*, eds. Scott MacDonald and Eleonore Stump (Ithaca, NY: Cornell University Press, 1999), 63–78; Joseph Boyle, "Toward Understanding the Principle of Double Effect" *Ethics* 90 (1980): 527–538.

A more thorough elucidation of Thomas' treatment of temperance can be found in Stephen J. Loughlin, *Aquinas' Summa Theologiae: A Reader's Guide* (New York: T&T Clark, 2010), 249–273.

Section 3

SPIRITUAL END (*TERTIA PARS* AND *SUPPLEMENTUM*)

9

CHRIST'S INCARNATION AND THE SACRAMENTS OF THE CHURCH

PREFACE

We have arrived at the *tertia pars*, Thomas' final and most theologically oriented part of the *Summa*. In the *prima pars*, Thomas argued that God is the source of all being and goodness, and explained how all created beings—including human beings—come forth (*exitus*) from God's creative activity. In the *secunda pars*, Thomas demonstrated that humanity's return (*reditus*) to the source of our existence, who we desire to know and be in loving communion with, is what our happiness consists in. He further elucidated how voluntary moral activity, in accord with the rationally discoverable principles of natural law and informed by theological and moral virtues, leads us on a path in this life toward that return. In order to complete this journey to our supernatural end, however, we require divine assistance to overcome the damaging effects of *original sin* and to infuse within us the *grace* necessary to take us beyond our natural intellectual and volitional limits. Thus, God chose to become *incarnate* in human flesh, suffer and die in atonement for humanity's sin, and thereby provide a fitting conduit for grace to lead us toward both our natural flourishing and supernatural beatitude.

In this chapter, we will first examine Thomas' *Christology*, including *why* God chose to become incarnate, *how* the divine and human natures are united in Christ, and *what* Christ accomplished from His life on earth, through His ascension into heaven, to His current seat at the Father's right hand. We will examine how the grace bestowed through Christ's passion is mediated through the *sacraments* instituted by Him and ministered through the Church. This part of the *tertia pars* was left incomplete upon Thomas' spiritual experience that led him to cease writing not long before his death. As noted in Chapter 1, Thomas' *socius*—what we would today call a secretary or research assistant—Reginald of Piperno, edited together a *supplementum*, treating the topics he knew his master was planning to cover, out of Thomas' commentary on the *Sentences* of Peter Lombard. While Reginald's efforts provide evidence of what Thomas *may* have written if he had completed the *Summa*, Thomas' *Sentences* commentary is one of his earliest writings from when he was completing his theological studies. Unfortunately, then, we do not have the benefit—aside from what he occasionally says in other writings—of knowing how Thomas' thoughts may have matured concerning these final topics.

QUESTIONS 1–26—WHY AND HOW GOD BECAME HUMAN

The incarnation of the Second Person of the Trinity—who, following St. John the Evangelist, is most properly called "the Word" (*Logos*) of God according to Thomas (Ia, q. 34, aa. 1–2)—as the historical man Jesus of Nazareth—whom Thomas refers to throughout as "Christ"— was primarily a response to humanity's Fall as a means of atoning for and repairing the defects in human nature caused by original sin: "the work of the Incarnation is principally ordained to the restoration of the human race by blotting out sin" (IIIa, q. 1, a. 5). Thomas contends that Christ's incarnation was not absolutely *necessary* since God, as omnipotent, could have redeemed humanity in myriad just and merciful ways (q. 1, a. 2; q. 46, a. 2); however, it was a most "fitting" (*conveniens*) way for God to establish humanity's redemption:

> To each thing, that is befitting which belongs to it by reason of its very nature . . . But the very nature of God is goodness . . . Hence, what belongs to the essence of goodness befits God. But it belongs to the essence of goodness to communicate itself to others . . . Hence it belongs to the essence of the highest good to communicate itself in the highest manner to the creature, and this is brought about by *His so joining created nature to Himself that one Person is made up of these three – the Word, a soul and flesh*, as Augustine says (*De Trinitate*, XIII). Hence it is manifest that it was fitting that God should become incarnate.
>
> (q. 1, a. 1)

Thomas further affirms the fittingness of Christ's incarnation insofar as human beings attain truth by means of sensory experience: "It would seem most fitting that by visible things the invisible things of God should be made known" (a. 1 *s.c.*). As discussed below, this same rationale underlies Christ's wisdom in instituting the sacraments of the Church as providing perceptible means for mediating divine grace.

Since the primary rationale for Christ's incarnation is for a being of both divine and human natures to "satisfy" the infinite debt of sin humanity owed to our creator (q. 1, a. 2 *ad* 2; q. 48, a. 2), Thomas affirms that the incarnation would not have happened if humanity had not sinned (a. 3); although God could still have chosen to become incarnate for other reasons—e.g. to provide an example of the fullness of moral virtue, as means of bestowing supernatural grace, or to confirm the inherent dignity of human nature by conjoining it with the divine nature. According to Thomas, it was most fitting for God—and particularly the Word as God's *wisdom*—to become incarnate in order to conjoin Himself with what He created in order to repair what had become defective in it—similar to a craftsman who, having designed something perfect in his mind and then built it, must then go into the structure he built to effect any repairs so as to bring it back in line with the original blueprint—as well as to invite human beings to share in His divine "sonship" and to reveal to us the "true knowledge" Adam and Eve had sinfully sought through their own pride against God's command (q. 3, a. 8).

Questions 2 through 6 explicate the mode of the *hypostatic union* of divine and human natures in the one person of Christ, who is thereby both the eternal Word of God and the historical Jesus of Nazareth. To pre-summarize the traditional position Thomas defends and seeks to rationally explain, which is still the orthodox Christian position today: All that can be said of God can be said of Christ, and all that can be said of human nature—in its perfect form without sin—can also be said of Christ (q. 16, a. 4). Thus, it can be said that God died on Calvary since Christ, as human, died on Calvary; conversely, it can be said that Jesus of Nazareth was omniscient since Christ, as divine, has perfect knowledge. It would be illogical, however, to attribute essential qualities of Christ's human *nature* to His divine *nature* insofar as the two natures—though united in a single *person*—remain essentially distinct (q. 16, a. 5). Hence, for example, Christ's human nature is essentially *mortal*—thus He could die (q. 50)—whereas, in His divine nature, Christ persisted during the three days His body laid in the tomb (q. 51), descended into hell (q. 52), and causally effected His own resurrection (q. 53, a. 4).

The early centuries of Christianity saw a variety of Christological theories promoted by various sects attempting to account for, within the limits of human understanding, the fundamental *mystery* of Christ as the "God-man." For example, adherents of *monophysitism* contended that Christ possessed only a single nature comprising both divine and human qualities: Christ's mind being that of the Word and His body being human. Defenders of *monothelitism* held that Christ possessed both divine and human natures, but only a divine *will* that determined His actions. More radically, followers of the archbishop Nestorius (*c.* 386–*c.* 450) argued that the divine and human natures of Christ yielded two distinct persons. These and various related views were declared heretical through a series of ecumenical councils, culminating in a Christological formula proclaimed at the Council of Chalcedon (451 AD) that affirmed Christ as having both divine and human natures united in one person:

> Following the saintly fathers, we all with one voice teach the confession of one and the same Son, our Lord Jesus Christ: the same perfect in divinity and perfect in humanity, the same truly God and truly human, of a rational [intellective] soul and body; consubstantial with the Father as regards his divinity, and the same consubstantial with us as regards his humanity; like us in all respects except for sin . . . at no

point was the difference between the natures taken away through the union, but rather the property of both natures is preserved and comes together into a single person and a single subsistent being; he is not parted or divided into two persons; but is one and the same only-begotten Son, God, Word, Lord Jesus Christ.

This is what Thomas accepts as the *orthodox* formula upon which he develops his detailed Christology. He proceeds to explicate what the gospels and Christian tradition, as encapsulated in the Chalcedonian formula, tell us about Christ's ontological make-up by utilizing Aristotelian metaphysical concepts and relations developed throughout his treatment of divine and human nature in the *prima pars*, as well as human moral psychology in the *secunda pars*.

In line with the Chalcedonian formula, Thomas contends that it can truthfully be said both that God is a human being (q. 16, a. 1) and that a human being—specifically, Jesus of Nazareth—is God (aa. 2, 11). Thomas understands the gospels to report accurately the nature of Christ's earthly life; thus, he takes it at face value—and not as merely figurative—that Christ experienced physical pain, emotions, temptations, friendships, etc., which are common to human experience, but *perfected* insofar as they accord with reason and His divine will. In this way, Christ illustrates humanity's proper mode of existence before the Fall. Hence, as a truly *human* being, it follows that Christ had a physical body (q. 5, aa. 1–2), had the capacity to experience physical pain (q. 15, a. 5) and emotional sorrow (a. 6)—along with other emotions such as fear (a. 7), wonder (a. 8), and anger (a. 9)—and that He acquired knowledge through sense experience (q. 9, a. 4; q. 12).

As one can imagine, navigating what can be predicated of Christ in His *unified* existence as a single person, and what can be predicated of Him relative to His *distinctive* natures, can be an excruciating exercise in metaphysical exactitude. For instance, Thomas affirms that, while the Second Person of the Trinity is *eternal*, this does not entail that Christ's human nature is eternal (q. 16, a. 9); rather, it was "assumed" by the Second Person of the Trinity at a particular historical moment (q. 3, a. 1), and it could occur again at another moment in time (a. 7). In referring to Christ as an *individual person*, Thomas utilizes the Aristotelian term *hypostasis* (Latin: *suppositum*), which refers to a substance bearing a specific nature or, in this special case, *two* specific natures (q. 2, a. 3). To be clear, as a *hypostasis*, there is only *one being* to whom we are referring in this discussion: Christ (q. 16, a. 12; q. 17, a. 2). Jesus of Nazareth is not a distinct human person from the Second Person of the Trinity; rather, the one person, Christ, is *both* the human Jesus and the divine Second Person conjoined in a "hypostatic union": one person subsisting in two natures.

Christ's human nature, insofar as it is ontologically united to the Second Person of the Trinity, functions as a *personal instrument* of divine action—see the discussion of Christ's power below. To accomplish the divine mission of redeeming humanity from sin, as well as serving as an exemplar of human moral perfection, Christ's human nature was infused with the same graces that other human beings require in order to attain both our natural and supernatural perfection (q. 2, a. 12; q. 7, a. 1)—including the theological virtue of charity and infused moral virtues (q. 7, a. 2), along with the gifts of the Holy Spirit (a. 5)—even the gift of "fear of the Lord," not insofar as Christ feared punishment due to sin, but rather due to the *reverence* He felt in his humanity for His divine Father (a. 6). Although it can be said that Christ possessed *all* the virtues necessary to perfect His human soul's capacities and activities, insofar as He also possessed a divine nature, Christ did not require the theological virtues of faith and hope (aa. 3–4). Possessing these graces in their fullness (aa. 9–10), Christ serves not only as a fitting *exemplar* of the perfection all human beings can attain through divine assistance, but also as the *mediator* through whom divine grace overflows into others (a. 1). As we will discuss below, the sacraments of the Church function as *instrumental causes* mediating this overflow of grace from Christ to the rest of humanity. Christ is thus "the first and chief teacher of spiritual doctrine and faith" since He knows the truth about God directly (a. 7).

Christ's primacy in possessing the *fullness* of grace, with the power to bestow grace upon others, places Him in the position of "Head of the Church" (q. 8, a. 1), comprising all of humanity (a. 3) and the angels (a. 4). The effects of Christ's grace include the healing and elevation of human nature, the institution of the Church, and the causal effectiveness of the sacraments—especially the Eucharist—in mediating divine grace to humanity. As Head of the Church, Christ is not a removed, absentee leader, but rather is intimately united with the Church insofar as the latter constitutes His "mystical Body" (aa. 5–6).

This is evidenced scripturally through Christ's promise to be *present* wherever "two or three are gathered in my name" (Matthew 18:20) and allows for the meritorious grace associated with Christ's passion to become ontologically manifest through the sacraments insofar as these are only performed when the Church—the Body of Christ—is gathered (q. 19, a. 4).

Thomas now moves to discuss specific features of Christ's nature during His earthly life: His knowledge, power, capacity to suffer physically, emotions, and will. With respect to His *knowledge*, Thomas holds that Christ, in his divine nature as the Word, possesses the Beatific Vision of the divine essence (q. 9, a. 2; q. 10). In His human nature, Christ possessed *infused* knowledge of all that can be known by the human intellect (q. 9, a. 3; q. 11), as well as knowledge *acquired* through sense experience (q. 9, a. 4; q. 12). To make sense of how Christ's human intellect could have knowledge in both of these ways, since the former would seem to preclude the latter, we must recall the distinction between the *habit* of knowledge and the actual *use* of what one knows. Thomas affirms that Christ's infused knowledge was habitual (q. 11, a. 5), which allows for His ability to use this knowledge to develop throughout His earthly life (q. 12, a. 2). Thus, Thomas can consistently affirm that Christ suffered no ignorance (q, 15, a. 3), and yet "Christ did not know everything from the beginning, but step by step, and after a time" (q. 12, a. 2 *ad* 1). This can be seen scripturally in the account of the 12-year-old Jesus teaching the elders in the Temple, thereby exhibiting the divinely infused knowledge He possessed, and yet upon returning home to Nazareth He continued to increase in wisdom (Luke 2:41–52).

Concerning his *power*, Thomas affirms that Christ's human soul was *not* omnipotent (q. 13, a. 1). In the subsequent articles, Thomas explains how Christ's *miraculous* works were accomplished by virtue of His divine nature working instrumentally through His human nature. Hence, Christ performs physical acts—speaking, touching, rubbing mud into a blind man's eyes—but such acts are not the *primary* efficient cause of the healing effected; rather, they are *personal instrumental causes* of His divine power at work. The qualifier "personal" denotes an instrumental cause that is *intrinsic* to the substance of the primary causal agent—as opposed to an *extrinsic* instrument that the agent may utilize. For example, a writer writes a sentence with a pen. The primary causal agent is the writer herself—or more specifically, her intellect and will. A personal instrumental cause would be her hand, which is an integral part of the substance of her body, moving the pen to write; while the pen, which is not part of the substance of her body, would be an extrinsic instrumental cause. Referring to Christ's miraculous healing of a leper (Matthew 8:1–3), Thomas states,

> to heal a leper is a proper work of the Divine operation, but to touch him is the proper work of the human operation. Now both these operations concur in one work, inasmuch as one nature acts in union with the other.
>
> (q. 19, a. 1 *ad* 5)

Christ's physical act of touching the leper is a personal instrumental cause of His divine act of healing; whereas, in the case of Christ mixing His spittle with dirt to make a mud that He applies to heal a blind man's eyes (John 9:1–7), the mud functions as an extrinsic instrumental cause.

Christ's capacity to *suffer physically* is part of the "fittingness" of His incarnation for various reasons. First, Christ took on the physical penalties of human sin to render appropriate satisfaction—though without taking on the guilt of sin itself (q. 15, a. 1). Second, Christ's capacity to suffer serves to render His incarnation *believable*—as well as His resurrection, as the story of "doubting Thomas" illustrates (John 20:24–29). Finally, Christ's suffering provides an exemplar for human beings of how to endure suffering patiently in our own lives (q. 14, a. 1; q. 15, a. 5). It is important to emphasize that Christ *willingly* assumed the capacity to suffer physically and endured His sufferings, as it was not *absolutely* necessary to effect humanity's redemption in this manner since God is omnipotent; although it was necessary *by supposition* insofar as God had eternally willed—which means that Christ, in His divine nature, had eternally willed—to redeem humanity in this way (q. 14, aa. 2–3; q. 46, aa. 1–2)—see the discussion of the distinction between these two types of necessity with respect to God's will in Chapter 2.

In addition to the capacity to suffer, Christ "had taken a true human nature, with all its natural affections" (q. 21, a. 2). Christ's human nature thus had both *concupiscible* and *irascible* sensory appetites—see the discussion of these appetites and their attendant passions in Chapters 4 and 6. He thereby desired to eat, drink, sleep, and satisfy other sensory appetites (q. 15, a. 2 *ad* 2). Unlike post-Fall human beings, however, Christ's passions never focused on illicit objects and were perfectly in line with His reason, providing an illustration of how humanity's reason, desires, and emotions were in line with one another in our pre-Fallen state. Hence, Thomas states that "the passions were in Christ otherwise than in us" (a. 4).

Finally, contrary to the monothelites—who claimed that Christ, though possessing a human nature in other respects, had only a divine will—Thomas contends that Christ possessed *both* a divine and a human will (q. 18, a. 1) and that the *freedom* of Christ's human will was not sublimated by His divine will: "He allowed all the powers of His soul to do what belonged to them" (a. 5). Nevertheless, the two wills are perfectly aligned such that Christ's human will, though it could be tempted in various ways at the level of His sensory appetites—as He is by Satan at one point (q. 41; Matthew 4:1–11)—is not disposed toward willing anything contrary to His divine will (q. 18, a. 6). Christ possessed both concupiscent and irascible desires (a. 2) as appropriate to human nature, but these desires were rationally ordered, perfectly moderated by the virtues Christ possessed. Praying in the garden of Gethsemane the night before His passion, Christ's concupiscent desire to avoid physical suffering and natural aversion to bodily death are expressed, but do not deter Him from freely willing to endure such suffering as He had divinely willed (q. 21, a. 3; q. 22, a. 2 *ad* 1). Employing the distinctions of persons in the Trinity, however, it would be more accurate to state that Christ willingly—through His free human will—endured suffering and death out of *obedience* to the Father—whose divine will He shares (q. 47, a. 2).

Through His freely willed acceptance of His passion, Thomas views Christ's suffering and death as constituting a "true sacrifice" that was "most acceptable to God, as coming from charity"—i.e. Christ's perfect love for humanity (q. 48, a. 3). In this way, Christ establishes Himself most perfectly in the role of *priest* (q. 22, a. 2). Thomas defines a "priest" as a "mediator between God and the people," who "bestows Divine things on the people" and "offers up the people's prayers to God, and, in a manner, makes satisfaction for their sins"

(a. 1). By freely offering the perfect sacrifice of *Himself* to the Father, Christ gained for humanity the *remission* of sin, with consequent *liberation* from the effects of sin, and *conversion* of each human being's heart toward loving union with God, thereby allowing us to attain *reconciliation* with God and complete our *reditus* through the now opened "gate of heaven's kingdom" (a. 3; cf. qq. 48–49).

Since Christ's priestly sacrifice required His own suffering and death, it is only insofar as He became *human* that Christ is able to function as mediator between God and humanity (q. 26, a. 2). Nevertheless, it is only insofar as Christ is *divine* that He should be adored and venerated (q. 25, a. 1). While it is appropriate to *honor* a human being of great virtue who willingly sacrifices herself for the sake of others, it would not be appropriate to *worship* such a person insofar as she is a human being; only *God* is to be worshipped. Thus, Thomas concludes that Christians do not worship Christ's flesh *as flesh*, even in the sacrament of the Eucharist—as we will discuss further below—but only insofar as it is the flesh *of God*. Furthermore, in response to the controversy among various Christian denominations regarding the veneration of *images* of Christ or sacred *relics*, Thomas defends the veneration of such physical items against the "iconoclasts" by distinguishing the worship of the Person whom such things *represent* from the worship of the things themselves (aa. 3–4, 6).

QUESTIONS 27–59—THE LIFE OF CHRIST

Thomas' treatment of Christ's life reflects the *exitus–reditus* structure of the *Summa* itself. Christ enters into the world (*ingressus*) (qq. 27–39), His earthly life unfolds (*processus*) (qq. 40–45), He then departs from this world (*exitus*) (qq. 46–52), and, in exaltation (*exaltatio*), returns (*reditus*) to the Father (qq. 53–59). Thomas begins with a brief discussion of Mary as the "Mother of God" (qq. 27–30), affirming—*contra* Nestorius—that this is indeed her appropriate title insofar as the child she conceived by the causal efficacy of the Holy Spirit (q. 32, a. 1), and to whom she gave birth, is *the numerically same person*—the same *hypostasis*—as the Second Person of the Trinity (q. 35, a. 4). As we have seen above, Christ's growth and earthly ministry depicted both the operation of His divine power, particularly in various miracles He performed (q. 43, a. 2), as well as the natural desires and emotions He felt as a human being.

Christ's earthy life culminates in His passion, which Thomas considers to be the most fitting way for God to have redeemed humanity—as opposed to God simply redeeming us out of His merciful goodwill—for several reasons: 1) to make us aware of the depth of God's love for us; 2) to set an example of various virtues essential for our salvation, such as obedience, humility, constancy, and justice; 3) to merit for us justifying grace and the glory of heavenly beatitude; 4) to strengthen humanity's obligation to refrain from sin; and 5) to dignify human nature through a human being conquering Satan, who had initially deceived humanity into falling into sin, and overcoming the consequent penalty of death through dying (a. 46, a. 3). Thomas further explains how *crucifixion* was also the most fitting way for Christ to suffer and die (a. 4).

Thomas describes Christ's passion as more profound than any other experience of human suffering. While Christ could not, of course, experience every *specific* type of human suffering—e.g. He could not be both drowned and burned as these are mutually exclusive—Thomas affirms that "He did endure every human suffering" *generically* (q. 46, a. 5). First, He endured suffering from *every class of humanity*—e.g. Gentiles and Jews, women and men, servants and rulers, the anonymous mob and his closest friends. Second, He was afflicted with *every type of suffering* a human being can experience: abandonment, dishonor, insults, loss of possessions, emotional sorrow, and physical injury. Finally, regarding the last category of suffering, Christ was wounded in *every part of His body* and tormented in *all five of His physical senses*. Furthermore, Christ suffered to the greatest extent possible not only *quantitatively*, but also *qualitatively* insofar as the perfection of His human nature increased the sensitivity of His body and soul (a. 6). Thus, Christ suffered to the greatest extent possible both physically and psychically (a. 7). Yet, Christ continued to enjoy the Beatific Vision even while dying on the cross due to His divine nature (a. 8), paving the way toward his exaltation.

Before Christ's exaltation in His resurrection and ascension, He experienced death, burial, and descent into hell. Thomas gives several reasons justifying the fittingness of each of these events. Christ's death 1) satisfied the penalty owed by humanity's sin, 2) demonstrated the truly physical nature of His body, 3) showed humanity that we need not fear death, 4) provided an example we may follow by dying *spiritually* to sin, and 5) through His rising from death instilled in us hope of our own future resurrection (q. 50, a. 1). Christ's burial fittingly 1) established the truth of His death, 2) gives hope that all those who are buried will rise again as He did, and 3) illustrates figuratively that those who die spiritually to their sins are "buried together with Christ" and thereby are "hidden away from the disturbance of men" (q. 51, a. 1). Finally, Christ's descent into hell 1) delivered us from the penalty of hell just as His death delivered us from death, 2) delivered holy men and women—such as Abraham, Moses, and Esther—made captive prior to Christ's incarnation who were nevertheless joined to His passion through *charity*, and 3) manifested Christ's lordship over both the living and the dead (q. 52, aa. 1, 5).

After one day and two nights in the tomb (q. 51, a. 4), Christ rose from dead on what Christians celebrate as Easter morning. Thomas provides five reasons for the necessity of Christ's resurrection: 1) as following from God's justice, which requires that those who humble themselves in obedience to God's will merit exaltation; 2) to instruct the faithful by confirming Christ's divine nature; 3) to inspire hope of humanity's sharing in Christ's resurrection; 4) to reorient the "new" lives of the faithful toward God and away from sin; and 5) to complete Christ's salvific work by not only enduring evil, but also advancing humanity toward the good (q. 53, a. 1). Thomas next emphasizes that Christ's resurrected body, while "glorified" (q. 54, a. 2), nevertheless was still a "true" human body (a. 1) with all of its natural physical parts (a. 3) and even the scars of His passion due to their spiritual significance (a. 4), as confirmed by the ways in which Christ manifested Himself to the disciples after His resurrection (q. 55). This is important to keep in mind as we consider Thomas' metaphysical account of our own resurrection in the next chapter, since he considers Christ's resurrection as both "the efficient and exemplar cause" of the future resurrection and glorification of our bodies (q. 56, a. 1 *ad* 3).

Christ's exaltation is completed by His ascension into heaven (q. 57, a. 1), which fosters the virtues of faith, hope, and charity in us, as well as our reverence for Christ "since we no longer deem Him an earthly man, but the God of heaven" (a. 6). Furthermore, Christ fulfills His role as humanity's "high priest" by entering God's holy sanctuary and interceding for us. Additionally, insofar as Christ is the Head of the Church (q. 8), His ascension causes our own since the members of Christ's "body" must be united with their "head" (q. 57, a. 6 *ad* 2). Christ now "sits at the Father's right hand," which refers figuratively to Christ 1) abiding eternally in divine beatitude, and 2) exercising God's judiciary power (q. 58, a. 1). The latter power extends not only from Christ's divinity, but also His humanity insofar as it is appropriate that whoever judges human beings share in our likeness, including our weaknesses to provoke compassionate judgment (q. 59, a. 2). Christ's judgment encompasses all voluntary moral actions of both angels (a. 6) and humans beings (a. 4) throughout the entire course of history, culminating in a final "general judgment" in which all the consequential effects of each moral choice made by every human being can be made manifest and taken into account (a. 5).

In sum, Thomas' account of Christ's hypostatic union and His incarnated life outlines several essential truths held by faithful Christians to this day:

1 God reveals himself to humanity in a "most fitting" way through the Second Person of the Trinity assuming a human nature.
2 Christ is *essentially* human, meaning that He has an intellective soul informing a material human body and possesses the constitutive capacities definitive of human nature—e.g. an intellective mind, free will, concupiscible and irascible appetites, passions, gender, etc. Thomas states, "Nothing that God planted in our nature was wanting to the human nature assumed by the Word of God" (q. 9, a. 4). Sin, however, is not constitutive of human nature as divinely intended, but only as a consequence of humanity's Fall. It is therefore not a feature of human nature as assumed by Christ: "the truth of His human nature is not proved by sin, since sin does not belong to human nature, whereof God is the cause" (q. 15, a. 1).
3 Christ's human nature includes *perfections* wrought by infused divine graces that are necessary for Him to function both as humanity's redeemer, as well as an ideal exemplar of moral virtue living in accord with God's eternal law: "Christ's action is our instruction" (q. 40, a. 1 *ad* 3). Thus, for instance, Christ's concupiscible and irascible desires and passions are moderated in ideal harmony with His perfect rational understanding of God's law.

4   Christ's human nature includes *defects* that are a consequence of humanity's original sin—although Christ does not share in original sin itself—in order for Him to exist in solidarity with humanity and to offer the redemptive sacrifice of His suffering and death.

5   Finally, combining all of these elements, it can be said that Christ, as the historical man Jesus of Nazareth, lived an *authentically human life*: He was born, grew as child and adolescent, ate, drank, slept, loved family and friends, got angry at those who offended Him, feared physical suffering and death, was wounded physically by various torments, as well as emotionally by rejection and abandonment, died, and rose in a glorified—yet still physically human—form. We will discuss further the metaphysical implications of this final manifestation of Christ's humanity as prefiguring our own future transformation in Chapter 10.

QUESTIONS 60–65—THE SACRAMENTS IN GENERAL

Thomas succinctly defines a *sacrament* as "the sign of a holy thing so far as it makes men holy" (q. 60, a. 2). The broad meaning of a sacrament as a "sign" includes not only the seven sacraments Thomas understands to have been instituted by Christ, but also various rites recorded in the Hebrew Scriptures insofar as they *prefigure* Christ's sacrifice and the grace that flows therefrom (q. 60, a. 2 *ad* 2; q. 60, a. 6 *ad* 3; q. 61, a. 3; q. 62, a. 6). Thomas even allows for certain sacramental rituals to have been present prior to the revelation of God's law to the Hebrew people due to an "inward instinct" to worship God (q. 60, a. 5 *ad* 3), which coheres with his understanding of *natural law*, as a manifestation of God's *eternal law*, having been written into the hearts and minds of all human persons (Ia–IIae, q. 94, a. 4). The specifically *Christian* sacraments differ from these others insofar as they are not only signs, but also *instrumental causes* of divine grace being bestowed upon individual human persons (IIIa, q. 62, a. 1). Thomas thus summarizes a sacrament as "a reminder of the past, i.e. the passion of Christ; and an indication of that which is effected in us by Christ's passion, i.e. grace; and a prognostic, that is, a foretelling of future glory" (q. 60, a. 3).

The reason Christ instituted the sacraments follows directly from humanity's *hylomorphic* nature as both rational and animal, with the consequence that our natural mode of deriving intellective knowledge is through sense-perception of material objects—see Chapter 4. Furthermore, our sensory appetites are oriented toward sensible objects as goods we are inclined to pursue—see Chapter 6; a consequence of original sin is our *inordinate* inclination toward sensible objects, along with other defects in our nature, which must be repaired through the grace merited by Christ's passion. Finally, as bodily creatures, we are inclined toward performing physical actions, including in our modes of worship, and thus sacramental rituals provide us with an alternative to superstitious practices (q. 61, a. 1). In short, through the mediation of physical sacraments God meets us where we are at in order to bring us to where He is, and thus every sacrament involves something *sensible* (q. 60, a. 4): "Sacraments are necessary for man's salvation, in so far as they are sensible signs of invisible things whereby man is made holy" (q. 61, a. 3).

The *principal effect* of the sacraments is the conferral of divine grace upon the recipient (q. 62, a. 1), which *incorporates* one into the Body of Christ and also *perfects* one's soul through infusion of theological and moral virtues, as well as the gifts of the Holy Spirit (a. 2). The *primary efficient cause* of grace is Christ's passion insofar as it is *the* salvific act that atones for, and thereby redeems humanity from, original sin: "The Church is said to be built up with the sacraments *which flowed from the side of Christ while hanging on the cross*" (q. 64, a. 2 *ad* 3; cf. q. 62, a. 5; q. 64, a. 3; q. 66, a. 3 *ad* 3). The grace merited by Christ's passion, however, is communicated through the sacraments as *extrinsic instrumental causes*—except in the case of the Eucharist, which functions as a *personal* instrumental cause for reasons discussed below. The sacraments are akin to a writer's pen, which writes only because of the primary casual activity of the writer, but which also has a specific form that allows it to function as an instrument appropriate for writing: "But if we hold that a sacrament is an instrumental cause of grace, we must needs allow that there is in the sacraments a certain instrumental power of bringing about the sacramental effects" (q. 62, a. 4). Thus, each sacrament has its own casual efficacy due to the determinate objects, actions, and words that constitute it (q. 60, aa. 5–7). Nevertheless, just as a pen cannot write without the principal action of the writer, no sacrament can cause grace without the principal action of Christ behind it:

> Now the principal efficient cause of grace is God Himself, in comparison with Whom Christ's humanity is as a united [*personal*] instrument, whereas the sacrament is as a separate [*extrinsic*] instrument. Consequently, the saving power must needs be derived by the sacraments from Christ's Godhead through His humanity.
>
> (q. 62, a. 5)

In addition to these active causes of divine grace, there is also the necessity of a *passive power* to receive grace on the part of recipients (q. 63, a. 2).

In the case of certain sacraments— namely, Baptism, Confirmation, and Orders (q. 63, a. 6)—not only are specific graces conferred, but an *indelible change of character* is effected. Thus, even if a baptized person were to renounce her Christian affiliation and further proclaim that God does not exist, the spiritual "imprint" of her Baptism cannot be removed, just as enlisted soldiers used to be indelibly tattooed with a mark of their service (a. 1). This spiritual imprint allows recipients not only to receive divine grace but also to bestow grace upon others (a. 2). All baptized individuals participate in the *priesthood* of Christ (a. 3); while some individuals are further instituted to confer the *plenitude* of graces through the sacrament of Orders—comprising the offices of deacon, priest, and bishop, as well as four non-sacramental "minor" orders (a. 6; Supp., q. 37).

Ministers of divine grace should not be conceptualized merely as "antennae" channeling God's power through themselves to others, but as persons who are *fundamentally changed* in the "essence of [their] soul" through their ministerial service (q. 63, a. 2 *ad* 3; a. 4 *ad* 2; a. 5 *ad* 1). Nevertheless, as emphasized above, the primary efficient cause of the sacraments is Christ Himself, who, as Head of the Church (q. 8), becomes present with the body of the gathered faithful through the *instrumental* mediation provided by the sacramental minister acting "in the person of Christ" (*in persona Christi*).

Addressing the question of why there are *seven* Christian sacraments, Thomas continues to refer to humanity's hylomorphic nature and thereby the appropriateness of comparing one's spiritual journey to her physical journey through life: "For spiritual life has a certain conformity with the life of the body" (q. 65, a. 1). Thomas identifies two essential dimensions of human life: first, with respect to oneself insofar as she is a *rational animal*; second, with respect to one's community insofar as she is a *social animal*. Turning to the first dimension, he notes that human survival and flourishing requires both seeking what one needs to live, grow, and maintain her health, as well as removing hindrances, such as illness or other forms of physical weakness. He then proceeds to relate his analysis of the essential dimensions of, and necessities for, human life to the sacraments in the context of the spiritual life:

> Now the life of the body is perfected *directly*, in three ways. First, by generation whereby a man begins to be and to live: and corresponding to this in the spiritual life there is Baptism, which is a spiritual regeneration . . . Secondly, by growth whereby a man is brought to perfect size and strength: and corresponding to this in the spiritual life there is Confirmation, in which the Holy Ghost is given to strengthen us . . . Thirdly, by nourishment, whereby life and strength are preserved to man; and corresponding to this in the spiritual life there is the Eucharist.
>
> (a. 1)

A human body sometimes falls victim to physical infirmity and requires healing; analogously, one's soul may become afflicted by spiritual infirmity, sin, and thereby require spiritual healing:

> One is the healing that restores health: and corresponding to this in the spiritual life there is Penance . . . The other is the restoration of former vigor by means of suitable diet and exercise: and corresponding to this in the spiritual life there is Extreme Unction, which removes the remainder of sin, and prepares man for final glory.
>
> (a. 1)

Finally, there are the sacraments related to the *communal* dimension of human life:

> In regard to the whole community, man is perfected in two ways. First, by receiving power to rule the community and to exercise public acts: and corresponding to this in the spiritual life there is the sacrament of Order . . . Secondly in regard to natural propagation. This is accomplished by Matrimony both in the corporal and in the spiritual life: since it is not only a sacrament but also a function of nature.
>
> (a. 1)

Thomas also notes that the seven sacraments may be related to various ways by which they remedy spiritual defects caused by sin. Additionally, they may be related to specific virtues or how they safeguard against certain vices.

QUESTIONS 66–SUPP. 68—THE SACRAMENTS IN PARTICULAR

The first group of sacraments listed above—Baptism, Confirmation, and Eucharist—are sometimes referred to as the sacraments *of initiation* insofar as they function collectively to bring a person into full communion with the Body of Christ. Baptism is the primary sacrament through which the stain of original sin is washed away by the grace of Christ's passion (q. 66, a. 2). It also effects the removal of all individual sins committed prior without requiring penance (q. 69, a. 1), as well as the infusion of grace and virtues (aa. 4–6), thereby opening the "gates of the heavenly kingdom" to the recipient (a. 7).

Insofar as Baptism denotes a "washing" (a. 1), Thomas affirms that the proper material sign of this spiritual effect is the use of *water* (aa. 3–4) along with the spoken formula, "I baptize thee in the name of the Father, and of the Son, and of the Holy Ghost" (a. 5). Since, as noted above, Baptism confers an *indelible character* upon the recipient and removes once and for all the stain of *original sin*, such that the recipient spiritually "dies" with Christ and "rises" to a new life oriented toward God, Baptism can be conferred only *once* in a person's lifetime (a. 9). While the grace conferred in Baptism does not guarantee that the recipient will never sin again as an individual—and thus the need for the sacrament of Penance—the original sin endemic to human nature due to the Fall has been permanently removed.

Although Baptism by water with the spoken formula invoking the Trinity is the *suitable* form of the sacramental ritual (a. 10), Thomas acknowledges that the spiritual effect can be realized in other forms (a. 11). First, a person who willingly suffers for love of Christ is baptized by virtue of sharing in Christ's passion—termed "Baptism of Blood." Second, a person who is moved by faith and charity, as infused by the Holy Spirit, toward belief in and love of God, with concomitant repentance of her sins, is said to be "Baptized by Repentance." Although Thomas considers an ordained priest or bishop to the appropriate minister of Baptism (q. 67, a. 2), he acknowledges that urgent circumstances, in which an unbaptized person is near death and an appropriate minister is not readily available, a lay person—preferably baptized herself, but even if unbaptized, may baptize another (aa. 3–5). This allowance is due to Thomas' recognition of the *necessity* of Baptism for salvation insofar as the salvific grace merited by Christ's passion can be conferred only through this sacrament (q. 68, a. 1); nevertheless, he allows multiple ways in the which the sacrament may take form and thus salvific grace could be conferred upon anyone who *freely desires* it "but by some ill-chance he is forestalled by death before receiving Baptism" (a. 2).

Due to the essential nature of this sacrament for salvation, Thomas affirms that its conferral should not be delayed in the case of children (q. 68, a. 3). It can be reasonably delayed, however, in the case of adults so that the Church can be assured of the sincerity of their conversion, provide appropriate instruction in the teachings of the faith (q. 71, a. 1), and welcome them into the Body of Christ at an appropriate communal celebration—typically at Easter or Pentecost. Thomas affirms the practice of baptizing children (a. 9), which is a point of debate among Christian denominations to this day; however, he considers it "contrary to natural justice" to baptize a child against his parents' will until the child attains the maturity to make his own *voluntary rational decision* (a. 10). Thomas' emphasis here on the importance of one's voluntary rational decision for Baptism—despite his allowance of infant baptism in cases where this is desired by the child's parents—also factors into his consideration of conferring the sacrament on those who have lost the use of their rational faculties such that they can no longer make an informed voluntary decision. In such cases, Thomas exhorts the Church to follow the individual's previously expressed wishes and thus to baptize *only if* one had expressed such a desire while possessing the use of reason: "If, on the other hand, while sane they showed no desire to receive Baptism, they must not be baptized" (a. 12).

Especially since Baptism may be conferred upon a child, who has not yet attained rational maturity, by the will of her parents, but even in the case of adults for whom Baptism is the *initial* sacrament through which they are welcomed into the Body of Christ, Thomas affirms the necessity of Confirmation as a sacrament by which one's communion with the Body of Christ is brought to fruition, exemplifying *maturity* in one's spiritual development (q. 72, a. 1). The visible matter involved in this sacrament is perfumed oil—termed "chrism"—that has been previously blessed and is administered by an ordained bishop on the recipient's forehead with the accompaniment of certain formal words (aa. 2–4, 9, 11). This *anointing* signifies the imprint of a spiritual character by which one may live her faith to the fullest extent in a public manner (a. 5).

The Eucharist, according to Thomas, is *the central* sacrament of the Christian community through which the members of the Church— the Body of Christ—are *unified* with each other and with Christ as their Head (q. 73, a. 2). Thomas considers the Eucharist to be the "consummation of the spiritual life" (a. 3), for it comprises the past— in commemorating Christ's passion—the present—in gathering the Church into unity—and the future—in prefiguring the "eternal glory" of humanity's loving union with God in heaven (q. 73, a. 4; q. 79, a. 2). Thomas conceptualizes the Eucharist as "spiritual food" (q. 73, a. 1; q. 79, a. 1) given to humanity directly by Christ in order to sustain and strengthen us in divine grace (q. 80, a. 10). Although it is not *necessary* for salvation in the way that Baptism is (q. 73, a. 3), he sees it as fulfilling the initiation into the Christian life that Baptism begins insofar as one who is baptized ought to desire to receive Christ in the Eucharist (q. 80, a. 11). Thomas' own desire for the Eucharist was so intense that he composed a full set of prayers and hymns for the feast of Corpus Christi—e.g. *Tantum ergo* and *Panis angelicus*—which can still be heard in Roman Catholic liturgical celebrations today.

The assertion that *Christ Himself* is present in the Eucharist stands in need of metaphysical explication. Thomas' importing of Aristotelian ontological concepts helps him to account for the reasonability of believing that when one receives bread and wine consecrated by an ordained priest or bishop (q. 82, a. 1) in the celebration of the Eucharist, one is actually—and not merely figuratively—receiving the body and blood of Christ (q. 75, a. 1). The metaphysical term describing the instantaneous change (q. 75, a. 7) that occurs when a priest or bishop speaks the formula of the words of consecration (q. 78) is *transubstantiation*: "The whole substance of the bread is changed into the whole substance of Christ's body, and the whole substance of the wine into the whole substance of Christ's blood" (q. 75, a. 4).

In natural occurrences of *substantial change*, a being composed of form and matter loses its substantial form, as when a human being dies because her body is no longer informed by her intellective soul—her body now identified, not as a "human body," but as a "corpse"—or a piece of wood, consumed by fire, ceases to bear the form of wood and has become a pile of ash. The *substance*—human being or wood—has ceased to exist and the matter that formerly composed the substance now constitutes a collection of decomposing organic parts or flakes of ash. In the case of Eucharistic transubstantiation, however, the *entire* form/matter composite that was once bread and wine becomes something completely different: the body and blood of Christ. While the bread and wine are not *annihilated* in this conversion—for then nothing at all would remain—they are *wholly* converted into Christ's body and blood, such that it would be improper to refer to what is present after the moment of consecration as either bread or wine (q. 75, a. 3). The only thing that persists through the change is a set of *accidental* qualities of dimension, texture, taste, odor, color, etc., such that the "appearance" of bread and wine remains (q. 75, a. 5; q. 77).

It is not as if Christ's body and blood are constantly being divided up in every Eucharistic celebration—as, say, the body of a saint may be divided into various relics placed in churches for veneration throughout the world. Rather, the sacramental presence of Christ's body and blood in the Eucharist is *without dimension* (q. 76, a. 4). Consider, by analogy, the color white as present in a volleyball, a blank piece of paper, or a flag of truce. There is no "supply" of whiteness from which these various items draw upon to instantiate this color in their matter. Furthermore, the whiteness *wholly* exists in each part of the colored surface area—cut off a small piece of a white flag and there is just as much whiteness in it as in the flag as a whole. Similarly, Thomas holds that Christ is wholly present in each consecrated piece of bread or drop of wine (aa. 1–3); and this does not detract from the simultaneous presence of His resurrected body in the heavenly kingdom after the ascension, since the Eucharistic presence is without dimension. Hence, it would be improper to say that Christ's body is *spatially located* in the consecrated bread (a. 5), such that it could be *moved* about (a. 6) or be *visible* except through the "spiritual eye" of one's intellect illuminated by faith (a. 7). The transubstantiated bread and wine, on the other hand, maintain their "dimensive quantity," by which they may bear the persistent accidental qualities of taste, color, etc., as well as being spatially located, moved about, and sensible (q. 77, a. 2).

While Thomas' account of Eucharistic transubstantiation may sound like metaphysical gerrymandering, consider the change of a living human body to a corpse. It is reasonable to construe the moment of death as a substantial change in which one thing—a living body composing a human person—has ceased to exist, and another thing—a collection of organic parts that will eventually disassociate from each other, i.e. a corpse—has come into existence. We certainly treat corpses very differently than we do living human bodies, even when the latter is quite close to death; and there are evident physical changes that ensue within a short time after death evidencing that a substantial, and not merely accidental, change has occurred. Nevertheless, the *moment* of death is not directly observable—physicians do not certify the moment of death, but rather the moment when it is certain that death *has* occurred at some past moment. At the moment death *actually* occurs, and for a short time thereafter, there may not be any perceptible change in the body under observation—particularly if certain vital functions are being artificially sustained but death has nonetheless occurred due to total absence of neurological function (see Chapter 11).

In short, a human body at the moment of death undergoes a substantial change without any evident change in various observable accidental qualities, such as dimension, color, texture, etc.—although a change in certain observable qualities is necessary in order to be able to declare death. Similarly, at the moment of consecration bread and wine undergo a substantial change—becoming the body and blood of

Christ—without any evident change in observable accidental qualities. Thomas admits that this change can be known only through *faith* since it is not perceptible and the natural mode of human knowing is through sense-perception: "The presence of Christ's true body and blood in this sacrament cannot be detected by sense, nor understanding, but by faith alone, which rests upon Divine authority" (q. 75, a. 1). He nonetheless defends the *reasonability* of believing that such a change occurs just as it is reasonable to believe that a living human body converts immediately into a corpse while evidently preserving various accidental qualities.

The next two sacraments—Penance and Extreme Unction— involve the administration of spiritual *healing* that is necessary due to human beings' propensity to commit individual sins even after the washing away of original sin through Baptism. Thomas likens these sacraments to the need for medical interventions to heal bodies that succumb to illness or injury. The sacrament of Penance—typically termed today "Reconciliation"—is offered regularly for the remission of sins for which one is sincerely repentant throughout the course of human life. Extreme Unction is intended solely for those approaching death as a means of ultimate reconciliation with God.

Penance is not essential for salvation in the way Baptism is insofar as a person only needs to avail herself of this sacrament if she should sin after having been baptized (q. 84, a. 5). Nor is it essential unless one has committed a *mortal* sin that has the effect of fundamentally disrupting one's relationship with God (q. 86, a. 2); although a form of everyday penance—which is a constituent of the celebration of the Eucharist—is essential for the remission of *venial* sin (q. 87, a. 1). Thomas also defines a *virtue* of penance whereby a penitent person is divinely infused with the disposition to regret her sin and so not be inclined to commit the same—or another—mortal sin again (q. 85). Nevertheless, cognizant that even a virtuous disposition does not necessarily entail virtuous action, Thomas acknowledges that the sacrament of Penance may be repeated as needed when one falls into a state of mortal sin (q. 84, a. 10).

Thomas defines three essential parts of the sacrament of Penance: contrition, confession, and satisfaction (q. 90, a. 2). These three parts are integrally related to each other (a. 3), which is evident in Thomas' definition of *contrition* as "an assumed sorrow for sins, together with the purpose of confessing them, and of making satisfaction for them" (Supp., q. 1, a. 1). The sins in question do not include original sin, the stain of which is removed through Baptism (q. 2, a. 2); nor can one be contrite about sins one has not yet committed (a. 4) or sins committed by someone else (a. 5). Thus, one should be contrite about all actual sins one has voluntarily committed himself (a. 3), especially mortal sins that fundamentally disrupt one's relationship with God (a. 6). It is essential, Thomas asserts, that one be contrite for the *sins* one has committed, and not simply be *fearful* of the punishment one may experience on account of his sins (a. 1). Finally, Penance is oriented not only toward the past insofar as one is sorry for the sins one has committed, but also toward the future insofar as the truly contrite person will be resolved—even though he may fail—not to sin again: "Now it belongs to penance to detest one's past sins, and to purpose, at the same time, to change one's life for the better, which is the end, so to speak, of penance" (IIIa, q. 90, a. 4).

Confession is another essential element for the forgiveness of actual mortal sins following upon contrition. Thomas likens Penance to Baptism insofar as both function for the remission of sins; and just as Baptism involves the mediation of the minister of the Church as an instrumental cause of divine grace being conferred, confession to a priest is a necessary instrumental cause of divine forgiveness being bestowed (Supp., q. 6, a. 1; q. 8, a. 1). The necessity of Penance being administered through the Church—as opposed to an individual penitent merely appealing to God for forgiveness through private petition—is recognized by Thomas to follow scripturally from when Christ bestows upon Peter, as the first of the Apostles, the "keys of the kingdom of heaven" (Matthew 26:19), thereby authorizing the Apostles and their successors "the power of binding and loosing" the faithful from their sins (q. 17, aa. 1–2). Thomas further affirms that the ordinary minister of Penance is an ordained priest, upon whom is conferred the power to "absolve [the penitent] from any sins whatever" (q. 20, a. 2); nevertheless, just as in the case of Baptism, any lay person could be an appropriate minister in case of necessity when no priest is present (q. 8, a. 2). Confession, followed by the absolution conferred through the minister of divine grace, delivers the penitent from sin and any concomitant punishment, thereby opening to her the gates of heaven and providing her with hope of salvation (q. 10).

The third essential element of Penance is *satisfaction*, in which the penitent renders to God some due recompense for his sin as a matter of justice (IIIa, q. 86, a. 4; Supp., q. 12, a. 2). Performing such works preserves the forgiven penitent from eternal punishment; however, *temporal* punishments—in this life or in purgatory (see Chapter 10)—may still be appropriate in order to purify one's soul before entering into loving communion with God (Supp., q. 14, a. 5). Temporal punishments may be mitigated, however, through the granting of spiritual "indulgences" (q. 25), which became a scandal for the Church when such indulgences were being sold for financial profit, leading to the righteous complaint of Martin Luther (1483–1546).

Extreme Unction is a sacrament aimed at "the healing of the disease of sin" (q. 29, a. 1), specifically to prepare one "for glory immediately, since it is given to those who are departing from this life" (a. 1 *ad* 2). It is more commonly known today as the sacrament of "Anointing of the Sick" since it is no longer administered only in cases where the recipient is near death, contrary to the practice in Thomas' time (q. 32, a. 2). Also contrary to Thomas' exhortation is the current practice of anointing a sick individual even if she is not lucid or conscious at all, as well as anointing children (aa. 3–4).

As with Confirmation, the material used in the sacrament is oil—although olive oil in this case signifying the soothing effects of a healing balm (q. 29, a. 4)—which has been consecrated by a bishop (aa. 5–6), accompanied by a spoken formula petitioning God to forgive the recipient's sins (aa. 7–9). As a "petition," the effect of this sacrament differs from the sacrament of Penance insofar as the forgiveness of sin is assured in the latter by the words of absolution spoken by the priest as the minister of God's grace in response to the penitent's sincere contrition and confession of her sins. In the case of Extreme Unction, however, insofar as it is administered to a dying person, the sincerity of her repentance is presumed rather than known, and thus God's forgiveness is *asked for* rather than bestowed by the minister's words—the appropriate minister being an ordained priest or bishop (q. 31).

Thomas notes that, while the primary effect of Extreme Unction is remission of sin (q. 30, a. 1), the sacrament may have a secondary effect of bodily healing insofar as the latter may be required—according to divine reason—for the former to occur (a. 2). One may conjecture, for example, that administration of this sacrament to a conscious or semi-conscious individual, aware of the minister having prayed for the forgiveness of her sins, provides a calming effect on both her body and psyche, such that she more willingly repents of her sins, accepts her impending death, and thereby becomes ready to enter into the divine presence. Whereas an individual suffering physical or emotional torment as he nears death, without the benefit of this sacrament, may despair of hope in God's forgiveness and thereby deprive himself of reconciliation before his death, as well as a peaceful transition.

The final two sacraments involve the basic social structuring of the Church and human society. The sacrament of Orders defines those upon whom specific graces are conferred so that they may in turn confer graces upon others through the sacraments, as well as delineating a hierarchy of ecclesiastical authority within the institution of the Church. Matrimony is the sacrament that defines the most basic social unit of human society— namely, the *family*—and thus refers not only to the loving union of two consenting individuals, but also to the begetting of children within the marital union.

Thomas defines Orders—sometimes termed "Holy Orders"—as the sacrament whereby the ordained becomes "the dispenser of the other sacraments" (q. 34, a. 3). He conceptualizes each ordained ministry—deacon, priest, and bishop—to fulfill specific spiritual tasks, just as different parts of the human body perform certain operations (a. 1; q. 37, aa. 1–2). He understands this sacrament to result in an indelible imprint upon one's character insofar as "each Order sets a man above the people in some degree of authority directed to the dispensation of the sacraments" (q. 35, a. 2). It is worth emphasizing that the type of authority to which Thomas refers relates directly to the administration of the sacraments; hence, while appropriate *ecclesiastical* authority is conferred on those ordained, it is not a *political* authority. Furthermore, such authority is not a reward for merit (a. 36, a. 3), and there is great responsibility on the part of both the ordained and he who ordains—namely, a bishop (q. 38, a. 1)— not to confer this office while conscious of the recipient being in a state of mortal sin (q. 36, aa. 1, 4), as well as for the ordained not to exercise his office while in a state of mortal sin (a. 5).

Insofar as it constitutes a position of ecclesiastical authority, Thomas holds that women cannot receive this sacrament (q. 39, a. 1), even though he recognizes that women can and do hold positions involving "temporal power" (a. 1 *ad* 2–3). Thomas' historically conditioned reasoning for his position does not bear on the question of women's ordination in the Church today. Furthermore, while his disallowance of boys who have not yet attained an age of mature reasoning to be ordained is premised upon a sound rationale of informed consent (a. 2), and his disallowance of those who are guilty of homicide makes sense given the ordained minister's role as a moral exemplar (a. 4); other reasons for disbarment from this sacrament are not so soundly based and are no longer followed in the Church today, such as being of illegitimate birth (a. 5) or lacking external bodily parts such that one's appearance is not "comely" (a. 6).

Thomas considers the sacrament of Matrimony to be a natural mode of relation for human beings for two primary reasons: 1) for the good of offspring, and 2) for the mutual services married individuals render each other in the household community (q. 41, a. 1), the latter of which includes spouses' *mutual faithfulness* to each other (q. 49, a. 2). As such, he sees it not merely as a "remedy against sin"—like all the other sacraments (q. 42, a. 1)—but also as a natural constituent of human society given the original complementarity of the male and female sexes even before the Fall (a. 2); thus, in the story of Genesis, Adam and Eve could be said to have been married in the Garden (a. 2 *ad* 4).

The efficient cause of Matrimony is the *expressed consent* of the parties being conjoined (q. 45, aa. 1–2), which is premised upon the "inward consent" of each (a. 4), such that one may not be forced into a marriage—whether out of compulsion or fear—who does not consent to it, even if he or she were to express insincere words of consent publicly (q. 47). Since one's internal consent cannot be perceived by external authorities in order to recognize the existence of a marriage, Thomas affirms the necessity of *sexual consummation* as an external sign of both parties having consented to marriage (q. 46, a. 2). Nevertheless, Thomas is clear that consent to marriage includes only "implicit" consent to sexual union, thereby requiring further consent for the latter (q. 48, a. 1). This leaves open the possibility of sinful sexual activity—e.g. rape—within the marital context.

Furthermore, Thomas considers sexual activity, even within the marital context, to be sinful if it is not done with an *actual* or *habitual* intention of potentially conceiving a child and in a spirit of mutual faithfulness, but rather only in pursuit of individual pleasure (q. 49, aa. 4–6). The distinction between "actual" and "habitual" intention refers to the marital couple being able to engage in sexual intercourse licitly either with the (actual) intention of attempting to conceive a child deliberately or with the (habitual) intention not to interfere deliberately with the natural process by which conception might occur (a. 5 *ad* 1). Thus, a couple need not deliberately intend to try to conceive a child with each and every sexual act. In contrast to objectors who claim that "consent to pleasure is a mortal sin" (a. 6 *obj.* 2) and thus a married couple cannot have sex "for mere pleasure" (*obj.* 1), Thomas acknowledges the inherent goodness of pleasure when concomitant with a morally good act. He thereby concludes that a married couple may engage in intercourse for the immediate purpose of sexual gratification, so long as the act stems from mutual faithfulness and the couple retains the habitual intention of procreation. While the validity of Thomas' viewpoint is debatable, it perseveres today as an underlying rationale—though not the only one—for the Roman Catholic Church's teaching against the use of artificial means of contraception.

Since marriage is a sacrament not effected externally by the ordained minister, who functions as the Church's *witness* to the sacrament, but rather internally by the mutually consenting spouses, there may be certain impediments to the sacramental union (q. 50). First, one party may not be in a position to freely consent due to either being forced into the union or being ignorant of certain information that would affect his or her decision to marry their intended spouse (q. 51)—e.g. that the latter is a drug addict or alcoholic, or has a violent criminal record; or one of the potential spouses may not be able to voluntarily consent due to either mental illness (q. 58, a. 3) or immaturity (a. 5). Second, there may be physical inability to consummate the marriage, since the sexual act is an intrinsic part of marriage for the sake of begetting offspring (q. 58, a. 1); of course, there are medical treatments to remedy such conditions today and it is not directly evident how Thomas would have considered cases of infertility—although some contemporary Thomists have taken up this question in light of Thomas' general principles. Third, one may be legally inhibited from entering into marriage due to a vow of celibacy (q. 53)—as in the case of an ordained priest or bishop—or because he or she is already married to another, as Thomas holds bigamy and polygamy to be contrary to the essential nature of marriage (qq. 65–66). Fourth, Thomas considers "disparity of worship" to be an impediment to marriage, such that a faithful Christian cannot marry an unbeliever (q. 59, a. 1). Another impediment he affirms is close familial relationship: whether by blood (*consanguinity*) (q. 54); by law, e.g. one's sister-in-law (*affinity*) (q. 55) or adopted child (q. 57); or by sacrament, e.g. one's godparent (q. 56). Finally, he considers having previously engaged in an adulterous relationship with one's intended spouse to be an impediment to a valid sacramental marriage.

All of the above-named impediments prevent one from entering into a valid sacramental marriage. Thus, if two persons marry despite the presence of one of these impediments—regardless of whether they are of aware of it—their marriage is not considered valid and they could attain a public declaration of such by the Church—known as an "annulment." To clarify, an annulment does not invalidate a marriage, but rather declares that there was not a valid marriage in the first place due to the presence of one of the above impediments. If a validly married couple decide to legally divorce each other for some reason—e.g. one of the spouses is unfaithful (q. 62, a. 3)—neither spouse may marry another unless grounds for annulment are discovered (a. 5). Marriage, however, lasts only until death; thus, an individual may validly marry again after the death of his or her spouse (q. 63).

The sacraments of the Church function as instrumental causes mediating the infusion of divine grace merited through Christ's passion. The incarnation and passion of the Second Person of the Trinity, while not absolutely necessary to effect humanity's salvation from original sin, was deemed by divine wisdom to be the most appropriate way of providing us with the justification and sanctification necessary for us to be able to fulfill our natural inclination toward happiness in this life and beatitude in God's loving presence in the next. We will now turn to Thomas' discussion of how our life after death—as prefigured by Christ's resurrection—comes about and what form it takes for various individuals as judged by divine providence.

SUGGESTIONS FOR FURTHER READING

Helpful resources for Thomas' Christology and sacramental theology can be found in Rik van Nieuwenhove and Joseph Wawrykow, eds.,

The Theology of Thomas Aquinas (Norte Dame, IN: University of Notre Dame Press, 2005); Joseph Bobik, *Veritas Divina: Aquinas on Divine Truth* (South Bend, IN: St. Augustine's Press, 2001), Chs. 6–9; and Matthew Levering and Michael Dauphinais, eds., *Rediscovering Aquinas and the Sacraments* (Chicago: Hillenbrand Books, 2009). Another excellent and thorough resource for Thomas' overall theological and spiritual worldview is Jean-Pierre Torrell, *Saint Thomas Aquinas – Vol. 2: Spiritual Master*, trans. Robert Royal (Washington, D.C.: Catholic University of America Press, 2003).

The Chalcedonian Christological formula can be found in its complete statement in Norman Tanner, ed., *Decrees of the Ecumenical Councils* (Washington, D.C.: Georgetown University Press, 1990), vol. 1, p. 86.

For a thorough treatment of Christ's experience of human passions in IIIa, q. 15, see Nicholas E. Lombardo, *The Logic of Desire: Aquinas on Emotion* (Washington, D.C.: Catholic University of America Press, 2011), Ch. 7.

A detailed explication of Thomas' metaphysical account of Eucharistic transubstantiation is provided by Reinhard Hütter, "Transubstantiation Revisited: *Sacra Doctrina*, Dogma, and Metaphysics" in *Resourcement Thomism: Sacred Doctrine, the Sacraments, and the Moral Life*, eds. Reinhard Hütter and Matthew Levering (Washington, D.C.: Catholic University of America Press, 2010), 21–79.

A contemporary analysis of Thomas' view of the nature of marriage and sexual morality is provided by John Finnis, "The Good of Marriage and the Morality of Sexual Relations: Some Philosophical and Historical Observations" *American Journal of Jurisprudence* 42 (1998): 97–134.

10

LIFE AND JUDGMENT
AFTER DEATH

PREFACE

Thomas provides an account of human immortality, bodily resurrection, and final judgment intended to be both faithful to Christian Scripture and philosophically sound in light of the Aristotelian view of human nature. Unfortunately, while we have the benefit of Thomas' arguments for a human soul's persistence beyond its body's death in the *prima pars*, he died before completing the final part of the *Summa*, and so we lack what would have been his most mature thinking on the doctrine of bodily resurrection and the ultimate disposition of the dead once raised. Instead, a *supplementum*—appended by his secretary, Reginald of Piperno—reproduces the latter half of Thomas' commentary on Book Four of the *Sentences* of Peter Lombard, which is one of Thomas' earliest works. The English-language edition translated by the English Dominican Fathers—from which I have drawn the quotations used in this guidebook—also includes two brief appendices comprising two questions and a couple of additional articles compiled by another of Thomas' students from his *Sentences* commentary. These appendices concern, first, the now defunct theological concept of "limbo" for those who die in a state of original sin alone— e.g. unbaptized children (App. I, q. 1)—and, second, purgatory (App. I, q. 2; II, aa. 1–2). Due to the lack of a definitive final statement on these various topics, it remains an open question for contemporary Thomistic scholars how his view of the resurrection's metaphysical mechanics and the implementation of divine justice may have developed from his earlier treatment.

SUPP. QUESTIONS 69–86—IMMORTALITY OF THE HUMAN SOUL AND BODILY RESURRECTION

Thomas' definition of a human being's death is premised upon an intellective soul's *unitive* function as its body's substantial form (Ia, q. 76)—bringing all of a human body's heterogeneous parts into a functionally integrated whole. *Corruptibility* follows, however, insofar as an intellective soul does not *perfectly* inform its body; Thomas considers this a consequence of the Fall (Supp., q. 75, a. 1 *ad* 5), as well as resulting from the natural progression of time (Supp., q. 86, a. 2 *ad* 1). As a result, material defects can arise in the body that eventually make it unsuitable for being informed by an intellective soul, through its becoming unable to actualize the soul's vegetative capacities. The observable criterion for determining the occurrence of this metaphysical event is the cessation of respiratory activity: "The union of soul and body ceases at the cessation of breath, not because this is the means of union, but because of the removal of that disposition by which the body is disposed for such a union" (Ia, q. 76, a. 7 *ad* 2).

Death occurs the moment one's soul ceases to inform her body, entailing a *substantial change*. The remaining matter no longer composes a "human body," but a "corpse" subject to decay. The soul, as a subsistent immaterial form, continues to function intellectively and eventually re-informs its resurrected body (Ia, q. 75, a. 6; q. 89). Thomas' account of human post-mortem existence thus has two components. First, at death, one's intellective soul separates from its body but continues to exist and function intellectively and volitionally; since the intellect and will do not require a bodily organ in order to function (Ia, q. 75, a. 2; q. 76, a. 1 *ad* 1; q. 80, a. 2 *ad* 2). After the soul's separation, the body—now a corpse—no longer has substantial unity, but is reduced to its constituent elements that will separate from each other as it decays (Ia, q. 76, a. 8). The second component is *resurrection*, in which the soul informs matter provided by God to compose the numerically same human being in her *perfected* state. In this state, her soul fully informs her body, such that the body is now "glorified" and thereby takes on qualities it did not have during its earthly life due to sin. Hence, there will be significant qualitative differences between one's pre-mortem and post-resurrection body. Such differences, however, will not result in the resurrected body being non-physical in nature or unrecognizable as that of a particular human being (Supp., qq. 81–85).

Thomas contends that a separated intellective soul can, by virtue of its own intrinsic capacities, reflect upon intellectual knowledge it had already gained in its pre-mortem life and thereby gain insight and new knowledge by reaching conclusions through discursive reasoning (Ia, q. 89, aa. 5–6). Additionally, with divine assistance, it can cognize new intelligible forms directly infused in it by God (Ia, q. 89, a. 1 *ad* 3); and, upon being granted knowledge of the divine nature, it can will to love God as the source of perfect happiness (Ia, q. 82, a. 2; Ia–IIae, q. 3, a. 2).

Thomas nevertheless argues that resurrection is metaphysically necessary insofar as a separated soul does not possess the complete nature of the human species; for the human essence includes both an intellective soul and a material body the soul informs in order to exercise its vegetative and sensitive capacities. Thomas thus conceives of a separated soul, due to its essentially being the substantial form of a particular human body, to have a natural "longing" for reunion with its body (Ia, q. 76, a. 1 *ad* 6); although the reverse is not the case, the decomposed elements of one's body do not have a natural inclination toward reunion with the same soul (Supp., q. 78, a. 3). Accepting as a basic principle of Aristotelian metaphysics that no natural desire can persist forever in vain, Thomas concludes that a separated soul must be reunited to the body at some point. Nevertheless, Thomas contends that since matter on its own does not have the capacity to unite itself with an intellective soul, it must be provided to the soul by God (Supp., q. 78, a. 3). Once provided with matter to inform, the soul functions as the *formal cause*—the "blueprint," one could loosely say—for the qualitatively and numerically same body to be resurrected out of such matter (Supp., q. 79, aa. 1–2).

That a quantity of matter composes a *human* resurrected body is sufficiently formally caused by virtue of its being informed by an intellective soul, due to the soul's essential function as the "blueprint" for its body: "whatever appears in the parts of the body is all contained originally, and, in a way, implicitly in the soul" (Supp., q. 80, a. 1). The soul's formal plan for its body guarantees that the matter provided to compose the resurrected body conforms to what Thomas refers to as "the truth of human nature":

> What is in man materially, is not directed to the resurrection, except in so far as it belongs to the truth of human nature, because it is in this respect that it bears a relation to the human souls. Now all that is in man materially belongs indeed to the truth of human nature in so far as it has something of the species, but not all, if we consider the totality of matter; because all the matter that was in a man from the beginning of his life to the end would surpass the quantity due his species . . . Wherefore the whole of what is in man will rise again, if we speak of the totality of the species which is dependent on quantity, shape, position and the order of parts, but the whole will not rise again if we speak of the totality of matter.
>
> (Supp., q. 80, a. 5)

Thomas thus explains why a resurrected body need not be composed of *all* the matter that had previously composed it throughout its earthly life. On this view, a resurrected body is composed of all that is essential to the specific nature of a human body: it will have all the requisite organs properly functioning; all the parts of the body will be spatially related to one another in the right way; and the body will be such that an intellective soul is able to reanimate it and carry out all of its essential functions for which it needs the body's organs.

Not only is all of the matter that composed one's pre-mortem body not needed to compose one's resurrected body, but also matter may compose one's resurrected body which had never previously composed one's pre-mortem body (Supp., q. 80, a. 4 *ad* 3). Thomas notes that the material constituents of a living organism are in continuous flux. Organisms undergo cellular decay, and food is taken in and transformed by digestion into raw material to generate new cells and other bodily components:

Now it is manifest that the human form can cease to exist in this (particular) matter which is its subject . . . Consequently it can begin to exist in another matter, so that something else be changed into true human nature.

(Ia, q. 119, a. 1)

As long as there is material *continuity*, the same substantial form and the same body persist through such changes in micro-level constituents. Thomas compares the "ebb and flow" of an organism's constituents to a fire:

[W]hen a certain matter is directly transformed into fire, then fire is said to be generated anew: but when matter is transformed into a fire already existing, then fire is said to be fed. Wherefore if the entire matter together loses the form of fire, and another matter transformed into fire, there will be another distinct fire. But if, while one piece of wood is burning, other wood is laid on, and so on until the first piece is entirely consumed, the same identical fire will remain all the time: because that which is added passes into what pre-existed. It is the same with living bodies, in which by means of nourishment that is renewed which was consumed by natural heat.

(Ia, q. 119, a. 1 *ad* 5; cf. Supp., q. 79, a. 3; q. 80, a. 4)

Of course, a human being loses all of her matter at death, and so there is no continuity of material constituents between her pre-mortem and resurrected body as in the case of a continuously burning fire. Thomas nevertheless asserts that matter can be "changed into true human nature" by virtue of being informed by an intellective soul (Supp., q. 80, a. 4). He further contends that Christ's resurrection provides testimony of God's omnipotence in this regard:

Christ rose from the tomb by Divine power, which is not narrowed within bounds. Consequently, His rising from the grave was a sufficient argument to prove that men are to be raised up by Divine power, not only from their graves, but also from any dust whatsoever.

(IIIa, q. 51, a. 3 *ad* 3)

A pertinent theological question raised by this passage regards whether Christ's resurrected body is composed of the same material constituents that had composed it at death. In other words, if Christ's soul could have informed *any* matter to constitute His resurrected body, then what happened to the matter composing the body that lay in the tomb for three days? It should first be noted that although God may utilize any matter to constitute one's resurrected body, Thomas clearly asserts that God *could* utilize the same material constituents as had composed one's body at death (Supp., q. 78, a. 2; q. 79, a. 1 *ad* 3–4; q. 79, a. 3 *ad* 2). Furthermore, Thomas contends that Christ's body did not suffer decomposition as do other dead bodies (IIIa, q. 51, a. 3). Hence, to use one of Thomas' favorite terms, it seems only "fitting" that God would have resurrected Christ through His soul re-informing the exact same matter composing the body lying in the tomb. The phrase, "God would have resurrected Christ," is somewhat tortured insofar as, according to Thomas, Christ effected His own resurrection insofar as He is God; nevertheless, Thomas allows for this phrasing when the reunification of Christ's soul and body is viewed within the context of the power of created nature (IIIa, q. 53, a. 4).

Perhaps, then, the same will follow for all other human beings whose bodies are preserved somewhat intact on the Day of Resurrection— for example, particular saints whose bodies have been miraculously preserved *incorruptible*. Note, however, that while Thomas affirms that Christ's dead and resurrected body remains identical insofar as Christ did not separate from His body at death (IIIa, q. 50, a. 2)— although His soul did separate and descend into hell—Christ's body did not remain identical insofar as it ceased to be a *living* body upon His death and life is an *essential* property of a human body (IIIa, q. 50, a. 5). Since the latter condition would follow for all other human beings, but not the former, we cannot cross-compare without qualification the metaphysics of resurrection for Christ and for other human beings. Nevertheless, the fact that Christ's resurrection prefigures— and in fact is the mediating cause of—our own provides some basis for comparison when appropriate (Supp., q. 76, a. 1). Furthermore, when the question arises whether Christ's body was a "true body" after His resurrection, Thomas does not appeal to the sameness of the material constituents composing both the body in the tomb and the resurrected body that appeared to Mary Magdalene, the Eleven, *et alia*; rather, he appeals to the sameness of *form* (IIIa, q. 54, a. 1). In sum, the numerically same soul is sufficient for the numerically same body to be resurrected by virtue of the soul informing matter provided by God to constitute the resurrected body, just as it suffices for the numerically same human being to persist through time and change.

What does Thomas say about the nature of the disembodied intellective soul persisting between death and resurrection? Does a person *survive* between death and resurrection composed of her soul alone, or is a person *corrupted* at death and only her soul exists through this interim state until the person returns to existence upon her body's resurrection? This is actually a matter of interpretive debate among contemporary Thomistic scholars, some of whom affirm the former position ("survivalism"), while others affirm the latter ("corruptionism").

On one hand, Thomas attributes many "personal" qualities to a separated human soul, such as enjoying the rewards of heaven or suffering the pains of hell, being capable of understanding and choosing, as well as appearing to the living and responding to their prayers (Supp., q. 69, aa. 2–5; q. 70, aa. 2–3; q. 72, a. 2). He does make a curious equivocation, though, when it comes to the question of *prayer*. At one point, he responds to an objection without denying the objector's claim that,

> the soul of Peter is not Peter. If therefore the souls of the saints pray for us, so long as they are separated from their bodies, we ought not call upon Saint Peter, but on his soul, to pray for us.
>
> (IIa–IIae, q. 83, a. 11 *obj.* 5)

But Thomas asserts at another point that "prayer is an act, and acts belong to particular persons" (Supp., q. 72, a. 2 *ad* 3).

It is arguable that an intellective soul's persistent existence is *sufficient* for a person's existence. Thomas holds that an intellective soul communicates its existence to a material body such that there is one existence of a composite substance—a human person:

> But the human soul retains the being of the composite after the destruction of the body: and this because the being of the form is the same as that of its matter, and this is the being of the composite. Now the soul subsists in its own being . . . It follows, therefore, that after being separated from the body it has perfect being, and that consequently it can have a perfect operation; although it has not the perfect specific nature.
>
> (Ia–IIae, q. 4, a. 5 *ad* 2)

The persistent "being of the composite" in the separated soul also partly accounts for the numerical identity of the resurrected body. Thomas thus concludes, "Consequently there has been no interruption in the substantial being of man, as would make it impossible for the selfsame man to return on account of an interruption in his being" (Supp., q. 79, a. 2 *ad* 1).

The question remains, however, whether the persistence of "the substantial being of man" in the separated soul suffices for the soul to count as *the person*? For Thomas emphatically asserts that a human person is not identical to her soul (Ia, q. 75, a. 4). Contemporary Thomists thus continue to debate not only whether "survivalism" or "corruptionism" is the proper way to understand Thomas' explicitly held view, but also which is the more metaphysically coherent position to hold.

Regardless of the resolution of this interpretive debate, Thomas clearly holds that the capacities for intellective thought and volition can be had by an intellective soul itself (Ia, q. 77, a. 5). Nevertheless, he thinks that, even if certain capacities belong to a soul itself, it is still to a human being that their actual operations are attributable (Ia, q. 75, a. 2 *ad* 2)—hence, Thomas' assertion that, because prayer is an *act*, it is ascribed to particular persons. Thomas finds this to be important for the sake of a human being's moral responsibility for her actions: "Operation, properly speaking, is not ascribed to the part but to the whole, wherefore the reward [or punishment] is due, not to the part but to the whole" (Supp., q. 79, a. 3 *ad* 3). Thomas thus considers bodily resurrection to be *morally*, as well as metaphysically, necessary (Supp., q. 75, a. 1 *ad* 3). Thomas allows, however, for a separated soul to experience reward or punishment on its own prior to the resurrection since the soul has in itself the capacities for intellection and volition from which all moral acts (*actiones humanae*) proceed (Ia–IIae, q. 1, a. 1).

SUPP. QUESTIONS 87–99—THE WORLD TO COME: HEAVEN, HELL, AND PURGATORY

Thomas deals extensively with not only the resurrection of a human person's body, but the necessity of such in order that persons may experience either perfect happiness (*beatitudo*) in the Beatific Vision, temporal purification for sins prior to the final state of *beatitudo*, or eternal punishment merited through their pre-mortem existence. Of particular concern to Thomas is his notion that the human body's resurrection is necessary for judgment of the dead to occur and divine justice to be properly fulfilled (Supp., qq. 87–90); the human soul alone not being a sufficient recipient of judgment. Nevertheless, as discussed above, Thomas holds that the soul experiences an *interim state* between the death and resurrection of the body: "the resurrection of men will be delayed until the end of the world when the heavens shall be broken" (Supp., q. 77, a. 1 *s.c.*). There is thus a *temporal gap* between the body's death and resurrection during which the soul exists separate from its body. The next question concerns whether the soul *experiences* anything during this interim period, or whether it exists in a state of "sleep" awaiting its body's resurrection.

For Thomas, the separated soul is anything but asleep. Although the body's resurrection will not occur for some time after death, the soul "receives at once its reward or punishment . . . as soon as the soul is set free from the body it is either plunged into hell or soars to heaven" (Supp., q. 69, a. 2). The soul's "reward or punishment" consists of the Beatific Vision in heaven (Supp., qq. 92–96), the "fire" of hell (Supp., qq. 97–99), or a period of "cleansing" in purgatory before its final ascension into heaven (App., I, q. 1; II, aa. 1–2). Thomas contends that the souls of the damned not only proceed immediately to hell, but suffer *corporeal* hellfire by being conjoined to the matter of the fire by God's power in order to fulfill divine justice:

corporeal hellfire is enabled as the instrument of the vengeance of Divine justice thus to detain a spirit; and thus it has a penal effect on it, by hindering it from fulfilling its own will, that is by hindering it from acting where it will and as it will.

(Supp., q. 70, a. 3)

Thomas thus recognizes a very distinctive type of experience for a separated soul consigned to hell. It suffers the pain of corporeal fire by being joined to the matter of the fire as it was previously joined to the matter of its body; however, it is not joined in the same *mode* as it was joined to its body. The soul does not *inform* the matter of the fire, but rather is joined to it as *in a place*: "In this way created incorporeal spirits are confined to a place, being in one place in such a way as not to be in another" (Supp., q. 70, a. 3). Thus, the soul experiences torment in the sense that the "body" of the fire fetters the soul to it, through divine power, and makes it such that the separated soul cannot exercise one of its fundamental attributes as a spiritual substance—namely, to be able to move itself from place to place unfettered by matter.

Thomas describes a similar type of distinctive experience of joyous reward by the separated souls of the blessed. They experience perfect happiness in the Beatific Vision of God's pure essence (Supp., q. 92). Thomas, here, reflects the accounts given in Scripture: "For now we see in a mirror dimly, but then we will see face to face. Now I know in part; then I will know fully, even as I have been fully known" (1 Corinthians 13:12); "they will see his face, and his name will be on their foreheads" (Revelation 22:4). For souls in purgatory, Thomas describes a twofold punishment: delay of the Beatific Vision and punishment by corporeal fire for the expiation of sin (App., I, q. 2, a. 1).

Because the separated soul is able to have such experiences, Thomas must provide a metaphysical mechanism by which the soul is able to have an intellectual understanding of these types of experiences: whether corporeal fire or God's essence. In our pre-mortem life, Thomas requires the body's sensory organs to provide the intellect with particular sensible objects from which it abstracts universal intelligible concepts (Ia, q. 85, a. 1). How, then, can a separated soul experience either corporeal fire or the Beatific Vision as intelligible concepts without bodily sense organs? Thomas responds that such post-mortem experiences are *directly* experienced by the soul in the same way that angels—as purely intellectual substances—are able to apprehend intelligible objects: that is, through direct *infusion* by God (Ia, q. 89, a. 1). Thomas emphasizes, however, that this is not the soul's *normal* mode of understanding, and so maintains the appropriateness of bodily resurrection for the soul to intellectively function in its proper mode.

Divine justice requires that each human person, after death, receive reward or punishment related to her having lived either a virtuous or a sinful life. Thomas contends that the soul alone, in which the powers of understanding and volition are exercised, is a proper recipient of such reward or punishment. Nevertheless, the soul alone does not fully constitute the nature of a human person. Hence, although it could be said in one sense that a soul itself wills to sin, since the power of volition belongs to the soul; it is more properly said that a *person* sins, through her body actualizing the volitions of her soul. Without a body, a soul's volition to murder someone would have no effect. Thus, it should be said that the *whole* person is the agent of either virtue or sin and, therefore, that the person-as-a-whole is the proper recipient of divine justice:

> The soul is compared to the body, not only as a worker to the instrument with which he works, but also as form to matter: wherefore the work belongs to the composite and not to the soul alone ... And since to the worker is due the reward of the work, it behooves man himself, who is composed of soul and body, to receive the reward of his work.
>
> (Supp., q. 75, a. 1 *ad* 3)

Thomas thereby concludes that "the resurrection is necessary in order that those who rise again may receive punishment or reward according to their merits" (Supp., q. 75, a. 2).

The fulfillment of divine justice, the experience of reward or punishment, is manifested in two ways relative to the two types of merit. If a person merits reward, she enjoys the full perfection of her human nature and the Beatific Vision. For the other type of merit, the punishment of hell for sinful persons, Thomas argues that the hellfire experienced by the separated soul is not sufficient to account for the whole sinful person experiencing punishment. For the damned to be properly punished according to divine justice, bodily resurrection must occur. Thomas further asserts that the suffering of a resurrected damned person will be *corporeal* as well as spiritual:

> whatever we may say of the fire that torments the separated souls, we must admit that the fire which will torment the bodies of the damned after the resurrection is corporeal, since one cannot fittingly apply a punishment to a body unless that punishment itself be bodily.
>
> (Supp., q. 97, a. 5)

A question now arises concerning the nature of the resurrected bodies of the damned. Thomas affirms two essential requirements of such a body: 1) that it be *incorruptible*, since punishment is eternal (Supp., q. 86, a. 2); and 2) that it be *passible*—i.e. it is capable of suffering corporeal hellfire (a. 3). According to basic natural physics, these two requirements are incommensurable, because fire affects bodies by *consuming* them. Hence, it would seem that corporeal hellfire would eventually consume the resurrected body, and thus it would pass into non-existence. It would be corruptible.

Thomas responds that the resurrected bodies of the damned will not suffer corruption for two reasons. First, the soul *perfectly* informs the resurrected body (Supp., q. 81, a. 1). As noted above, in the pre-mortem state, the body undergoes changes that eventually result in its being an unsuitable recipient of the soul's vegetative powers and death ensues. This is a result of humanity's sinful nature, in which the soul *imperfectly* informs the body. Post-resurrection, God provides for the soul's perfectly informing the body such that it could never be altered in any way not proper to the soul's powers; the soul's power of informing its resurrected body cannot be overcome by any external material agent. This conclusion applies to the resurrected bodies of the damned as well as the blessed (Supp., q. 86, a. 1); hence, the resurrected bodies of the damned cannot be consumed by hellfire. Second, Thomas argues that the damned can suffer from hellfire in terms of receiving the *form* of the fire—with its essential burning characteristics—without taking on the *nature* of the hellfire itself—i.e. being consumed by means of the fire converting the body's matter into the matter of fire (Supp., q. 86, a. 3).

CONCLUSION

This concludes our exploration through Thomas Aquinas' *Summa theologiae*. With the overcoming of original sin through the grace conferred by means of Christ's salvific sacrifice and mediated through the sacraments of the Church, the return (*reditus*) of a human being to the source of her creation—loving union with God—is made possible. Actualizing this possibility, however, requires each human being to understand intellectually what goods she ought to pursue in order to realize her flourishing as a rational animal in her pre-mortem life, as well as to open herself up to divine grace that will allow her to attain perfect happiness in the life to come. Having a proper understanding of what is objectively good for her to pursue, she must then exercise her will accordingly, not allowing inordinate passion or vice to preclude her willful pursuit of happiness/beatitude. Ordering her passions accordingly and eliminating vices from her moral character requires the cultivation of specific virtues—most essentially the cardinal virtues of prudence, justice, fortitude, and temperance—in cooperation with divinely infused moral virtues and the preeminent theological virtues of faith, hope, and charity. In brief, the universe, as well as each person who populates the universe, has been created as an act of divine love; and it is only through willful love that each one of us will attain the perfect fulfillment of our natural desire to be united with the loving source of our existence. This is the overarching take-home lesson of Thomas' *Summa*.

SUGGESTIONS FOR FURTHER READING

For a contemporary rendering of Thomas' understanding of a human being's death, see Jason T. Eberl, "A Thomistic Understanding of Human Death" *Bioethics* 19:1 (2005): 29–48.

An in-depth analysis of Thomas' account of the human soul's immortality can be found in J. Obi Oguejiofor, *The Philosophical Significance of Immortality in Thomas Aquinas* (New York: University Press of America, 2001).

A collection of accounts of the "incorruptible" bodies of various saints can be found in Joan Carroll Cruz, *The Incorruptibles: A Study of the Incorruption of the Bodies of Various Catholic Saints and Beati* (Rockford, IL: TAN Books, 1977).

Representative articles of each side of the "survivalism" versus "corruptionism" debate include Eleonore Stump, "Resurrection, Reassembly, and Reconstitution: Aquinas on the Soul" in *Die menschliche Seele: Brauchen wir den Dualismus?*, eds. Bruno Niederbacher and Edmund Runggaldier (Frankfurt: Ontos Verlag, 2006), 151–171; Patrick Toner, "St. Thomas Aquinas on Death and the Separated Soul" *Pacific Philosophical Quarterly* 91 (2010): 587–599; Christopher M. Brown,

"Souls, Ships, and Substances: A Response to Toner" *American Catholic Philosophical Quarterly* 81 (2007): 655–668; Turner C. Nevitt, "Survivalism, Corruptionism, and Intermittent Existence in Aquinas" *History of Philosophy Quarterly* 31:1 (2014): 1–19.

Part III

THE *SUMMA* TODAY

11

CONTEMPORARY THOMISTIC PHILOSOPHY

PREFACE

At the end of Chapter 1, we saw how a variety of Thomistic schools of thought evolved throughout the 20th century, whose adherents continue to explore Thomas' rich philosophical and theological legacy into the 21st century. Contemporary Thomistic scholarship has a twofold purpose. First, *historical* analysis elucidates our understanding of Thomas' explicitly held views, as framed within the context in which he lived and wrote. Second, what we could call "*applied* Thomism" seeks to reconstruct Thomas' views in light of contemporary scientific, philosophical, and theological understanding, thereby facilitating engagement with alternative complementary or opposing viewpoints. *Analytical Thomism* represents one of these approaches to bringing Thomas into both creative and critical conversation with contemporary philosophical theories on issues in metaphysics, epistemology, ethics, political philosophy, logic, philosophy of science, and philosophy of religion.

In this chapter, instead of providing a comprehensive overview of how Thomists have addressed issues in all of these areas—which would require a whole other book—we will focus on a few select areas in which Thomistic scholarship is currently active or has had a significant impact in shaping contemporary thought. First, we will examine how Thomas' metaphysical account of human nature—his *philosophical anthropology*—offers an understanding of the ontological make-up of human beings in comparison to various alternative theories promoted by contemporary metaphysicians. Next, we will see how Thomas' *natural law* ethic provides a theoretical foundation for the existence of objective human rights, and how Thomistic philosopher and political theorist Jacques Maritain (1882–1973) played a crucial role in the development of the United Nations' *Universal Declaration of Human Rights* in the aftermath of the Second World War. Finally, we will analyze how various Thomists have applied Thomas' philosophical anthropology and ethical theory to devise defensible viewpoints on questions regarding the beginning and end of human life, the moral status of non-human animals, and our ethical duty toward the environment.

PHILOSOPHICAL ANTHROPOLOGY: DUALISM, MATERIALISM, AND HYLOMORPHISM

The question of what metaphysically constitutes *human nature* has been a central concern throughout the history of philosophy, with multiple accounts having emerged of what constitutes the *essence* of human nature. In the West, the Greek philosophers Plato and Aristotle each offered a distinct view of what a human being fundamentally is. For Plato, a human being is identical to an immaterial soul that is "imprisoned" for a time in a material body before death sets it free, either to be united with another body or to spend eternity contemplating the source of all being, truth, and goodness. Aristotle conceived of a human being as a composite unity of an immaterial soul and a material body—a view known as *hylomorphism*.

This basic controversy regarding a human being's relationship to her material body has continued to drive debate among philosophers throughout the ensuing centuries into the present day. Numerous accounts that have been proffered identify the human essence as an immaterial soul or mind, a living animal body, a functioning brain, or a bundle of psychological states, to cite some of the principal views.

Depending on which of these theses one favors, the criterion of a human being's identity through time and change consists in sameness of soul or mind, continuity of biological life processes, continuity of neural functions, or some form of psychological continuity involving memory, personality traits, or self-consciousness.

The debate between philosophers who reduce human nature to either its physical or psychological properties, those who hold that human nature includes both types of properties, and those who argue that human nature transcends such properties has focused on three distinct camps. *Substance dualists* maintain a contemporary version of Plato's view that a human being is identical to an immaterial soul that is conjoined to a material body during one's earthly life. *Reductive materialists* contend that human nature is nothing "over and above" the biological and neurophysiological facts which are subject to empirical scientific investigation; all the physical and psychological states of a human being can be wholly explained in virtue of the physical properties had by one's body. Finally, *non-reductive materialists* take seriously the data provided by empirical science, while nevertheless maintaining that there are some aspects of human nature which cannot be wholly explained in terms of physical properties alone.

Thomas adds a comparable historical voice to the contemporary debate by formulating and defending a detailed version of Aristotelian hylomorphism—as elucidated in Chapter 4. It is notoriously difficult, however, to classify Thomistic hylomorphism among the traditional categories of dualism and materialism, for it clearly is neither without qualification. Thomas explicitly denounces Plato's substance dualist construal of human nature, in which a human being is *identified* with her soul alone. Yet, as we saw in Chapter 10, Thomas understands a human being to be capable of existing after the death of her body as *composed of* her soul alone. Thomas' claim that a human being can survive her body's death clearly sets him apart from any reductive materialist view of human nature, which identifies a human being with her physical body. Nevertheless, he contends that a human being is essentially an *animal*.

Thus, depending upon how certain claims Thomas holds are stressed, Thomistic hylomorphism can be construed either as a type of dualism or as a type of non-reductive materialism. One thing which is clear is Thomas' position that the existence of a human being entails the existence of a *person*, having adopted Boethius' definition of a person as "an individual substance of a rational nature" (Ia, q. 29, a. 1; IIIa, q. 16, a. 12 *ad* 1). Despite Thomas' affirmation of the existence of *non-human* persons— namely, God and the angels (Ia, qq. 29–30)— you and I could not exist as such beings. You and I are essentially *human persons*. In short, while, for Thomas, there are non-human persons, there are no non-person humans. Nevertheless, Thomas does not identify the existence of a human being with that of a living body of the species *Homo sapiens*. While a human being's existence *naturally* includes having such a physical body, it is not *essential* to one's existence. As described in Chapter 10, a defensible interpretation of Thomas' view of life after death is that it is possible for a human being to exist in the absence of her biologically "human" body.

Several *desiderata* may be defended that an adequate account of human nature ought to satisfy. First, *it is possible that human beings survive bodily death*. While only those who believe in the possibility of post-mortem existence may hold this desideratum, it is a fundamental belief held by a significant percentage of human beings. As such, an account of human nature that takes this belief seriously, and can account for its metaphysical possibility, will be stronger for it. Second, *it is acknowledged that human beings are biological organisms*. Third, *it is recognized that human beings are persons*, and thus add a significant ontological category of self-conscious, free, and moral beings to the universe. Fourth, *a human being exists as a unified entity*, as both a person and an animal.

While various theories of human nature may satisfy some of these desiderata, most fail to satisfy the entire set. For example, *substance dualism* satisfies the first insofar as it understands a person to be essentially an immaterial soul that survives its body's death; this view does not, however, satisfy the fourth desideratum insofar as one's soul and body are construed as distinct substances that merely interact in some fashion. A *reductive materialist* account, on the other hand, would stress the second desideratum, but—depending on the particular theory—may not satisfy the first or third.

From the Thomistic hylomorphic perspective, it is clear that the first desideratum is satisfied by Thomas' arguments that not only does an intellective soul survive separation from its body and can alone compose a human being, but also a human being will experience a resurrection in which her soul re-informs its body—see Chapter 10. The second is satisfied by Thomas' definition of a human being as a "rational *animal*" and his further description of a human being as naturally composed of a body informed by an intellective soul. A human being exists as an animal organism both when she is composed of her material body, and also when she is composed of her soul alone by virtue of her soul's possessing all the capacities proper to animal existence and serving as the "blueprint" for her material body.

Thomas' recognition that human beings are *persons*, by virtue of being "individual substances of a rational nature," satisfies the third desideratum (IIIa, q. 16, a. 12 *ad* 1). Every existence of a human being entails the existence of a person. The significance of being a person is defined by Thomas in terms of how a person's intellective capacity, and the volitional freedom that follows from this capacity, represents the highest form of existence that is possible for material beings. Human beings, as persons, occupy the highest level in the ontological hierarchy of beings composed of both matter and form, and thus have the largest set of causal capacities through which they are able to affect their surrounding environment:

> Further still, in a more special and more perfect way, the particular and the individual are found in the rational substances which have dominion over their own actions; and which are not only made to act, like others; but which can act of themselves; for actions belong to singulars. Therefore also individuals of a rational nature have a special name even among other substances; and this name is *person*.
>
> (Ia, q. 29, a. 1)

Additionally, Thomas asserts, "*Person* signifies what is most perfect in all nature – that is, a subsistent individual of a rational nature" (a. 3).

The satisfaction of the final desideratum is brought about by Thomas' rejection of Platonic dualism's division of a human being into a "mover"—a soul—and that which it moves—a body. Thomas complains that Platonic dualism does not allow for a human being to exist as "one unqualifiedly" (*unum simpliciter*) any more than one would say a sailor and the ship he pilots are "one unqualifiedly" (Ia, q. 76, a. 1). Thomas' description of an intellective soul as something that is not a substance, but something merely subsistent that is the substantial form of a human body and thus only one part of the human species, allows him to assert an immediate unity of body and soul in the composition of a human being.

Thomistic hylomorphism adds a distinctive voice to the contemporary debate concerning the nature of human persons. Furthermore, Thomas' hylomorphic account has certain advantages when compared with alternative substance dualist or reductive materialist accounts, satisfying certain desiderata the other theories do not, which contribute toward a proper understanding of human nature. While Thomistic hylomorphism may not offer *the* best account of human nature, it at least provides an excellent foundation for developing one, thus meriting serious attention and further analysis.

ETHICS: FROM NATURAL LAW TO NATURAL RIGHTS

Human-made laws, and the rights they protect, of any nation in the modern world may be judged by internationally agreed-upon standards including, most especially, the United Nations' (UN) *Universal Declaration of Human Rights* (UDHR). The rights enumerated in the UDHR were not conceived *ex nihilo*, but are grounded in traditions of moral theory represented by those who drafted or consulted in the drafting of the UDHR. An historical overview of the drafting of the UDHR evidences the significant influence of Thomistic natural law theory in validating the rights contained therein. While there continues to be controversy about the notion of "rights," the concept of universally valid human rights may be defended based on sound rational argumentation and not mere stipulation through the *fiat* of international organizations such as the UN. Thomism, as we will see, provides rigorous philosophical foundation upon which human rights, such as those enumerated in the UDHR, may be justified even in the face of disagreement or blatant lack of recognition of such rights by individual nations.

The conception, drafting, and adoption of the UDHR followed an extraordinary set of events in human history. The Second World War had concluded with staggering death tolls—an estimated 50–70 million—of both armed forces and civilians. During the war, the Allies, recognizing the failures of the League of Nations in stopping the military buildup of Nazi Germany and the outbreak of war, established the

UN as a world organization to prevent future wars; 51 nations signed the UN Charter. In 1946, the UN's Economic and Social Committee established a commission on human rights, which consisted of members from Australia, Belarus, Belgium, Chile, China, Egypt, France, India, Lebanon, Panama, the Philippines, Ukraine, the United Kingdom, the United States, Uruguay, the U.S.S.R., and Yugoslavia. The commission's members represented Chinese, Islamic, and Hindu perspectives, as well as a variety of Western philosophical, political, and religious views.

One of the commission's first tasks was to examine philosophical thought and religious traditions from around the world to identify foundational principles that would justify human rights. The commission gave this task to a "philosophical committee." A dichotomous view regarding the establishment of a philosophical foundation for universal human rights is represented by the chairman of this committee, French Thomistic philosopher Jacques Maritain, who, in response to a query regarding how individuals of such varied ideologies could agree on a list of "universal" human rights, quipped, "Yes, we agree about the rights but on condition no one asks us why."

Maritain's somewhat tongue-in-cheek response obscures the fact that he was one of the foremost modern natural law theorists, who influentially defined the "common good" in terms of the good of *each individual person* who constitutes a given society—as opposed to defining it in terms of an *aggregate* amount of goodness, as in the ethical theory of *utilitarianism*, in which the good of a smaller number of individuals may be overridden by consideration of the good of the majority. He thus had his own answer to the question of why certain rights should be established universally in the UDHR:

> In my opinion any rational justification of the idea of the rights of man, as of the idea of law in general, demands that we should rediscover the idea of natural law . . . in its true metaphysical connotations, its realistic dynamism and the humility of its relation with nature and experience. We are then able to understand how a certain ideal order, rooted in the nature of man and of human society, can impose moral demands valid throughout the world of experience, history and fact, and can establish, for the conscience as for the written law, the permanent principle and the elementary and universal criteria of rights and duties.

Maritain's Thomistic account of natural law provides both a "global language" for defining rights that are *transcultural*, and yet preserves some degree of *pluralism* in how such rights are construed and practically enforced within the context of particular social, political, economic, and cultural conditions.

As we saw in Chapter 6, Thomas defines the fundamental "good" for human beings as consisting in our *flourishing*, which is the fulfillment of our shared *nature* (Ia–IIae, q. 18, a. 5; q. 49, a. 2; q. 71, a. 1). Human nature is defined by a set of *capacities* relative to our existence as living, sentient, social, and rational animals. Human flourishing involves actualizing these definitive capacities of the human species, such that each of us becomes the most *perfect*—i.e. most complete or fully actualized—human being we can be. To achieve this end, Thomas claims that all human beings have a set of *natural inclinations* to pursue whatever we perceive to be good—i.e. what is desirable to us and will help actualize our definitive capacities. The natural law thus includes a set of principles which, if followed, will satisfy a human being's natural inclinations and thus lead to her perfection according to her nature as a human being.

A key question for natural law, and other universal rights, theorists concerns the conception of "human nature" upon which various rights and duties are supposed to be founded. One advantage of the Thomistic account of natural law is that it is premised upon a relatively basic conception of human nature in which the only common features identified are life, sentience, sociability, and rationality. Of course, each of these features must be defined and such definitions, as they become more specific, may be controversial. But a high degree of specification is not required to define certain general natural law precepts. For example, sentience may be understood broadly to refer to human beings' capacity to sense their environment and respond to it, along with the correlative experiences of pleasure and pain. One could then deduce that depriving a person of any of her senses—say, by blinding her—or causing her unwarranted pain would be bad for her; hence, there is an obligation to avoid intentionally or negligently depriving a person of her senses or causing her undue pain. On the positive side, restoring a blind person's sight, should she desire it, or causing a pleasurable experience would be good and thus worth pursuing.

As is the case with the rights enumerated in the UDHR, natural law principles are quite general so as to be universally applicable to all human beings, no matter what their cultural background or station in life. Thomas thus recognizes the need for what he terms "human law," which is the particular determination of general natural law principles made by human legislators using prudent practical judgment. Human laws are crafted with respect to particular communities to help educate each community's members in becoming morally virtuous; such laws can thus be considered *culturally relative*, because the same human laws would not be appropriate for every community (q. 95, a. 2 *ad* 3). Thomas further notes the important role that the *customs* of different communities play in specifying and applying natural law principles (q. 97, a. 3).

Nevertheless, human laws must be crafted in accordance with the general principles of natural law that are universal and thus binding upon all human beings regardless of culture or circumstance. Any valid human law, Thomas contends, must be somehow derived from the natural law; otherwise, it would be a "perversion of law" (q. 95, a. 2). Respect for cultural diversity thus has limits imposed by the basic conception of human nature outlined above. For example, the cultural practice of "female circumcision" would not be justified due to its negative effects of causing physical pain and depriving victims of the capacity for sexual pleasure—following from our sentient nature—of being a sign and instrument of sexual discrimination—following from our social nature—and of violating victims' autonomy insofar as they do not choose this for themselves—following from our rational nature as Thomas links this with our capacity for self-determination (Ia, q. 83, a. 1). Thomistic natural law theory thus provides an informative foundation for universally valid human rights, by means of which specific laws of various states may be evaluated as ethically valid or invalid, and which respects intercultural differences within reasonable limits imposed by a defensible philosophical anthropology.

APPLICATION: BIOETHICS AT THE MARGINS OF HUMAN LIFE

In addressing bioethical issues at the beginning of human life, such as abortion, human embryonic stem cell research, and cloning, a primary concern is to establish when a developing human embryo or fetus can be considered a "person"; for it is typically held that only persons are the subjects of moral rights, such as a "right to life." As noted above, Thomas asserts that all human beings are persons according to the Boethian definition (IIIa, q. 16, a. 12 *ad* 1); however, he contends that an embryo or fetus is not a human being until its body is informed by an *intellective soul*. Thomas' account of human embryogenesis has been generally rejected today due to its dependence upon medieval biological information. A number of scholars, however, have attempted to combine Thomas' basic metaphysical account of human nature with current embryological data to develop a contemporary Thomistic account of a human being's beginning. Some Thomists argue that an early-term human embryo lacks the necessary intrinsic qualities for it to be informed by an intellective soul until it reaches a certain point in its biological development. Others contend that there is nothing about a human embryo's biological nature, from the moment the process of fertilization is complete, that disallows its being informed by an intellective soul.

In Chapter 4, we explicated Thomas' account of *successive ensoulment* in a developing human embryo and fetus. He holds that the immediate product of conception is a body informed by a vegetative soul—i.e. an organism that is alive at the most basic level. Later, as the embryo develops into a fetus with sense organs and a rudimentary neural structure, it becomes informed by a sensitive soul. Once the fetus has developed a sufficiently complex neural structure to support intellectual operations, it becomes informed by an intellective soul (Ia, q. 76, a. 3 *ad* 3; q. 118, a. 2 *ad* 2). Akin to Thomas' explicitly stated view, some contemporary Thomists argue that intellective ensoulment occurs only when a fetus has developed a functioning *cerebral cortex* insofar as it is the organ of a human being's sensitive and imaginative capacities, and cerebral neural activity is correlated with intellectual operations.

This view has been challenged by appeal to Thomas' distinction between *active* and *passive potentiality* (q. 48, a. 5; q. 76, a. 4 *ad* 1)—as discussed in Chapter 4. In brief, an active potentiality is a quality intrinsic to a substance which the substance can actualize without requiring any further change wrought by an external agent. The actualization of an active potentiality may be *immediate*, as when a native

Spanish-speaker immediately begins to speak in Spanish; or it may require an *internally driven developmental process*, as when an acorn grows into a mature oak tree. A passive potentiality, on the other hand, requires an agent external to the substance to actualize it. For example, a piece of wood may become a table, but only if it is altered by a carpenter; or a non-Spanish-speaker may become a Spanish-speaker, but only if she is taught by a teacher, a textbook, or some sort of language-learning program.

The change required for something to actualize an active or passive potentiality is brought about by its *proper active principle*. An active principle is required because a potentiality can be actualized only by something that is already in a state of actuality. Something can be moved from a state of potentiality to a state of actuality only by some active principle that is either internal or external to it. A sufficient condition for something's having an active potentiality is if it can actualize the potentiality by some active principle *internal* to it; whereas the active principle in the case of a passive potentiality is *external* to it. Contrary to the focus on a cerebral cortex to provide the necessary material foundation for an immediately exercisable active potentiality for intellective thought, some Thomists emphasize that, from conception onwards, a human embryo has a complete human genome and other material factors that are sufficient—given a nutritive uterine environment—for it to develop a functioning cerebral cortex supportive of sensation and intellectual operations. One can thus infer that a human embryo, well before it forms a functioning cerebral cortex, possesses an active potentiality for sensation and intellective thought insofar as it has an intrinsic active principle to develop the requisite material foundation for such operations.

Thomas' account of a human being's death is premised upon an intellective soul's *unitive* function as its body's substantial form. Death occurs the moment one's soul ceases to inform her body, entailing a *substantial change*. The remaining matter no longer composes a "human body," but a "corpse" subject to decay. As we saw in Chapter 10, the soul, as a subsistent immaterial form, continues to function intellectively and eventually re-informs its resurrected body (Ia, q. 89). Thomas understands death to occur because a pre-mortem human body is not *perfectly* informed by its soul as an effect of *original sin* (Ia–IIae, q. 85, a. 5). Material defects can thus arise that eventually render the body unable to actualize the soul's basic vegetative capacities.

To determine the physical sign of death's occurrence, Thomas notes in a short treatise entitled *De motu cordis* ("On the movement of the heart") that the soul operates through the heart as a *primary organ* to holistically integrate the body's various organic systems, governing them as a ruler orders a city through laws. Contemporary Thomists appeal to evidence that the brain—particularly the brainstem—fulfills this role by stimulating and regulating the body's vital autonomic functions to support integrative organic activity. Thomists generally reject the so-called "higher-brain" concept of death in which a human *person*—understood in the post-Cartesian sense as a conscious, thinking subject—is claimed to have died if only the neo-cortical structures of the brain irreversibly cease to function, as with patients in a "persistent vegetative state," such as the well-publicized case of Terri Schiavo. Some Thomists, however, have defended this concept of death as a reversal of the successive ensoulment process Thomas describes at the beginning of human life.

Thomas does not speak directly about proper medical care for terminally ill persons, other than validating the administration of the sacrament of Extreme Unction for those in danger of death for the purpose of spiritual healing and remission of sin (IIIa, q. 32, a. 2). He does, however, morally condemn any killing of the innocent, including suicide (IIa–IIae, q. 64, aa. 5–6); and it is reasonable to extrapolate that he would thereby condemn both *euthanasia* and *physician-assisted suicide*. Some contemporary bioethicists have appealed to Thomas' incipient form of the "principle of double-effect" (a. 7) as justifying the use of *palliative treatment* that may *indirectly* hasten a patient's death—but without the direct intention of killing the patient—as well as not utilizing "extraordinary" medical treatment that is deemed either futile or disproportionately burdensome compared to the expected health benefits.

APPLICATION: ENVIRONMENTAL AND ANIMAL ETHICS

Despite the attitude of "mastery over nature" that dominated Christian thinking for millennia and remains influential among many Christians to this day, there are strands within the Christian tradition—particularly those that may be influenced by Thomistic thought—that are deeply concerned with the status of the environment, not only insofar as environmental damage may negatively impact human interests, but also due to the *intrinsic* value of the environment itself. As we saw in Chapter 3, Thomas understands the created universe to manifest God's *being*, *goodness*, and *beauty*. In God, these qualities are *infinite*, so they could not be replicated exactly by anything that is not God. Nevertheless, Thomas writes,

> [God] brought things into being in order that His goodness might be communicated to creatures, and be represented by them; and because His goodness could not be adequately represented by one creature alone, He produced many and diverse creatures, that what was wanting to one in the representation of the divine goodness might be supplied by another. For goodness, which in God is simple and uniform, in creatures is manifold and divided and hence the whole universe together participates in the divine goodness more perfectly, and represents it better than any single creature whatever.
>
> (Ia, q. 47, a. 1)

God saw fit to create not just one form of finite goodness—human beings—but a plentitude consisting of innumerably different forms and degrees of created goodness. One could thus argue that the extinction of species has a direct and negative impact on the manifestation of the divine in nature, especially given Thomas' assertion that "God is in all things, and innermostly" (Ia, q. 8, a. 1). Distinct from the *pantheistic* view this quotation seems to imply, God's essential nature is to be a *transcendent* creator, present to all beings as the source of their existence. But Thomas believes that God is also "present" within created beings in another way, as the source of an internal motivation that inspires them to strive to be as much like their creator as they can within the limits of their own essential nature, calling forth whatever forms of being, goodness, and beauty are proper to the *flourishing* of each species. "Flourishing" refers to the actualization of a creature's essential capacities, living the sort of life for which it was meant.

To manifest the qualities of God in nature, it is not enough that many different types of beings exist. Each individual member of each species must seek to *perfect* itself—striving to "be all that it can be" (in the spirit of the U.S. Army slogan of the 1980s). Hence, each plant strives to be the best plant it can be, by seeking nourishment and other necessities for its survival and reproduction. Each animal seeks not only its own survival and reproduction, but also pleasure and the avoidance of pain as part of its *sentient* animal nature. As one moves up the evolutionary chain, various capacities distinctive of each species emerge, which animals instinctively seek to exercise and perfect. Such activities may serve ends like survival and reproduction, but they are also activities that animals may come to value for their own sake, as essential components of a good life for that species. Finally, each human being seeks perfection as a living, sentient, social, and rational animal. Thus, everything in creation is seeking the divine in its own way. In the words of Thomas, "All things, by desiring their own perfection, desire God" (Ia, q. 6, a. 1 *ad* 2).

The premise that everything in the universe has its own intrinsic purpose—its own immanent striving toward both its own flourishing and the flourishing of other beings with whom it shares its environment—provides an initial foundation for the idea that everything also possesses its own intrinsic *value*. Thomas holds that any being's existence is good or valuable in itself, since he understands the properties of *being* and *goodness* to be *commensurate* (Ia, q. 5, a. 1). This means that the greater degree of existence a being enjoys, the greater its intrinsic value and the value of any act that supports its flourishing. It is good that any being continues to exist and flourish; the world is richer for it. Nevertheless, an inanimate substance is a lower grade of being than a living organism; while a merely living organism is a lower grade of being than a sentient animal, which in turn is a lower grade of being than a rational animal. Hence, the existence and flourishing of a rational animal is worth more than that of a non-rational animal, which in turn is worth more than the existence and flourishing of an organism that is neither rational nor sentient. But all creatures have some degree of goodness, so actions that support the life and health of any plant or animal will have a positive moral value, while actions that threaten life and health will have a negative moral value. From a moral point of view, when we evaluate our treatment of sentient beings capable of feeling pleasure and pain, we need to take into account whether our actions cause them needless suffering or bring them greater pleasure. Being and goodness are also commensurate with *beauty*: the more a being flourishes, the greater its inherent, objective beauty (Ia–IIae, q. 27, a. 1 *ad* 3). A healthy plant or animal is more beautiful than a sickly specimen of the same species. Likewise, a healthy, flourishing environment is more beautiful than a landscape that has been ravaged by strip mining. The natural and inescapable *aesthetic* reaction we have to the natural world also constitutes recognition of the intrinsic value of those beautiful natural objects, living and non-living alike, that compose the biosphere.

We have thus far defined three aspects of the Thomistic ecological worldview: the variety of beings as a manifestation of God's nature in the created universe; the interrelated and interdependent nature of the elements and creatures that comprise the biosphere; and the inherent goodness of allowing beings of all types to flourish in their essential natures. Collectively they provide a foundation for the moral duties of human beings toward other animals and the rest of the biosphere that sustains our existence.

Thomas believes in a hierarchy of living beings with plants at its base, non-rational animals distributed along the middle rungs, and rational animals perched at its apex. We may not want to treat these as *sharp* categorical distinctions, however. Some non-rational animal species have only the most rudimentary capacity for sensory awareness and self-motivated activity, making them little better—functionally—than higher levels of plant species. Others have a high degree of cognitive, affective, and volitional capacity that puts them right on the dividing edge between "non-rational" and "rational." Thomas links gradations in *value* with increasing capacity for volitional action, reserving the ultimate moral category of "person" to signify "what is most perfect in all of nature"—i.e. rational beings—whom he believes are inherently endowed with "high dignity" (Ia, q. 29, a. 3). This hierarchical view leads Thomas to reduce the value of all non-rational creatures to mere resources to be exploited by rational beings. Thomas does concede that cruelty to the other animals is wrong, but not because of any duties we owe them. His sole concern is that cruelty to non-rational animals might instill habits in us that would make it easier to act cruelly to our fellow human beings (Ia–IIae, q. 102, a. 6 *ad* 8).

Even if rational animals sometimes need to use non-rational animals for the sake of their survival and flourishing, this doesn't mean that the latter have only an instrumental value—that their existence is only meaningful insofar as they may serve the purposes of persons. Rather, it is evident that non-sociopathic human beings recognize at some level the intrinsic value of other animals whenever we feel *pity* for their suffering. The capacity to feel pity is premised on an implicit recognition of a "kinship" between rational and non-rational animals—the fact that we have a shared capacity to suffer. This does not entail that we may never cause other animals to suffer if doing so is necessary for the sake of human survival or flourishing; however, any necessary use or killing of other animals must be done in the most *humane* way possible—causing the least amount of suffering.

Many non-vegetarians prefer to live in blissful ignorance of the factory-farming techniques and other forms of unnecessary suffering animals experience before arriving at their dinner table. It is not that they are unaware such suffering is occurring; they just do not want to confront those facts directly because they know it will invoke a reaction of pity that may take the fun out of a family dinner at their favorite steakhouse. For the same reason, people who do not want to be motivated to give money to charities that provide food for starving children turn the TV channel or the magazine page when faced with a full-color image of a five-year-old orphan with a distended belly. This sort of *deliberate ignorance* does not excuse those who elect to eat meat or neglect their duty to support charitable causes, since their choice to avoid stimuli that would awaken appropriate moral emotions is itself a blameworthy decision (Ia–IIae, q. 6, a. 8).

According to Thomas' hierarchy of being, human beings may justifiably use non-rational animals to support their own life. It would thus be permissible for a human being to kill an animal for food (IIa–IIae, q. 64, a. 1) or to save her own life from a predatory attack *if* there are no other viable options. But some contemporary Thomists have argued that it would not be justified to kill an animal for food if vegetarian options were available or to kill an animal in self-defense if non-lethal means were feasible. Even when violence is justified to secure a higher good, only the least amount of violence necessary should be tolerated. Anything beyond that minimum, any *disproportionate* violence, is morally unjustifiable (a. 7). It goes without saying that any purely arbitrary—and certainly any outright *cruel*—treatment of animals is summarily ruled out.

Thomas describes how before the Fall animals followed the commands of human beings "of their own accord"—as *subjects* following a leader, not as *slaves* obeying a master (Ia, q. 91, a. 1 *ad* 4). He further notes that in the pre-Fall world we did not need to eat animals to survive (a. 1 *ad* 3). In the Book of Genesis, immediately after setting human beings over the other animals, God announces that all plant life has been "given" to human beings and the other animals for food (Genesis 1:29–30). No mention is made of other animals also having been given to us for food. God does grant Adam the power to *name* the different types of animals as an exercise of humanity's rational capacity (Genesis 2:19); but this does not entail an absolute moral superiority that justifies any sort of use of other animals according to mere human whim. In fact, Genesis implies an initial state of *vegetarianism* that was later rescinded, post-Fall, at the time of Noah—apparently, as a concession to the violent tendencies of fallen human beings (Genesis 9:1–3).

According to Thomas, through the grace bestowed by God by means of Christ's redemptive sacrifice, a future restoration of the pre-Fall *harmony*—i.e. the coming of the "Kingdom of God"—is now made possible although it has yet to be realized. Thomas contends, however, that the establishment of the Kingdom of God will restore the harmony only among all *rational* beings: God, angels, and human beings. Plants and animals will no longer exist due to the fact that time will have ceased and there will be no further purpose to their existence (Supp., q. 91, a. 5).

Building on the moral worldview inherited from Thomas and others in the Christian tradition, theologians and philosophers have begun to emphasize an ordering of living beings in the natural world that is not premised on human beings possessing a "manifest destiny" to use and abuse other animals however we see fit. Rather, both rational moral reflection and our natural capacity for sympathy should lead each of us to recognize the intrinsic value not only of other animals, but of all living things and the biosphere as a whole. All reflect, to varying degrees, the being, goodness, and beauty of God.

SUGGESTIONS FOR FURTHER READING

Works explicitly focused on Analytical Thomism include John Haldane, ed., "Analytical Thomism" *The Monist* 80:4 (1997); Haldane, ed., *Mind, Metaphysics, and Value in the Thomistic and Analytical Traditions* (Notre Dame, IN: University of Notre Dame Press, 2002); Craig Paterson and Matthew S. Pugh, eds., *Analytical Thomism: Traditions in Dialogue* (Burlington, VT: Ashgate, 2006).

For Plato's and Aristotle's respective views of human nature, see Plato, *Phaedo*, in *The Collected Dialogues of Plato*, eds. Edith Hamilton and Huntington Cairns (Princeton: Princeton University Press, 2005); and Aristotle, *De anima*, in *The Complete Works of Aristotle*, vol. 1, ed. Jonathan Barnes (Princeton, NJ: Princeton University Press, 1984).

A contemporary representative of a substance dualist construal of human nature is Richard Swinburne, *The Evolution of the Soul*, rev. ed. (New York: Oxford University Press, 1997).

A representative reductive materialist account of human nature is provided by Eric T. Olson, *The Human Animal: Personal Identity Without Psychology* (New York: Oxford University Press, 1997).

Other contemporary discussions of dualist and materialist views of human nature include Lynne Rudder Baker, *Persons and Bodies: A Constitution View* (New York: Cambridge University Press, 2000); Mark C. Baker and Stewart Goetz, eds., *The Soul Hypothesis: Investigations into the Existence of the Soul* (New York: Continuum, 2011); Kevin Corcoran, ed., *Soul, Body, and Survival: Essays on the Metaphysics of Human Persons* (Ithaca, NY: Cornell University Press, 2001); Stewart Goetz and Charles Taliaferro, *A Brief History of the Soul* (Malden, MA: Wiley-Blackwell, 2011); William Hasker, *The Emergent Self* (Ithaca, NY: Cornell University Press, 1999); Hud Hudson, *A Materialist Metaphysics of the Human Person* (Ithaca, NY: Cornell University Press, 2001); Robert C. Koons and George Bealer, eds., *The Waning of Materialism* (New York: Oxford University Press, 2010); Nancey Murphy, *Bodies and Souls, or Spirited Bodies?* (New York: Cambridge University Press, 2006); Eric T. Oslon, *What Are We? A Study in Personal Ontology* (New York: Oxford University Press, 2007); Klaus Petrus, ed., *On Human Persons* (Frankfurt: Ontos Verlag, 2003); Peter van Inwagen and

Dean Zimmerman, eds., *Persons: Human and Divine* (New York: Oxford University Press, 2007).

Contemporary reconstructions of Thomistic hylomorphism have been put forth by Eleonore Stump, "Non-Cartesian Substance Dualism and Materialism without Reductionism" *Faith and Philosophy* 12 (1995): 505–531; Robert Pasnau, *Thomas Aquinas on Human Nature* (New York: Cambridge University Press, 2002); Gyula Kilma, "Man = Body + Soul: Aquinas's Arithmetic of Human Nature" in *Thomas Aquinas: Contemporary Philosophical Perspectives*, ed. Brian Davies (New York: Oxford University Press, 2002), 257–274; and Jason T. Eberl, "Aquinas on the Nature of Human Beings" *Review of Metaphysics* 58:2 (2004): 333–365.

This history of the development of the UDHR and the role of Maritain's "philosophical committee" is chronicled in Mary Ann Glendon, *A World Made New: Eleanor Roosevelt and the Universal Declaration of Human Rights* (New York: Random House, 2001). See also UNESCO, *Human Rights: Comments and Interpretations* (New York: Columbia University Press, 1949); Jacques Maritain, "Communication with regard to the Draft World Declaration on the Rights of Man" (June 18, 1947): http://unesdoc.unesco.org/images/0012/001243/124341eb.pdf (accessed May 26, 2015).

For further insight into Maritain's Thomistic moral and political theorizing, see his *Man and the State* (Chicago: University of Chicago Press, 1951); *The Person and the Common Good*, trans. John J. Fitzgerald (South Bend, IN: University of Notre Dame Press, 1966); *Natural Law: Reflections on Theory and Practice*, ed. William Sweet (South Bend, IN: St. Augustine's Press, 2001).

For a comprehensive overview of contemporary Thomistic interpretations of the beginning and end of human life, see Fabrizio Amerini, *Aquinas on the Beginning and End of Human Life*, trans. Mark Henninger (Cambridge, MA: Harvard University Press, 2013); and Jason T. Eberl, *Thomistic Principles and Bioethics* (New York: Routledge, 2006).

Thomists who argue that a human person does not exist until after the cerebral cortex has developed include Robert Pasnau, "Souls and the Beginning of Life: A Reply to Haldane and Lee" *Philosophy* 78 (2003): 521–531; and Joseph Donceel, "Immediate Animation and Delayed Hominization" *Theological Studies* 31 (1970): 76–105.

Thomists who argue that a human person begins to exist at conception include John Haldane and Patrick Lee, "Aquinas on Human Ensoulment, Abortion and the Value of Life" *Philosophy* 78 (2003): 255–278; Benedict Ashley and Albert Moraczewski, "Cloning, Aquinas, and the Embryonic Person" *National Catholic Bioethics Quarterly* 1 (2001): 189–201; and Stephen Heaney, "Aquinas on the Presence of the Human Rational Soul in the Early Embryo" *The Thomist* 56 (1992): 19–48.

Thomistic arguments defending the "higher-brain" concept of death have been offered by William A. Wallace, "St. Thomas on the Beginning and End of Human Life" in *Sanctus Thomas de Aquino Doctor Hodiernae Humanitatis* (Vatican City: Libreria Editrice Vaticana, 1995), 394–407; D. Alan Shewmon, "The Metaphysics of Brain Death, Persistent Vegetative State, and Dementia" *The Thomist* 49 (1985): 24–80; and Eike-Henner Kluge, "St. Thomas, Abortion and Euthanasia: Another Look" *Philosophy Research Archives* 7 (1981): 312–344.

Criticisms of the "higher-brain" interpretation of the Thomistic account of human death have been offered by J. P. Moreland and Stan Wallace, "Aquinas versus Locke and Descartes on the Human Person and End-of-Life Ethics" *International Philosophical Quarterly* 35 (1995): 319–330; and Philip Smith, "Brain Death: A Thomistic Appraisal" *Angelicum* 67 (1990): 3–35.

For further discussion of care for terminally ill persons from a Thomistic ethical perspective, see Jason T. Eberl, "Aquinas on Euthanasia, Suffering, and Palliative Care" *The National Catholic Bioethics Quarterly* 3 (2003): 331–354.

For contemporary treatments of Thomistic environmentalism, see Peter P. Cvek, "Thomas Aquinas, Natural Law, and Environmental Ethics" *Vera Lex* 1 (2000): 5–18; Jill LeBlanc, "Eco-Thomism" *Environmental Ethics* 21 (1999): 293–306; John Haldane, "Admiring the High Mountains: The Aesthetics of Environment" *Environmental Values* 3:2 (1994): 97–106; and Montague Brown, "Natural Law and the Environment" *Proceedings of the American Catholic Philosophical Association* 63 (1989): 221–234.

For Thomistic arguments concerning the ethical treatment of non-human animals, see Andrew Tardiff, "A Catholic Case for Vegetarianism" *Faith and Philosophy* 15:2 (1998): 210–222; Peter

Drum, "Aquinas and the Moral Status of Animals" *American Catholic Philosophical Quarterly* 66 (1992): 483–488; Judith Barad, "Aquinas's Inconsistency on the Nature and the Treatment of Animals" *Between the Species* 4 (1988): 102–111. Another good resource for a Christian theological defense of animal rights is Charles Camosy, *For Love of Animals: Christian Ethics, Consistent Action* (Cincinnati, OH: Franciscan Media, 2013).

Bibliography

An exhaustive list of the available Latin editions, English translations, commentaries, and secondary literature on Thomas' *Opera omnia* would constitute a whole book in itself. Below is a selected bibliography comprising works that have been referenced throughout this guidebook.

EDITIONS OF THE *SUMMA THEOLOGIAE*

Aquinas, Thomas, *Summa Theologica*, trans. Fathers of the English Dominican Province (New York: Benziger Brothers, 1947–8).
—— *Summa Theologiae: A Concise Translation*, ed. Timothy McDermott (Notre Dame, IN: Christian Classics, 1989).
—— *Summa Theologiae* (Latin-English), 60 vols. (New York: Cambridge University Press, 2006).

COMMENTARIES ON THE *SUMMA THEOLOGIAE* OR SPECIFIC PARTS THEREOF

Davies, Brian, ed., *Aquinas's Summa Theologiae: Critical Essays* (New York: Rowman & Littlefield, 2006).
—— *Thomas Aquinas's Summa Theologiae: A Guide and Commentary* (New York: Oxford University Press, 2014).

Henle, R. J., ed., *The Treatise on Law* (Notre Dame, IN: University of Notre Dame Press, 1993).

Kenny, Anthony, *The Five Ways: St. Thomas Aquinas' Proofs of God's Existence* (New York: Routledge, 1969).

—— *Aquinas on Mind* (New York: Routledge, 1993).

Loughlin, Stephen J., *Aquinas' Summa Theologiae* (New York: T&T Clark, 2010).

Pasnau, Robert, *Thomas Aquinas on Human Nature* (New York: Cambridge University Press, 2002).

—— *The Treatise on Human Nature* (Indianapolis, IN: Hackett, 2002).

Pope, Stephen J., ed., *The Ethics of Aquinas* (Washington, D.C.: Georgetown University Press, 2002).

Shanley, Brian J., *The Treatise on Divine Nature* (Indianapolis, IN: Hackett, 2006).

te Velde, Rudi, *Aquinas on God: The "Divine Science" of the Summa Theologiae* (Burlington, VT: Ashgate Publishing, 2006).

Torrell, Jean-Pierre, *Aquinas's Summa: Background, Structure, and Reception*, trans. Benedict M. Guevin (Washington, D.C.: Catholic University of America Press, 2005).

OTHER WORKS BY THOMAS WITH COMMENTARIES

Aquinas, Thomas, *Summa contra Gentiles*, 5 vols. (Notre Dame, IN: University of Notre Dame Press, 1975).

Kretzmann, Norman, *The Metaphysics of Theism* (New York: Oxford University Press, 1997).

—— *The Metaphysics of Creation* (New York: Oxford University Press, 1999).

—— "The Metaphysics of Providence" *Medieval Philosophy and Theology* 9:2 (2000): 91–213.

McInerny, Ralph, *Aquinas against the Averroists: On There Being Only One Intellect* (West Lafayette, IN: Purdue University Press, 1993).

BIOGRAPHIES OF THOMAS AQUINAS

Chesterton, G. K., *Saint Thomas Aquinas: "The Dumb Ox"* (New York: Doubleday, 1956).

Pieper, Josef, *Guide to Thomas Aquinas*, trans. Richard and Clara Winston (San Francisco, CA: Ignatius Press, 1991).

Torrell, Jean-Pierre, *Saint Thomas Aquinas – Vol. 1: The Person and His Work*, trans. Robert Royal (Washington, D.C.: Catholic University of America Press, 1996).

—— *Saint Thomas Aquinas – Vol. 2: Spiritual Master*, trans. Robert Royal (Washington, D.C.: Catholic University of America Press, 2003).

Turner, Denys, *Thomas Aquinas: A Portrait* (New Haven, CT: Yale University, Press, 2013).

Weisheipl, James A., *Friar Thomas d'Aquino: His Life, Thought, and Work* (Garden City, NY: Doubleday, 1974).

HISTORY OF SCHOLASTICISM

Gilson, Etienne, *The Spirit of Medieval Philosophy* (New York: Charles Scribner's Sons, 1936).

Kretzmann, Norman, Anthony Kenny, and Jan Pinborg, eds., *The Cambridge History of Later Medieval Philosophy* (New York: Cambridge University Press, 1982).

McGrade, A. S., ed., *The Cambridge Companion to Medieval Philosophy* (New York: Cambridge University Press, 2003).

Pieper, Josef, *Scholasticism: Personalities and Problems of Medieval Philosophy* (New York: Pantheon Books, 1960).

Rubenstein, Richard, *Aristotle's Children: How Christians, Muslims, and Jews Rediscovered Ancient Wisdom and Illuminated the Dark Ages* (San Diego, CA: Harcourt, 2003).

GENERAL GUIDES TO THOMAS' THOUGHT

Chenu, Marie-Dominique, *Toward Understanding Saint Thomas*, trans. Albert M. Landry and Dominic Hughes (Chicago: Henry Regnery, 1963).

Dauphinais, Michael, Barry David, and Matthew Levering, eds., *Aquinas the Augustinian* (Washington, D.C.: Catholic University of America Press, 2007).

Davies, Brian, *The Thought of Thomas Aquinas* (Oxford: Clarendon Press, 1992).

—— *Thomas Aquinas: Contemporary Philosophical Perspectives* (New York: Oxford University Press, 2002).

—— and Eleonore Stump, eds., *The Oxford Handbook of Aquinas* (New York: Oxford University Press, 2012).

Gilson, Etienne, *The Christian Philosophy of St. Thomas Aquinas* (New York: Random House, 1956).

Kretzmann, Norman and Eleonore Stump, eds., *The Cambridge Companion to Aquinas* (New York: Cambridge University Press, 1993).

Pasnau, Robert and Christopher Shields, *The Philosophy of Aquinas* (Boulder, CO: Westview Press, 2004).

Stump, Eleonore, *Aquinas* (New York: Routledge, 2003).

CLASSICAL AND CONTEMPORARY THOMISM

Brezik, Victor B., *One Hundred Years of Thomism: Aeterni Patris and Afterwards* (Houston, TX: Center for Thomistic Studies, 1981).

Cessario, Romanus, *A Short History of Thomism* (Washington, D.C.: Catholic University of America Press, 2005).

Haldane, John, ed., "Analytical Thomism" *The Monist* 80:4 (1997): 485–618.

—— *Mind, Metaphysics, and Value in the Thomistic and Analytical Traditions* (Notre Dame, IN: University of Notre Dame Press, 2002).

Knasas, John F. X., *Being and Some Twentieth Century Thomists* (Bronx, NY: Fordham University Press, 2003).

McCool, Gerald A., *From Unity to Pluralism: The Internal Evolution of Thomism* (Bronx, NY: Fordham University Press, 1992).

—— *The Neo-Thomists* (Milwaukee: Marquette University Press, 1994).

Paterson, Craig and Matthew S. Pugh, eds., *Analytical Thomism: Traditions in Dialogue* (Burlington, VT: Ashgate, 2006).

ADDITIONAL SECONDARY LITERATURE ON SPECIFIC TOPICS IN THOMAS' THOUGHT

METAPHYSICS AND EPISTEMOLOGY

Amerini, Fabrizio, *Aquinas on the Beginning and End of Human Life*, trans. Mark Henninger (Cambridge, MA: Harvard University Press, 2013).

Ashley, Benedict and Albert Moraczewski, "Cloning, Aquinas, and the Embryonic Person" *National Catholic Bioethics Quarterly* 1 (2001): 189–201.

Brown, Christopher M., "Souls, Ships, and Substances: A Response to Toner" *American Catholic Philosophical Quarterly* 81 (2007): 655–668.

Donceel, Joseph, "Immediate Animation and Delayed Hominization" *Theological Studies* 31 (1970): 76–105.

Eberl, Jason T., "Aquinas on the Nature of Human Beings" *The Review of Metaphysics* 58:2 (2004): 333–365.

—— "A Thomistic Understanding of Human Death" *Bioethics* 19:1 (2005): 29–48.

Haldane, John, "The Metaphysics of Intellect(ion)" *Proceedings of the American Catholic Philosophical Association* 80 (2006): 39–55.

—— and Patrick Lee, "Aquinas on Human Ensoulment, Abortion and the Value of Life" *Philosophy* 78 (2003): 255–278.

Heaney, Stephen, "Aquinas on the Presence of the Human Rational Soul in the Early Embryo" *The Thomist* 56 (1992): 19–48.

Kerr, Gaven, "Essentially Ordered Series Reconsidered" *American Catholic Philosophical Quarterly* 86:4 (2012): 541–555.

Klima, Gyula, "Man = Body + Soul: Aquinas's Arithmetic of Human Nature" in *Thomas Aquinas: Contemporary Philosophical Perspectives*, ed. Brian Davies (New York: Oxford University Press, 2002): 257–274.

Kluge, Eike-Henner, "St. Thomas, Abortion and Euthanasia: Another Look" *Philosophy Research Archives* 7 (1981): 312–344.

Kreeft, Peter J., *Angels (and Demons): What Do We Really Know about Them?* (San Francisco, CA: Ignatius Press, 1995).

Lonergan, Bernard, *Verbum: Word and Idea in Aquinas*, ed. Frederick E. Crowe and Robert M. Doran (Toronto: University of Toronto Press, 1997).

MacDonald, Scott, ed., *Being and Goodness: The Concept of the Good in Metaphysics and Philosophical Theology* (Ithaca, NY: Cornell University Press, 1991).

McInerny, Ralph, *Aquinas and Analogy* (Washington, D.C.: Catholic University of America Press, 1996).

Moreland, J. P. and Stan Wallace, "Aquinas versus Locke and Descartes on the Human Person and End-of-Life Ethics" *International Philosophical Quarterly* 35 (1995): 319–330.

Nevitt, Turner C., "Survival, Corruptionism, and Intermittent Existence in Aquinas" *History of Philosophy Quarterly* 31:1 (2014): 1–19.

Oguejiofor, J. Obi, *The Philosophical Significance of Immortality in Thomas Aquinas* (New York: University Press of America, 2001).

Pasnau, Robert, *Theories of Cognition in the Later Middle Ages* (New York: Cambridge University Press, 1997).

—— "Souls and the Beginning of Life: A Reply to Haldane and Lee" *Philosophy* 78 (2003): 521–531.

Pegis, Anton, *St. Thomas and the Problem of the Soul in the Thirteenth Century* (1934; reprint, Toronto: Pontifical Institute of Mediaeval Studies, 1978).

Shewmon, D. Alan, "The Metaphysics of Brain Death, Persistent Vegetative State, and Dementia" *The Thomist* 49 (1985): 24–80.

Smith, Philip, "Brain Death: A Thomistic Appraisal" *Angelicum* 67 (1990): 3–35.

Stump, Eleonore, "Non-Cartesian Substance Dualism and Materialism Without Reductionism" *Faith and Philosophy* 12:4 (1995): 505–531.

—— "Aquinas's Account of Freedom: Intellect and Will" *The Monist* 80:4 (1997): 576–597.

—— "Resurrection, Reassembly, and Reconstitution: Aquinas on the Soul" in *Die menschliche Seele: Brauchen wir den Dualismus?*, ed. Bruno Niederbacher and Edmund Runggaldier (Frankfurt: Ontos Verlag, 2006), 151–171.

Toner, Patrick, "St. Thomas Aquinas on Death and the Separated Soul" *Pacific Philosophical Quarterly* 91 (2010): 587–599.

Wallace, William A., "St. Thomas on the Beginning and End of Human Life" in *Sanctus Thomas de Aquino Doctor Hodiernae Humanitatis* (Vatican City: Libreria Editrice Vaticana, 1995), 394–407.

Wippel, John, *The Metaphysical Thought of Thomas Aquinas* (Washington, D.C.: Catholic University of America Press, 2000).

ETHICS

Barad, Judith, "Aquinas's Inconsistency on the Nature and the Treatment of Animals" *Between the Species* 4 (1988): 102–111.

Boyle, Joseph, "Toward Understanding the Principle of Double Effect" *Ethics* 90 (1980): 527–538.

Bradley, Denis J. M., *Aquinas on the Twofold Human Good: Reason and Human Happiness in Aquinas's Moral Science* (Washington, D.C.: Catholic University of America Press, 1999).

Brock, Stephen L., *Action and Conduct: Thomas Aquinas and the Theory of Action* (Edinburgh: T&T Clark, 1998).

Brown, Montague, "Natural Law and the Environment" *Proceedings of the American Catholic Philosophical Association* 63 (1989): 221–234.

Cates, Diana Fritz, *Aquinas on the Emotions: A Religious-Ethical Inquiry* (Washington, D.C.: Georgetown University Press, 2009).

Cavanaugh, Thomas A., "Aquinas's Account of Double Effect" *The Thomist* 61 (1997): 107–112.

Cessario, Romanus, *The Moral Virtues and Theological Ethics*, 2nd ed. (Notre Dame, IN: University of Notre Dame Press, 2008).

Cvek, Peter P., "Thomas Aquinas, Natural Law, and Environmental Ethics" *Vera Lex* 1 (2000): 5–18.

DeYoung, Rebecca Konyndyk, Colleen McCluskey, and Christina Van Dyke, *Aquinas's Ethics: Metaphysical Foundations, Moral Theory, and Theological Context* (Notre Dame, IN: University of Notre Dame Press, 2009).

Drum, Peter, "Aquinas and the Moral Status of Animals" *American Catholic Philosophical Quarterly* 66 (1992): 483–488.

Eberl, Jason T., "Aquinas on Euthanasia, Suffering, and Palliative Care" *The National Catholic Bioethics Quarterly* 3 (2003): 331–354.

—— *Thomistic Principles and Bioethics* (New York: Routledge, 2006).

Finnis, John, *Aquinas: Moral, Political, and Legal Theory* (New York: Oxford University Press, 1998).

—— "The Good of Marriage and the Morality of Sexual Relations: Some Philosophical and Historical Observations" *American Journal of Jurisprudence* 42 (1998): 97–134.

Flannery, Kevin L., *Acts Amid Precepts: The Aristotelian Logical Structure of Thomas Aquinas's Moral Theory* (Washington, D.C.: Catholic University of America Press, 2001).

Goyette, John, Mark S. Latkovic, and Richard S. Myers, eds., *St. Thomas Aquinas and the Natural Law Tradition: Contemporary Perspectives* (Washington, D.C.: Catholic University of America Press, 2004).

Haldane, John, "Admiring the High Mountains: The Aesthetics of Environment" *Environmental Values* 3:2 (1994): 97–106.

Jensen, Steven J., *Living the Good Life: A Beginner's Thomistic Ethics* (Washington, D.C.: Catholic University of America Press, 2013).

Keys, Mary M., *Aquinas, Aristotle, and the Promise of the Common Good* (New York: Cambridge University Press, 2006).

Koritansky, Peter Karl, *Thomas Aquinas and the Philosophy of Punishment* (Washington, D.C.: Catholic University of America Press, 2012).

LeBlanc, Jill, "Eco-Thomism" *Environmental Ethics* 21 (1999): 293–306.

Lisska, Anthony J., *Aquinas's Theory of Natural Law: An Analytic Reconstruction* (New York: Oxford University Press, 1996).

Lombardo, Nicholas E., *The Logic of Desire: Aquinas on Emotion* (Washington, D.C.: Catholic University of America Press, 2011).

Lonergan, Bernard, *Grace and Freedom: Operative Grace in the Thought of Thomas Aquinas*, ed. Frederick E. Crowe and Robert M. Doran (Toronto: University of Toronto Press, 2000).

MacDonald, Scott and Eleonore Stump, eds., *Aquinas's Moral Theory: Essays in Honor of Norman Kretzmann* (Ithaca, NY: Cornell University Press, 1999).

McInerny, Ralph, *Ethical Thomistica: The Moral Philosophy of Thomas Aquinas*, rev. ed. (Washington, D.C.: Catholic University of America Press, 1997).

Miner, Robert, *Thomas Aquinas on the Passions* (New York: Cambridge University Press, 2009).

Nelson, Daniel Mark, *The Priority of Prudence: Virtue and Natural Law in Thomas Aquinas and the Implications for Modern Ethics* (University Park, PA: Pennsylvania State University Press, 1992).

O'Rourke, Fran, *Pseudo-Dionysius and the Metaphysics of Aquinas* (Notre Dame, IN: University of Notre Dame Press, 2005).

Pieper, Josef, *The Four Cardinal Virtues* (Notre Dame, IN: University of Notre Dame Press, 1966).

—— *Faith, Hope, and Love* (San Francisco, CA: Ignatius Press, 1997).

Porter, Jean, *Nature as Reason: A Thomistic Theory of the Natural Law* (Grand Rapids, MI: Eerdmans, 2005).

Tardiff, Andrew, "A Catholic Case for Vegetarianism" *Faith and Philosophy* 15:2 (1998): 210–222.

THEOLOGY

Bobik, Joseph, *Veritas Divina: Aquinas on Divine Truth* (South Bend, IN: St. Augustine's Press, 2001).

Emery, Giles, *The Trinitarian Theology of St. Thomas Aquinas*, trans. Francesca Aran Murphy (New York: Oxford University Press, 2007).

Hütter, Reinhard and Matthew Levering, eds., *Resourcement Thomism: Sacred Doctrine, the Sacraments, and the Moral Life* (Washington, D.C.: Catholic University of America Press, 2010).

Jenkins, John I., *Knowledge and Faith in Thomas Aquinas* (New York: Cambridge University Press, 1997).

Levering, Matthew and Michael Dauphinais, eds., *Rediscovering Aquinas and the Sacraments* (Chicago: Hillenbrand Books, 2009).

Smith, Timothy L., *Thomas Aquinas' Trinitarian Theology* (Washington, D.C.: Catholic University of America Press, 2003).

Stump, Eleonore, *Wandering in Darkness: Narrative and the Problem of Suffering* (New York: Oxford University Press, 2010).

van Nieuwenhove, Rik and Joseph Wawrykow, eds., *The Theology of Thomas Aquinas* (Notre Dame, IN: University of Notre Dame Press, 2005).

OTHER HISTORICAL TEXTS CITED

Anselm, *Proslogion*, trans. Thomas Williams (Indianapolis, IN: Hackett, 1995).

Aristotle, *The Complete Works of Aristotle*, ed. Jonathan Barnes (Princeton, NJ: Princeton University Press, 1984).

—— *Nicomachean Ethics*, trans. Terence Irwin, 2nd ed. (Indianapolis, IN: Hackett, 1999).

Augustine, *On Free Choice of the Will*, trans. Thomas Williams (Indianapolis, IN: Hackett, 1993).

Averroes, "On the Harmony of Religions and Philosophy" in *The Philosophy and Theology of Averroes*, trans. Mohammed Jamil-al-Rahman (Baroda: A. G. Widgery, 1921), 14–19.

Bentham, Jeremy, *An Introduction to the Principles of Moral and Legislation* (Oxford: Clarendon Press, 1907).

Hume, David, *Enquiry Concerning the Principles of Morals*, ed. P. H. Nidditch (Oxford: Clarendon Press, 1975).

——, *Dialogues Concerning Natural Religion*, ed. Richard H. Popkin, 2nd edition (Indianapolis: Hackett, 1998).

John Paul II, *Fides et ratio* (1998): http://w2.vatican.va/content/john-paul-ii/en/encyclicals/documents/hf_jp-ii_enc_14091998_fides-et-ratio.html (accessed May 26, 2015).

Kant, Immanuel, *Groundwork of the Metaphysics of Morals*, ed. Mary Gregor (New York: Cambridge University Press, 1997).

Leo XIII, *Aeterni patris* (1879): http://w2.vatican.va/content/leo-xiii/en/encyclicals/documents/hf_l-xiii_enc_04081879_aeterni-patris.html (accessed May 26, 2015).

Mill, John Stuart, *Utilitarianism*, ed. George Sher, 2nd ed. (Indianapolis, IN: Hackett, 2001).

Plato, *The Collected Dialogues of Plato*, ed. Edith Hamilton and Huntington Cairns (Princeton, NJ: Princeton University Press, 2005).

Seneca, *De ira*: http://www.sophia-project.org/uploads/1/3/9/5/13955288/seneca_anger.pdf (accessed May 26, 2015).

Tanner, Norman, ed., *Decrees of the Ecumenical Councils* (Washington, D.C.: Georgetown University Press, 1990).

UNESCO, *Human Rights: Comments and Interpretations* (New York: Columbia University Press, 1949).

ADDITIONAL SOURCES CITED

Baker, Lynne Rudder Baker, *Persons and Bodies: A Constitution View* (New York: Cambridge University Press, 2000).

Bealer, Mark C. and Stewart Goetz, eds., *The Soul Hypothesis: Investigations into the Existence of the Soul* (New York: Continuum, 2011).

Camosy, Charles, *For Love of Animals: Christian Ethics, Consistent Action* (Cincinnati, OH: Franciscan Media, 2013).

Cavanaugh, T. A., *Double-Effect Reasoning: Doing Good and Avoiding Evil* (New York: Oxford University Press, 2006).

Corcoran, Kevin J., ed., *Soul, Body, and Survival: Essays on the Metaphysics of Human Persons* (Ithaca, NY: Cornell University Press, 2001).

Cruz, Joan Carroll, *The Incorruptibles: A Study of the Incorruption of the Bodies of Various Catholic Saints and Beati* (Rockford, IL: TAN Books, 1977).

Finnis, John, *Natural Law and Natural Rights* (New York: Oxford University Press, 1980).

Glendon, Mary Ann, *A World Made New: Eleanor Roosevelt and the Universal Declaration of Human Rights* (New York: Random House, 2001).

Goetz, Stewart and Charles Taliaferro, *A Brief History of the Soul* (Malden, MA: Wiley-Blackwell, 2011).

Hasker, William, *The Emergent Self* (Ithaca, NY: Cornell University Press, 1999).

Hudson, Hud, *A Materialist Metaphysics of the Human Person* (Ithaca, NY: Cornell University Press, 2001).

Koons, Robert C. and George Bealer, eds., *The Waning of Materialism* (New York: Oxford University Press, 2010).

Maritain, Jacques, "Communication with regard to the Draft World Declaration on the Rights of Man" (June 18, 1947): http://unesdoc.unesco.org/images/0012/001243/124341eb.pdf (accessed May 26, 2015).

—— *Man and the State* (Chicago: University of Chicago Press, 1951).

—— *The Person and the Common Good*, trans. John J. Fitzgerald (South Bend, IN: University of Notre Dame Press, 1966).

—— *Natural Law: Reflections on Theory and Practice*, ed. William Sweet (South Bend, IN: St. Augustine's Press, 2001).

Murphy, Nancey, *Bodies and Souls, or Spirited Bodies?* (New York: Cambridge University Press, 2006).

Oderberg, David S. and Timothy Chappell, eds., *Human Values: New Essays on Ethics and Natural Law* (New York: Palgrave Macmillan, 2004).

Olson, Eric T., *The Human Animal: Personal Identity Without Psychology* (New York: Oxford University Press, 1997).

—— *What Are We? A Study in Personal Ontology* (New York: Oxford University Press, 2007).

Petrus, Klaus, ed., *On Human Persons* (Frankfurt: Ontos Verlag, 2003).

Rommen, Heinrich A., *The Natural Law: A Study in Legal and Social History and Philosophy*, trans. Thomas R. Hanley (St. Louis, MO: Herder, 1948).

Swinburne, Richard, *The Evolution of the Soul*, rev. ed. (New York: Oxford University Press, 1997).

van Inwagen, Peter and Dean Zimmerman, eds., *Persons: Human and Divine* (New York: Oxford University Press, 2007).

Woodward, P. A., ed., *The Doctrine of Double Effect: Philosophers Debate a Controversial Moral Principle* (Notre Dame, IN: University of Notre Dame Press, 2001).

INDEX